*Dedicated to the event doers around the world who want to
deliver excellent events no one will ever forget.
I hope you wear out the pages.*

And to my family, may you Keep On Going.

— Roger / Dad

THE ROGER C. IGO COLLECTION

Keep On Going:
The History of the Bell Tower on 34th

———

**The Official Handbook for Producing
Social Events, Weddings, and Corporate Parties:**
The Complete Guide for Pros, Amateurs,
and Everyone in Between

The Official Handbook for

PRODUCING SOCIAL EVENTS, WEDDINGS, AND CORPORATE PARTIES.

The Complete Guide for Pros, Amateurs, and Everyone in Between

ROGER C. IGO

IGO LUXURY COACHES LLC • HOUSTON, TEXAS

Name: Igo, Roger C., author.
Title: *The Official Handbook For Producing Social Events, Weddings, and Corporate Parties : The Complete Guide For Pros, Amateurs, and Everyone In Between* / Roger C. Igo.
Description: Houston, TX : Igo Luxury Coaches LLC, [2025] | Series: The Roger C. Igo collection. | Includes index.
Identifiers: ISBN: 978-1-966667-01-8 (Hardcover) | 978-1-966667-00-1 (Paperback) | 978-1-966667-02-5 (E-book) | LCCN: 2025900778
Subjects: LCSH: Special events—United States—Planning. | Special events—United States—Management. | Parties—United States—Planning. | Weddings—United States—Planning. | Office parties—United States—Planning. | Event planners—Handbooks, manuals, etc. | Special events industry—Handbooks, manuals, etc. | LCGFT: Handbooks and manuals. | Reference works. | BISAC: REFERENCE / Weddings. | REFERENCE / Event Planning. | REFERENCE / Etiquette. | REFERENCE / Personal & Practical Guides.
Classification: LCC: GT3406.U6 .I466 2025 | DDC: 394.2068—dc23

For information, contact:
Roger C. Igo
RogerIgo1@gmail.com
713-409-4000

Hardcover ISBN: 978-1-966667-01-8
Paperback ISBN: 978-1-966667-00-1
E-book ISBN: 978-1-966667-02-5

Contents

Meet Roger C. Igo. VII

At the Heart of Successful Events VIII

PARTIES AND SPECIAL EVENTS   1

1. Planning Large Gatherings 3

2. Seasonal Celebrations. 27

3. Milestones 41

4. Being Prepared. 73

5. Etiquette and Stationery 87

6. Celebration Food and Bar. 105

WEDDINGS   129

7. Wedding Planning 131

8. Celebrations Before and After the Wedding 161

9. The Bride and the Groom 179

10. Close Family and Wedding Party. 199

11. The Ceremony and Special Wedding Moments . . 219

12. Common Wedding Questions. 239

13. Event Planning Considerations 255

14. Preventing and Dealing with Event Challenges. . . 285

15. Food, Drinks, and Attendee Comfort 305

16. Event Tech, Trends, and Social Media 319

17. Music and Entertainment for Your Event 331

18. Event Décor. 341

My Commitment to Event Industry Success 349

Wedding and Events Glossary 351

Index 361

Meet Roger C. Igo

Event mastermind Roger Igo is the CEO of The Bell Tower on 34th, based in Houston, Texas, which delivers more than 300 events a year, including weddings, corporate gatherings, and large-scale landmark celebrations. Since Igo co-founded The Bell Tower on 34th in 2009, he has overseen approximately $100 million in events. At the time of publishing, the venue has garnered more than 1,000 five-star Google reviews under his leadership and received multiple industry awards for excellence.

Igo's debut book, *Keep on Going: The History of The Bell Tower on 34th*, shares his entrepreneurial journey and offers insights into the lessons that have shaped his approach to creating extraordinary events and cultivating a thriving business. Igo is a proud alumnus of both CEO Space International and The Disney Institute, where he honed his expertise in business and leadership.

He and his wife, Angela, live in Houston. The Igos have two grown children and are active in their community.

For speaking engagements, consultations, events, and more, contact him at RogerIgo.com or RogerIgo1@gmail.com.

At the Heart of Successful Events

I have a confession for you: Beyond my closest friends and family, I can't tell you who attended my wedding. It's not that I didn't appreciate everyone who was there for my wife, Angela, and me. But there were 500 people at our wedding, and 24 years later, I couldn't begin to tell you who all of them were.

What I do remember is what I experienced. How I felt when I saw Angela walking down the aisle. The songs we danced to, the smell of the flowers at the altar, and the taste of the rich chocolate groom's cake. Our wedding day was a symphony of experiences, emotions, and sensory details. It's these memories that have endured, and they've shaped stories we've passed along to our children.

And so, from an event-planning perspective, our wedding was a resounding success. The people who planned it, who put thought into the myriad special touches that shaped our event, achieved the pinnacle of creating an event: They made it memorable.

In the last 15+ years, since I became CEO of Houston venue The Bell Tower on 34th, I've seen thousands of people plan and execute events. My team and I have supported their efforts, and I can tell when the elements necessary to create an excellent event are in place. It's more than my perspective as a venue owner; it's also my experience as an event creator. Over the years as a musician, real estate professional, and entrepreneur, I've put together my share of excellent events. I know what works.

Creating a truly successful event is not about checking off certain boxes. It's not about inspiring everlasting connections (as in, everyone who attends is still in touch). At the end of the day, it comes down to inspiring memories. That's the magic that makes an awesome event, whether it's a wedding, a big party, or a corporate function.

While I've been able to achieve this for quite some time, it took me a while to be able to explain what separates an adequate two-dimensional event from a spectacular three-dimensional one. I started thinking about how events intersect with guests' lives and guests' experiences during their time at the event. I thought about what inspires good memories and about the noise or distractions that can interfere with memory-making (a dynamic I refer to as the "Memory Plane.")

It helped to think of events in terms of film productions. The event and reasons behind it were the plot, and things going on behind the scenes, from an ice machine on its last legs to personal circumstances in guests' lives, could be considered subplots. It's up to the person putting the event together to make sure the main plot is what captivates the guests and lives on in their memories. But how?

To answer that, I started identifying elements that are consistently found in highly successful events. In each case, the person creating the event, the "event doer," makes it a priority to deliver optimum sound, light, air/climate, and music (SLAM) for guests. The event doer makes painstaking efforts to make sure that, as much as possible, everything guests see, hear, taste, smell, and feel delights them. And it goes without saying that those wonderful sensory experiences are shaped, at least in part, by incredible food and beverages (FAB). All of these elements, combined, make up what I've come to think of as the "Vibe Dimension," and I believe this is paramount to making an event stand out. If you plan an event carefully and strategically, always with the Vibe Dimension in mind, then you can really cement the memories of your event into the hearts and minds of those who attend.

For several years now, I've been trying to help event doers achieve this by sharing tip-packed blog posts on The Bell Tower on 34th website. But I realized that this detailed advice would be even more impactful if it was organized in one easy-to-access resource. That's why I've compiled this blog post collection for you. Every suggestion can be applied to creating a Vibe Dimension that will make your event a long-standing memory in the minds of the people there. This includes my tips on things that take place before and after an event (from bridal showers to sending thank-you notes), which still have a role to play in shaping memories.

Apply these tips and strategies, and even if the people who attend your event can't recite the names of everyone who was there, they'll be speaking fondly about what they experienced long after they've said goodbye.

And then you, too, will have achieved true event-planning success.

PARTIES AND SPECIAL EVENTS

CHAPTER 1

Planning Large Gatherings

Courtesy of Becca Lee Photography

10 WAYS TO ACHIEVE THE CELEBRATION OF YOUR DREAMS AT A PRICE YOU CAN LIVE WITH

You want to throw a big, beautiful party, but your vision and your budget don't exactly match.

Not a problem: Contrary to what social media posts may have you believe, you don't need to shell out loads of cash to host a memorable party or special event.

In fact, there are lots of ways to cut costs while still getting most of what you want. It's simply a matter of creative thinking and a willingness to be flexible.

1. **Prioritize.** When it comes to keeping your spending in check, you have to know where you want your money to go. Have a discussion with everyone sharing planning duties, or whoever is footing the bill, and decide what elements are most important.

2. **Let go of Saturday.** There's no rule that says Saturday is the only day for a big celebration, but we can admit it's the go-to choice for many people, which explains why it's the most expensive. For your party, think about kicking off the weekend with a Friday night affair, or host a Sunday afternoon garden party. Either option will be loads cheaper than Saturday.

3. **Invite only your nearest and dearest.** Fewer folks to feed and house means savings—big ones. If you're hosting a big birthday celebration, or any kind of family affair, be sure to include parents, grandparents, and siblings and their spouses, along with a few of the honorees' friends, for an intimate and fun affair.

4. **Limit guests' plus-one.** Except for those who are married, engaged, or in a long-term relationship, don't allow guests to bring a date.

5. **Opt for e-vites.** Nowadays, digital invitations are commonplace, and the options are endless. Take advantage and choose your signature style.

6. **Host an adults-only celebration.** Specify that there are no children invited.

7. **Go with a DJ.** If you want music and dancing at your party, a band is a wonderful and lively feature, but you'll definitely pay the price. If you're simply looking for great music, a DJ is a less expensive, fun option that tons of people go with. Plus, with a DJ, you have a lot more freedom to pick your playlist than with a live band.

8. **Ask your caterer to serve in-season foods.** The easier it is for your caterer to source the food, the more affordable it will be to serve it to your guests.

9. **Skip the cocktails.** Every good party needs a few good refreshments and, in most situations, beer and wine will do the trick. Talk to your vendor or venue about budget-friendly beverage packages.

10. **Repurpose:** There's nothing wrong with repurposing decorations from previous events or holidays to fit the theme of your party. This approach will save you money, and it will add a nice personal touch to your celebration.

When you're thinking of ways to balance your budget while ensuring your celebration lives up to your expectations, there are endless options. So don't feel overwhelmed, but be deliberate in your choices. Decide where you can save and where you want to splurge, and go for it! The end result is sure to be all you're hoping for.

WHEN IT'S TIME TO DITCH YOUR DIY IDEAS

When you're preparing for a big event, do-it-yourself projects can be fun, fulfilling, and fantastic, especially when they turn out just as you'd envisioned. They can also be a way to keep costs under control. On the flip side, they can make for stress and disappointment when they don't. In most DIY instances, that is an expected part of the process, but I'd argue it's not something you want to subject yourself to when you're planning a special event.

Below are tasks best left to industry experts. Go on, give yourself a break, and bring in a pro.

Photography. No matter how many of your friends and/or family members consider themselves cell phone selfie experts or even boast an enviable Instagram portfolio, they are no substitute for a professionally trained and experienced photographer. Your photos likely will be one of the few lasting, tangible records of your celebration and the source of many of your memories. In other words, you should not be willing to take chances!

Videography. Like photography, videography may seem like something anyone with a good phone app can do, but in reality, achieving quality results requires expertise, experience, and the right equipment. Skilled videographers know how to capture key shots, deal with weather and light issues, and edit their footage.

Music. Again, many think cell phones and our many self-made playlists are up to par when it comes to setting the musical stage for an event, but your choice of music may not be a fit for a multigenerational guest list. If money is an issue, skip the band and go with a DJ, which is often more affordable. DJs, especially experienced ones, have a good idea about which songs get people moving—and which ones fall flat—and can play tunes that appeal to all age groups.

Catering. Many families can boast great cooks, no doubt, but it wouldn't be a good idea to rely on those folks to create a feast big enough to feed a large number of people. Catering is a difficult, stress-filled, time-consuming affair, and one best left to a seasoned chef who's handled large crowds and has experience directing under chefs and staff. They also know a thing or two about the proper way to store and transport food. What's more, a good caterer will likely have a backup plan if something goes wrong, and they can help you accommodate guests with dietary needs and restrictions.

Large-scale décor projects. True, it's not uncommon for people to set up their own centerpieces, signage, and other decorative touches for their parties. And while doing their own décor may save them money, these DIY projects consume valuable time and add stress on the day of the celebration. They may not achieve the desired results, either.

Another factor to consider: Your venue might restrict some of the brilliant décor ideas you had in mind, or they might require you to work with professional, insured vendors. Discuss your intentions with your venue in advance.

Putting together a big celebration requires the efforts of experienced vendors who've done it all before and have the resources to pull it off in a polished style. Your event might be filled with fun surprises, but it's best that those surprises don't revolve around food or photography catastrophes that could have been averted by relying on the pros.

ESSENTIAL DOS AND DON'TS FOR EVENT DOERS

One thing I never tire of as an event venue owner is the chance to have meaningful conversations with our customers. Conversations with couples who want advice on creating the wedding of their dreams. Conversations with event planners who are curious about the best events we've delivered here—and how they can achieve similar results. Conversations with families arranging parties who want a celebration that's as special as their loved ones.

What I've noticed during these conversations is that two words tend to come up repeatedly: "always" and "never." After more than a decade in the events business, I've gotten a good feel for essential planning steps and strategies. And I know the mistakes planners must avoid.

While I'm looking forward to many more conversations with customers on what I believe makes for an unforgettable event, I thought it would be helpful to make my top always-never items available to anyone who'd like to see them. Here they are:

Always Do These Things

I'm starting with the things I'd strongly advise you to do if you're planning an event of any kind. These are your keys to excellent, memorable events.

Always have all the essentials you need to deliver a successful event ready: food, sound equipment, just-in-case items (from a generator to an emergency kit for the bride), you name it. This includes plenty of service staff—talk with your venue about this. Make sure that whenever you throw a party or arrange an event, everything you and your guests might need will be on hand.

Always insist your food is prepared fresh and on-site if possible. Even when food is expertly prepared, serving it immediately will elevate your guests' experience and their perception of your event.

Always have access to up-to-date information about your event, day or night, 24/7. Staying on top of your event will give you peace of mind, encourage ongoing communication with everyone who is playing a role in it, and help you make sure nothing falls through the cracks. We've seen this for ourselves at The Bell Tower on 34th since we started providing an online portal for our customers so they can check event details, like their menu, seating plan, and payments, around the clock.

Always under-promise and over-deliver. This is an excellent strategy for delighting your guests. Give them the details they need to decide whether to attend your event, but keep the steps you plan to take to make your event truly magical for them—from the amazing food you'll be providing to the excellent service you've ensured they'll get—to yourself.

Never Do These Things

These are the choices and missteps you should be aware of and steer clear of. They're not just about hospitality for your guests—they're also about safeguarding your interests and your wallet.

Never pay for an entire day at a venue if you don't need it. Talk with venues about their policies and packages. Can you book for a half-day or for a set number of hours? Venues that don't require full-day reservations show that they understand their customers' diverse needs, budget constraints, and concerns.

Never ask your guests to pay for parking or expect them to walk a long distance to attend your event.

Never pay extra for the following:

- **Your cake-cutting:** This is often a simple service, but some venues charge for it.

- **Vendor buyouts:** These are fees imposed for bringing in outside vendors not on the venue's approved list. It's a charge that can significantly inflate your expenses and restrict your choices.

- **Beverage service:** Charges for passing drinks during your cocktail hour or refilling water or wine glasses during meals can add up quickly.

- **Rehearsals, bridal portraits, and tastings:** While these are standard parts of the wedding experience, some venues capitalize on them with additional fees.

Make Your Standards Clear

Keep these always-and-never items in mind as you research venues, and include them in your conversations with venue representatives. The people you interview should be able to tell you exactly how they'll accommodate you.

Believe me, these dos and don'ts are not unreasonable, and standing firm on them will have a tremendous impact on the success of your event.

HOW TO MAKE YOUR SPECIAL EVENT ACCESSIBLE FOR DISABLED GUESTS

Helping your guests—all of your guests—share the joy of your party or special event is one of your responsibilities as a host. And in most cases, accomplishing that goal is very doable, whether it calls for sending a Braille invitation to your visually impaired aunt or working with your venue to make sure that a guest who wears leg braces can safely navigate the grounds and building. I have some general accessibility guidelines and ideas for you, but generally, your guest(s) will be the best, and most important, source of information.

Communication Is Key

I strongly encourage you to initiate a conversation with your disabled guests early in your planning process. Asking them what you should know is not intrusive; it's a considerate and proactive way to make sure you're meeting their specific needs. In addition to asking guests to explain what they'll need at your special event, consider asking about the following:

- Seating considerations

- Dietary restrictions

- Hotel and transportation requirements

- The need for specific services, such as an American Sign Language interpreter

- Things that should be avoided, such as dance floor lights that could trigger seizures

To avoid communication mishaps—like a guest wrongly assuming that you know their plus-one has hearing loss—it wouldn't hurt to add wording to your RSVP card and/or event website encouraging guests to let you know how you can accommodate them. A blog post on One Fab Day (focused on weddings but applicable to all events) suggests wording your statement like this: "Our wedding is a day for everyone to enjoy so please let us know if you have any dietary restrictions or require special accommodations."

Venue Considerations

While most venues, by federal law, must comply with the Americans with Disabilities Act (ADA), it's still a good idea to make sure the location you're considering meets your disabled guests' specific needs. This is especially important if you're considering a historic venue built before the ADA went into effect in 1990.

When you tour potential sites, check for the following:

- **Bathrooms:** Do the stalls provide ample room for a motorized wheelchair? Are there grab bars?

- **Building and room entrances:** Will guests of all abilities be able to enter and exit easily?

- **Elevators:** Does the venue have them? Do they work? Does the venue have a contingency plan for malfunctions during events?

- **Outdoor settings:** If you plan to have some or all of your event outdoors, will all your guests have easy access to chairs, tables, and gathering areas?

Don't limit your tour to the rooms where your event will take place. If you see any potential obstacles or challenges for disabled guests, talk with the venue. Are they willing to work with you to address them?

Food and Beverages

Food and drink typically are major elements of an event, but this is an area where accessibility issues can sneak in. If you've been thinking about offering a buffet or mini food stations, be sure to have a plan in place so all of your guests can peruse the selections and make a plate. A staff member or volunteer guest should be able to help.

You'll also want to talk with your caterer in advance if any of your guests have food allergies or intolerances, so they have safe alternatives and know which dishes to avoid.

Seating Strategies

Depending on your guests' needs, you may need to work with your venue to provide an extra buffer of space for those in a wheelchair or scooter.

If anyone on the guest list is visually impaired or has hearing loss, try to provide optimal seating so they can enjoy the celebration, speeches, and special moments. Guests with hearing loss may want a sign language interpreter. If you're not sure where to find one, Accessibility. com recommends starting with the Registry of Interpreters for the Deaf (rid.org).

While these suggestions aren't comprehensive, they should help jump-start your planning process.

YOUR ROAD MAP TO ARRANGING EVENT TRANSPORTATION

Getting yourself and your guests to your special event or family celebration on time may not be one of the first things you think about when you start your planning, but it is an important consideration.

There are plenty of reasons to line up transportation services. Here are some of the most common ones:

- You'd like to provide transportation for close family (parents, siblings, grandparents).

- Out-of-town relatives are more than 30 minutes away from your venue.

- Elderly or disabled relatives will need a ride to and from the party.

- You'd like to make a group trip to the event a fun part of the celebration.

And if you do need transportation, there are more decisions to make, from how much to spend to how to find the right service.

I've covered some of those things below, along with tips for lining up and working with transportation services.

1. Wondering who should pay? The bill could go to you, as the event doer, but you also might be able to share it with other family members or close friends of the party honoree(s).

   In any case, I encourage you to think about transportation early in your planning process and include it in your budget. Your costs will depend on the number of people you need to transport, the season, your location, and the type of vehicle you're considering.

2. Your options for transporting guests include limos, passenger vans, cars, a trolley, a party bus (usually has fun amenities from disco balls to light shows), and even a school bus. (Yes, some people rent school buses.)

3. As you select vehicles, remember that your guests, who likely will be dressed up and might be carrying a gift, won't want to be packed in like sardines. Don't aim to max out the space in a limo for 12 to 14 people. Find an option that matches your budget and keeps your guests comfortable.

4. If you will need transportation services, try to book them as soon as possible: right after you line up your location. This is especially important if your event will take place during the prom season or the holiday season.

5. Don't consider a transportation service unless they can show that they're licensed, insured, and have a great safety record.

6. Ask your event venue if they can recommend any transportation services. They may even have an agreement or partnership that can help you get a discount.

7. While you're talking with your venue about transportation options, have a conversation about parking for guests who transport themselves. Will valet parking be provided? Is there anything your guests should know in advance? Is overnight parking an option for those who've been drinking?

8. As you request quotes from potential transportation services, ask them to include gas, mileage, and tips so you can make sure your final choice remains within your budget.

9. As you would with any contract, read your transportation service's agreement carefully, including their policies for cancellations, refunds, hour minimums, overtime, and pickup and drop-off times.

10. Keep the people you'll be transporting in the loop. If you'll be providing transportation, share details about what you've lined up and timetables. Provide contact information for the service provider.

11. If you opt to transport multiple guests in one vehicle, make sure the driver has a complete list of the people they'll be picking up, along with their addresses and phone numbers.

12. Unless you have the budget to provide transportation for all of your guests, you should connect the people coming to your party

with the resources they'll need to line up their own transportation. Include details about public transportation, nearby hotels that offer shuttle services, and your venue's parking information.

13. If you're counting on guests being able to request a ride from Uber or Lyft, consider your location and make sure there's no risk of spotty cell phone service or limited drivers there.

14. Look into discount codes. A number of transportation services, from limo companies to rideshare programs, offer discounts for groups and special events.

CREATING A SEATING PLAN

If you're arranging a large family celebration, your seating plan might be one of the most intricate planning puzzles you'll solve. Arranging who sits where requires balancing family politics, keeping friends comfortable, and setting the stage for an enjoyable event.

Though seating planning might sound stressful, it doesn't have to be. This guide will walk you through everything you need to know.

What Is a Seating Plan?

A seating plan determines where guests sit during your celebration's seated meal. It's typically shown through escort cards displayed alphabetically or a seating chart poster guiding attendees to numbered tables.

Some event doers skip assigned seats, but arrangements carry essential benefits:

- **Mingling:** Clustering compatible guests sparks conversation. You want your friends and family to be relaxed and chatting during the celebration, not anxious and isolated.

- **Logistics:** Assigned seating makes serving courses easier for your catering team and wait staff.

- **Thoughtfulness:** Your loved ones feel moved when you devote hard work to arranging an ideal seating chart. The time and care spent demonstrate affection. Thoughtfully assigned seats say "you matter" without words.

When Should You Start on a Seating Plan?

Ideally, you should aim to finalize your guest list six months before your celebration. Use your venue's floor plan to craft seating arrangements four months out. Order escort cards and your seating chart two months ahead to allow time for calligrapher corrections.

You'll tweak the chart until the big day to accommodate evolving RSVPs. That's a normal part of planning a large celebration. As responses trickle in, adjust tables to fill seats.

Staying Stress-Free While Planning

Here are tips for making seating arrangements while keeping your cool:

- **Know perfection is impossible:** Not everyone will love the plan. Manage expectations, do your best, and let go of the uncontrollable.

- **Neutralize powder kegs:** Identify potential landmines like divorced parents and feuding relatives before detonations occur. Separate if needed.

- **Remember what matters most:** Focus on family members blending harmoniously and supportive friends reuniting. Everything else is logistics.

- **Build in breathing room:** Spread out planning over a few weeks to prevent last-minute fire drills. You want wiggle room in case life happens and you need more time than expected to finish your seating plan.

Getting Help from Family

Close loved ones can provide insight into long-standing feuds and alliances in your community. Early on, ask parents, siblings, and grandparents to review arrangements and share feedback.

That said, know when to stand firm if family disputes arise. Kindly say you want the day focused on love, not old fights. Explain why resolutions now would mean so much. With calm compromise, seating sparring can give way to open hearts.

Seating Charts

When it's time for the meal, guests will need to know where their assigned seating is. This is where seating chart posters come in: They illustrate how guests will be arranged at each of the numbered tables. These framed charts should be stationed near your event entrance.

Escort Cards

If you've assigned guests to specific tables and are allowing them to pick their seats there, escort cards can serve as a guiding compass.

These place cards display attendee names calligraphed on tent-folded cards in alphabetical order at a table near the event room's entrance. Guests find their cards and then see the table number notated inside.

More Ways to Direct Guests

Here are some additional options to point your guests in the right direction.

- **Place cards:** Set these directly on tables to help guests locate their seats.

- **Apps and signage:** Incorporate QR codes on items leading to digital seating charts. Or install monitor slides that rotate attendee table assignments.

Crafting the Kids' Table

Children add joyful energy to celebrations, but including them does call for some extra planning. Some event doers find that a separate kids' table, complete with activities, can make the celebration more fun for them. Fill the kids' table with engaging diversions so parents can enjoy adult conversations nearby. Consider providing:

- Coloring books and crayons

- Stickers

- Bubble wands

- Picture books

- Age-appropriate board games

Etiquette Considerations

A graciously woven seating chart demonstrates care for guests' comfort. Follow traditional guidelines to avoid unintentional snubs:

- Allow elders and VIPs to sit with minimal walking.

- Separate combative family members or exes sensitively.

- Don't scatter solo guests randomly. Pair or cluster considerately.

- Place engaged or longtime couples together.

- Set parents/children, aunts/uncles, and siblings side by side.

CREATING A BEAUTIFUL BRUNCH GATHERING

Planning a big celebration? Brunch is becoming an increasingly popular choice for all kinds of events, and for good reason. It offers a more relaxed vibe than a formal dinner, and it can be easier on the budget, too.

I've put together some factors to consider before opting for a brunch event, along with tips and ideas for making your event shine.

What You Should Know

First of all, while brunch is often a meal we enjoy after sleeping in, brunch events don't work that way. Starting your celebration late in the morning or early in the afternoon means all of your preparations will start early in the day. I'm talking really early, before the crack of dawn.

If you go this route, you'll need to convey timelines clearly with your guests, your venue, and all of the vendors you'll be working with.

A few more thoughts about your guests: A morning celebration may pose a challenge for some of them, depending on their work and family obligations. I recommend touching base with the people you'd like to invite before committing to a morning event.

Upsides to Morning Events

If formal evening affairs aren't your style, brunch events can be a nice compromise. In most cases, they're more casual. That applies to dress, décor, table settings—everything that impacts the celebration's atmosphere. (Of course, if you want a formal morning affair, no one is going to call the event police. Whichever way you go, the key is to communicate what you have in mind with guests, party honorees, and the businesses you're working with.)

You might be able to save on your venue costs by passing on the popular Saturday-night time slot, and brunch menu items can be less expensive than dinner selections.

Also, a morning event can contribute to a more child-friendly atmosphere, if that's a priority.

Children, in many cases, will be well-rested in the morning and in a better mood than they might be in the evening, with bedtime nearing. If you are going to welcome children, consider offering activities geared toward them. Maybe giant tabletop dominoes or a large Jenga game. Other popular options are coloring and LEGO stations, a scavenger hunt, and a kids' photo booth.

Tips for Success

If you decide to move forward with a brunch event, these suggestions can help.

First of all, select an optimal venue. Some venues have gorgeous décor and gardens that are perfect for a brunch gathering. As you research possibilities, try to schedule morning or early afternoon tours. And, of course, make sure they're available for morning events.

Don't make your guests wonder what to wear. Be very clear about your dress code on your invitations and event website (if you have one). Also, keep in mind that the definition of casual attire varies from person to person, so offer examples of what you envision, from colorful dresses and jumpsuits for women to a sports coat or pants and a button-down shirt for men.

Offer caffeine. Lots of it. I recommend setting up coffee stations and/or an espresso bar at your event. You can also provide paper coffee cups with customized sleeves.

Create a morning vibe. You have plenty of creative options. Consider citrus, songbird, or coffee-themed centerpieces. Have fun with playful signage. Possibilities include "Sip Sip Hooray! It's Brunch Day," "Espresso Yourself" or "Brew-tiful Mornings Start Here" for a coffee station, and "Spread the Love with Bagels" for a bagel station.

Think about morning-friendly entertainment for your celebration. Possibilities include games, a photo booth, a caricature artist or on-site artist, or a flower crown station.

You could also select brunch-themed favors. Give guests coffee and tea packages, or think about mason jars with premeasured waffle, pancake, or muffin mix and mix-ins.

The Food!

What's a brunch celebration without scrumptious food? Here are some tips.

- Don't forget your guests' needs and preferences. Just like you would with a dinner menu, you'll need to consider food allergies and dietary restrictions. And you'll want to aim for a variety of food choices that can satisfy eclectic tastes and preferences.

- Ask your caterer about food stations. Your options for brunches are endless, from omelets, pastries, and crepes to fresh fruit, donuts, and bagel food stations.

- Have fun with your appetizers. Think about crab cakes, deviled eggs, chicken-and-waffle skewers, mini breakfast pizzas, or bacon planks (bite-sized sweet or savory foods wrapped in bacon).

- Egg it up. Yes, omelets are great, but guests might also enjoy quiche, frittatas, eggs Benedict, eggs Florentine, or egg casserole.

- Have you thought about smoothie bowls? According to Peppersartfulevents.com, smoothie bowls are a rising trend. They comprise a smoothie base with such toppings as chia seeds, berries and fruits, nuts, granola, and coconut.

- Don't limit the selection to breakfast foods. Include salads, finger sandwiches, and proteins like salmon or beef strata.

- Offer appealing drinks. Popular options include mimosas, screwdrivers, Bellinis, and Bloody Marys. Guests also will appreciate juice, smoothies, and other nonalcoholic drinks.

- For dessert, offer light choices, possibly angel food cake, coffee cake, fruit tarts, yogurt parfaits, lemon sorbet, berry pavlova (a meringue-based dessert topped with whipped cream and a mix of berries), and/or mango mousse.

What You Should Know About Sunday Events

Sundays are a hidden gem for special events. They offer a break from the usual hustle and bustle, creating a more relaxed and intimate atmosphere for your guests.

Here, we'll take a closer look at scheduling events on a Sunday, including some pros and cons, along with tips for planning success.

Sunday Event Pluses

Sunday events can save you money. Venues usually charge their highest rates for Saturday night events simply because those are the time slots in greatest demand. Some caterers offer lower rates on Sundays, too, freeing money for other priorities like special entertainment or a custom video.

Another reason to consider a Sunday event is the overall vibe that comes with it. If the party atmosphere associated with Saturday night events isn't your thing, you may enjoy creating a family-friendly event or enjoying a beautiful outdoor setting on Sunday.

Challenges To Be Aware Of

Sunday events can be wonderful, but they do pose a few challenges.

First of all, you may find it a bit more difficult to line up vendors. Some vendors, especially those who do a lot of wedding work, limit themselves to one client per weekend. That means that if the videographer you're interested in already has a Saturday wedding gig, they may turn you down for your Sunday event.

What's more, a Sunday event won't necessarily be convenient for out-of-town guests, unless your event is taking place during a three-day weekend or it's not a problem for them to take Monday off for their trip home. I suggest touching base with guests who would need to travel before you finalize your event date. Beyond that, prepare yourself for some guests to decline your invitation or to leave your event early so they can return home at a reasonable time.

A few more thoughts on three-day holiday weekends: Holding a Sunday event during Memorial Day or Labor Day weekend has its own pros and cons. Most out-of-town guests can travel home on Monday, but they also will have to budget for more expensive airfare and hotel rooms on a holiday weekend. And the more affordable, non-Saturday venue rate you were looking forward to may not be available on a holiday weekend, when demand tends to increase. I'm not saying you should rule out holiday weekends, but you will want to weigh your options carefully.

Tips for You

If Sunday sounds like a good fit for your event, here are a few suggestions for planning success.

If your Sunday event coincides with a holiday weekend, create an event website with hotel options so guests can find the right fit for their tastes and budgets — even when rates are higher than usual.

Provide transportation resources if your event falls on a holiday weekend that impacts travel plans. Offering a shuttle service can be helpful for out-of-town guests. (Guests also will appreciate information about local attractions if they're coming to town for a longer stay.)

Theme Ideas

If you do go with Sunday, you might want to customize your theme — assuming you want one. For example, instead of a Hollywood theme, you could go with "Sunday Matinee" with popcorn and candy stations and a retro movie theatre décor.

Looking for something more formal? A traditional Sunday tea party theme with lush flowers, china, delicate pastries, and creative signage allows you to keep things elegant but earlier in the day.

Want to get guests on the dance floor? A Sunday Funday theme sets the stage for an upbeat celebration, complete with beer, lawn games, and a killer playlist.

Or … create a festival-style event with rustic elements and carnival games. Offer fresh lemonade, sausage on a stick, and funnel cake.

Remember, there is no "wrong" day to hold an event, and there is no reason why your Sunday celebration can't be an excellent, unforgettable occasion.

YOUR GUIDE TO PHOTO BOOTHS FOR EVENTS

Photo booths aren't exactly new — the first photo booth made its debut at the 1889 World's Fair in Paris — but their ability to make magic is as strong as ever.

That could be one of the reasons why photo booths, for years now, have been a popular feature at special events.

With that popularity in mind, I've created a guide for you with insights and tips for providing photo booths at large parties, weddings, corporate gatherings, and other special events.

What Is an Event Photo Booth?

The photo booth business has evolved quite a bit since the 19th century. The booths used at events are equipped with digital cameras and a printer so guests can get all the digital images they take then and there.

Are Photo Booths a Good Idea for Events?

Like most event elements, the decision to offer photo booths depends on the hosts' personalities, preferences, and overall vision for their event.

Here are some pros and cons of photo booths to help you make an informed decision:

Photo Booth Benefits

Event photo booths provide guests with a fun and interactive experience, and many organizers say they find photo booths worth the investment. For one thing, they are a great way to break the ice and engage guests during an event. People chat while they wait in line to take photos, and they show one another their prints. And, if you provide fun props, your guests can get a little silly and relax.

A photo booth can also support your event theme and infuse a sense of whimsy and creativity into your celebration. If you have a Texas event theme, for example, you can provide such custom props as cowboy hats, a chalkboard sign that says "Howdy," and bluebonnet backdrops.

For a 1970s disco theme, you can provide platform shoes, a disco ball, and signs with 70s sayings. The creative possibilities are endless.

Photo booths allow you to give your guests unique keepsakes, bringing joy to them long after your event. Guests will leave with unique photos: images that have special meaning to them. If the booth is for an anniversary celebration or graduation party, you can also send guests home with prints of the honorees.

Also, these booths are a highly effective way to create lasting memories of an event. Booths allow guests to capture relaxed, silly, and intimate moments that a photographer could miss.

Photo Booth Downsides

Depending on your budget, you may not want the additional costs of a photo booth rental—and any extras associated with it. If you line up a photo booth company to provide your photo booth setup, there could be charges to cover their transportation and mileage, and you'll need to provide them with a meal. You might also pay extra web-hosting fees for the photos available for digital download, along with charges for custom backdrops, professional lighting, specialized photo booth props, or other add-ons.

In most cases, long lines form for photo booths. Depending on your guest count and the size of your venue, that could be a concern.

And, in some cases, the appeal of the photo booths can be considered a downside—sort of. Sometimes guests get so enamored with taking photos at the booth that it can be challenging to get them out on the dance floor.

Do Photo Booths Save Photos?

Many photo booths store images in a folder on their hard drive. That means that you get all the photos your guests took as your unofficial event photographers. Many photo booth rental services provide customers with an online gallery or a USB drive with the images.

How Would I Get a Photo Booth?

You have several options. You can arrange a rental from a photo booth company. Typically, these companies handle your setup and run the booth. Rental services also provide technical support during your event (and after if you opt for digital downloads).

I'd also like to mention that The Bell Tower on 34th has its own photo booth rental service, which means you don't have to worry about arranging for a vendor to come to you.

What Types of Photo Booths Can Be Rented?

Here are some of the options available today:

- **Traditional:** Guests go inside a simple booth—giving them a bit of privacy—and pose for the camera.

- **Open-air:** This popular option is essentially a station where guests can take photos of themselves—minus the booth. A camera is set up on a tripod or table. One plus of an open-air photo booth is that it allows for custom backdrops.

- **Mirror:** This booth appears to be a full-length mirror, but it's actually a touch screen that can be used as a selfie station.

- **Slow-motion video:** This option lets guests create short clips in slow motion for a dramatic or comedic effect.

- **Green screen:** Do you think your guests would enjoy photos set in a far-off locale? Or a fictional setting? A green screen photo booth will make it happen.

- **360-degree:** This allows your guests to see themselves from all sides during their photo session. Guests tend to love these booths, but they do take up a lot of space.

- **GIF:** Some photo booth companies allow guests to make animated GIFs that can be shared on social media. This option is always a hit.

Talk with your photo booth service about the options they offer, pricing details, and good fits for your particular event and location.

Tips for You
Here are a few suggestions to inspire you:

Be creative with backdrops. If you go with an open-air photo booth, you can set up a photo booth wall with a backdrop that complements the overall vibe of your event or supports your theme. Below are a few backdrop ideas:

- A beautiful quilt
- Balloons
- Greenery
- A flower wall
- Colorful art
- Neon signs

- Interactive backdrops (chalkboard wall for drawing or magnetic board for posting photos and printouts)

- Projected images

- Balloon arch

- Paper flowers

- Fabric draping

- Geometric shapes

- Upcycled materials (old doors, windows, pallets)

Offer creative props. Masks are popular photo booth props, but you don't have to stop there. Other possibilities include wigs, mustache and beard props (you can find printable versions online), crowns and tiaras, giant sunglasses, or costumes.

Invite guests to add their own creative touches. Offer your guests chalkboard signs and let them take it from there. You can also encourage them to bring props with special meaning—possibly an enlarged photo of a pet or loved one—to pose with. Include a notice on your event website.

CHAPTER 2

Seasonal Celebrations

MAKE YOUR HOLIDAY PARTY A FEAST FOR THE SENSES

Have you been put in charge of holiday party plans for your company, organization, or family?

Don't stress out. A memorable event is within your reach.

Many of the successful holiday parties I see are a feast for the senses. Think about surrounding your guests with tantalizing aromas, a gorgeous venue decked out in glowing lights, and classic holiday music. By setting the right mood, you'll be able to put your guests in the holiday spirit.

Not sure where to start? These tips and ideas might help.

Start planning the party now.

If possible, I encourage you to start your planning early — ideally in the summer. That gives you enough time to create a budget, develop your ideas, and make all of your arrangements. The more time you give yourself, the less stressful the planning process will be.

Send creative invitations.

Set the tone for your party from the very start with fun, festive invitations. Get creative with shapes like snowflakes, trees, wreaths, or ornaments.

You can include clever wording like "Let's sleigh the holidays together!" and details like "Ugly sweater contest to follow."

Or send e-invitations with animated images, holiday tunes, or video clips to build excitement.

Put a twinkle in your guests' eyes.

Have you noticed that, in recent years, more and more houses are being decked out in lights well before Thanksgiving? While some may grumble when they see decorations go up "early," I understand what drives people to put them up. Few things evoke the holiday season like the glow of lights. They help set the mood. They're like comfort food for the eyes.

And when you're holding a holiday party, lighting will be one of the most effective tools you have to get people in the spirit of the celebration. Here are a few tips:

- For a warm, intimate setting, consider soft lighting — which, as a bonus, will make guests look even better in photos — and complement it with twinkling strings of lights in strategic locations.

- Candles, possibly as table centerpieces, can add to the overall effect. But don't put them in high-traffic areas, such as near buffet tables, where there's a risk of lit candles getting bumped or knocked down.

- Weave in other decorative touches, from traditional garlands and winter elements to more personal items like photos of guests or shared memories from the previous year.

When it comes to food, go for the oohs and aahs.

Food is always a powerful way to enhance your guests' experience and make your celebration linger pleasantly in their memories. This is particularly true for holiday parties because we associate so many holiday foods with positive memories.

"If the holidays are a time for family, then food and tradition are the ties that squeeze those families together," John Ingold wrote for *The Denver Post*. "Recipes are passed down through generations. Sometimes they are changed or lost, then revived and learned again. The goal isn't nutrition but continuity, a bond across the years."

You may not be able to replicate Aunt Ruth's amazing Hanukkah latkes or the bûche de Noël recipe your boss remembers eating as a child, but if you offer a selection of sumptuously made holiday classics, mixed with a few creative options (possibly Eggnog Cinnamon Rolls or a pizza wreath) to keep things fresh, you'll have a lot of happy guests on your hands.

A few more thoughts on what you serve: Your beverage selection will add to the flavor of the party, too. Again, classics (like eggnog or punch) are always strong choices, along with appealing nonalcoholic options like hot chocolate or holiday mocktails.

Music will matter.

Since holiday parties are sensory experiences, music plays an important role in creating ambiance. You have the option of bringing in a DJ or band, but if your planning time or budget is nearly spent, ask your venue if they can help you. They may be able to pipe in holiday music or help you present your favorite holiday party playlist.

Speaking of playlists, you can find options created specifically for office parties on Spotify. Or you can poll your guests in advance and invite them to make song suggestions. Either way, try to aim for an eclectic mix of new and classical selections that will appeal to a variety of preferences.

Don't forget the fun and games.

While setting the mood is important for holiday party success, don't forget to encourage fun.

You can enlist help in the form of a comedian, magician, or other professional entertainers.

Additional options include a photo booth and games.

Here are some game and activity ideas:

- **Naughty and nice:** Add some playful humor with a "naughty and nice" superlative game. As guests arrive, have them secretly vote for who is "most festive," "best holiday stylist," "biggest Scrooge" and other silly titles from your list. Announce the winners and hand out funny gag gifts.

- **Holiday trivia:** Compose trivia rounds about holiday movies, songs, traditions, foods, and general holiday facts. Give out mini candy canes or other small prizes to winners of each round. To get everyone involved, have guests write their own trivia questions and take turns reading them.

- **Ornament exchange:** Here's a thoughtful way to create take-home memories: Host an ornament gift exchange. Ask each guest to bring one or two wrapped ornament gifts. Draw numbers for a 1:1 exchange.

- **Gingerbread house competition:** Tap into your guests' creative and competitive sides with a fun gingerbread house decorating contest. Provide graham cracker gingerbread house kits along with loads of candy, cookies, pretzels, and other edible decorations. Give awards for the most realistic, most whimsical, and most ginormous houses.

- **Holiday karaoke:** Belt out the holiday hits at a Christmas karaoke bash. Rent a machine and get the carols rolling with songbooks featuring all of the season's standards. Award prizes for the best singing performances.

- **Snowball toss:** Bring a little bit of outdoor fun inside with a snowball toss game. Set up a snowman target and give guests soft plush snowballs or crumpled-up paper "snowballs" to throw. Give holiday treats as prizes.

- **Reindeer ring toss:** Try this Christmas twist on a classic party game by using reindeer-shaped rings. Set up poles decorated like reindeer with antlers. Give each guest a set of reindeer ring "halos" and let them take turns trying to toss a ring around each reindeer topper.

- **Snow globe making:** Hand out mini snow globe kits so your guests can create miniature worlds. Provide clear plastic globes along with figurines, confetti, glue, and decorative embellishments. Set out samples made by you so they can see the potential magic.

- **Christmas movie screening:** Entertain guests throughout your holiday party by screening a continuous loop of favorite holiday movie moments (or full movies) on a projector, TV, or other large screen. Choose a mix of nostalgic and modern classics. Hand out popcorn or movie candy and encourage reactions like booing the villain and cheering the heroes.

Set up a candy cane calm-down corner.

Guests who find themselves a bit frazzled at the holiday season will appreciate a little oasis with a "calm-down corner" filled with relaxing holiday ambiance. Play soft instrumental Christmas music and adorn the corner with candy canes and electric candles. Provide hot cocoa and cookies, too.

Try a creative theme.

Themed parties are a great way to delight your guests and to inspire your party-planning creativity. Maybe you'd like to have a Christmas movie theme that you incorporate into invitations, centerpieces, décor, food, music, and games. (I'll leave it up to you to decide whether to include *Die Hard*.) Additional possibilities include pajamas, a winter wonderland, or a giving-focused celebration.

Ultimately, planning a holiday party doesn't have to be overly complicated or stressful. If you focus on creating a cozy, welcoming atmosphere, aim for quality food, and work some merriment and fun into the day, your holiday party is likely to be a true crowd-pleaser.

Are you planning a Hanukkah celebration?

Want to give your holiday party a Hanukkah twist? Here are some tips for putting together a lively latke-filled bash to celebrate the Festival of Lights:

- Decorate with hanukkiahs (menorahs), dreidels, gold coins, and banners with Hebrew letters.

- Serve traditional fare like latkes, sufganiyot (Israeli donuts), brisket, and matzo ball soup.

- Play dreidel and hand out chocolate gelt coins as prizes.

- Set up carnival games like a menorah ring toss or Star of David bean bag toss.

- Light the menorah together and say the Hanukkah prayer.

- Give out Hanukkah-themed gifts like candles, gelt, or homemade olive oil soap.

- Share the story of the Maccabees and the miracle of the oil lamps.

- Play music from Jewish artists like Matisyahu or The LeeVees.

- Encourage guests to wear ugly Hanukkah sweaters.

Enjoy!

As you plan your holiday party, focus on festive details, playful activities, great music, delicious food and drinks, and, most importantly, gathering special people for a joyful, spirited celebration.

SUMMER CELEBRATIONS: INSPIRING IDEAS YOUR GUESTS WILL LOVE

Summertime, with its long days and warm nights, provides the perfect backdrop for celebrating life's big moments. Milestone birthday parties. Family reunions. Graduation parties. These gatherings create memories that last a lifetime.

Looking for inspiration to make your event sparkle? Here are some ideas to start with, along with some practical tips, to help you create a truly unforgettable event.

Selecting a Summer Theme

You have endless creative ideas available if you want to incorporate a theme into your event. Here are some possibilities:

- **Boho:** Bohemian event themes celebrate freedom of expression. They tend to have a hippie, artsy, adventurous vibe. You can create a bohemian atmosphere at your event by bringing a bit of nature into your décor. Earthy ideas include displaying wildflowers or dried flowers and creating backdrops of natural materials like linens, wood, and burlap. Aim for a color palette with natural tones including beige, brown, and burgundy. Set up retro wicker chairs—or invite guests to sit on floor pillows. On your tables, try macramé or wicker placemats, heavy glass goblets, and ceramic plates.

- **Beach:** You can't go wrong with the beach for your summer event theme. Aim for a light color palette and neutral accents in your décor. To create your beachy vibe, work in items you'd find at the beach—sunglasses, sand, starfish, or seashells. Just remember, less is more when it comes to these items. You can also arrange wicker chairs and couches topped with white and pastel cushions. Create the feel of a beach picnic by offering burgers, grilled meats, veggie kabobs, and ice cream. You can even set up a lemonade stand.

- **Pastels:** Pastels may be associated with the spring, but they work for any season, including summer. Create an ethereal vibe with soft shades of pink, purple, blue, yellow, peach, and more. You can add pastel touches to your invitations, signage, food, décor, favors—the list goes on. Create pastel centerpieces, and offer a decadent, pastel signature cocktail, possibly a hibiscus gin sour, which is pink, or peach cocktails adorned with edible flowers.

- **July 4th:** (You don't have to hold your event on Independence Day to use these ideas. They are fun options for any summer celebration.) Create a red, white, and blue color combo with your dining area chairs, tablecloths, and table runners or napkins. Choose a red signature cocktail and top it with blueberries. You can also use berries to add patriotic coloring to your desserts and other dishes. Additional July 4th ideas include working red roses into your floral arrangements and serving barbecue, hot dogs, s'mores, and other summery favorites.

- **Summer movies:** Display photos and other elements from some of your favorite summer blockbuster movies, from "Star Wars" to "Grease." Or you can go with movies that make us think of summertime, like "Some Like It Hot" or "Dirty Dancing."

Outdoor Event Themes

An outdoor event offers beautiful possibilities for integrating creative themes that enhance your venue's natural surroundings. Here are some popular outdoor themes perfect for summer:

- **Campground:** Get playful with a sleepaway camp-inspired theme using gingham, garlands, twinkling lights, and lawn games. DIY s'mores favors add sweetness.

- **Sunflower field:** For bright summer cheer, celebrate in an area surrounded by sunflowers and decorate with burlap, mason jars, and yellow and green accents.

- **Fire and ice:** Cool blue and silver with candlelight and fire pits creates an elegant outdoor theme.

- **Carnival:** Carnivals are another beloved summer tradition that can inspire creative event ideas. Set up booths with carnival games. Put up colorful displays of string lights. Offer popcorn and candy stations. You can create carnival centerpieces for meal tables with pinwheels, old-fashioned lollipops, and stuffed animals. If your budget allows it, go all out and rent carnival rides, such as a carousel or Ferris wheel.

Plan for Games

If you are having an outdoor summer event, use the space for games. They'll help your guests get to know each other and inject more fun into your celebration. You can rent Twister, giant Jenga sets, lawn croquet, and more.

Cool and Creative Touches

- **Embrace summery color schemes.** You can, of course, choose any color scheme for your event, but why not have fun with your choices? Summer is a season of vibrant colors: fuchsia, yellows, oranges, and light blues. You can use them to inject a sense of joy and excitement into your décor. Even if you're aiming for a more elegant, formal atmosphere, you have lovely color options, including pale pink, lilac, and pale yellow.

- **Try creative centerpieces.** Flowers are always a gorgeous option for summer decorations, but if you're not sure how they'll handle the summer heat—especially if you're holding an outdoor event—consider other creative options like candles, fresh produce, or elements that tie in with your theme.

- **Select décor strategically.** Try incorporating elements that add to the visual appeal of your event space and can help guests beat the heat. One option would be topping each place setting with an attractive paper fan.

- **Use oversized balloons.** Either colorful or elegant white, balloons can add an element of fun to your event space. Another fun option is to use balloons for your signage or to share whimsical messages with your guests.

- **Offer light menu options.** Avoid heavy options on your menu, and offer guests grilled fish or chicken, fresh fruits and vegetables, and other light dishes. This will be especially appreciated if you're holding an outdoor event. It's also wise to offer vegetarian or plant-based menu items.

- **Set up drink stations.** Add to the fun and atmosphere of your event with drink stations. One option is to offer a spot for nonalcoholic beverages like iced tea, juice, coffee, lemonade, and soda. You can also offer themed stations like a margarita station or a mimosa bar.

- **Get creative with ice cubes.** Add a pop of color and flavor to the summer drinks you offer by including pleasant surprises in the ice cubes, such as vanilla beans, berries, edible flowers, or herbs, to name just a few. You can also make cubes with fruit juices or alcohol that would complement your guests' beverages.

- **Set the ambiance with lights.** Lighting is a highly effective way to enhance the atmosphere of your event and create an inviting vibe. Try adding strings of lights to trees for a summer festival effect, or arrange clusters of lights to dangle from tree branches. Another lighting option is to set up chairs and sofas around tables topped with lanterns.

Dance All Night to Summer Tunes

If you'll be encouraging guests to get out on the dance floor during your event, you might want to incorporate some feel-good summer music into the playlist.

A few of the many possibilities include "Dancing in the Moonlight" by Toploader, "California Girls" by The Beach Boys, "Señorita" by Justin Timberlake, "The Boys of Summer," by Don Henley, "Red Red Wine" by UB40, "Mine" by Bazzi, and "Walking On Sunshine" by Katrina and the Waves.

Keeping Your Guests Comfortable

Holding an event in the middle of a hot summer day isn't necessarily ideal, especially in areas known for broiling temperatures. Try to develop your event timeline carefully, possibly in the late morning (brunch, anyone?) or early evening, to shield guests from the hottest part of the day.

Combine your strategic timing with strategies to keep your guests cool: Offer water and nonalcoholic drinks frequently to keep people hydrated; provide cushioned seating so people don't burn their legs or bottom on hot surfaces; and put mini water misters in each guest's chair.

Guests will appreciate sunscreen and bug spray, too.

Keeping the Children Safe and Happy

If children are attending your event, consider offering juices, Gatorade, water, Popsicles, and other drinks that they're likely to enjoy so they don't get overheated or dehydrated.

And if you've planned to offer outdoor games, add a few options that children might enjoy, or set up a kids' tent with coloring books, LEGO sets, hula hoops, and other fun options. You can add bean bags, rugs, or cushions where they can sit down.

Pick What Speaks to You

I know I've included more ideas than you can possibly use, but I hope you find some that are a good fit—and that they inspire you, ease your planning, and help you create a memorable event.

HOW TO PLAN AN UNFORGETTABLE PROM

Proms create memories that can last a lifetime.

But when you're on a committee responsible for pulling a prom together, the idea of creating a perfect event can be daunting, to say the least.

With that in mind, I've put together guidelines to help you along the way. Follow them to plan an unforgettable prom that all of the attendees will rave about.

The Planning Process

Coordinating a prom takes organization, creativity, and a fair amount of time. Give yourself at least three to four months to plan so you have time to get everything just right. Here are some tips to guide you:

- **Recruit a prom committee.** Get a responsible group of students (and possibly faculty members) together to brainstorm and delegate tasks. Aim for five to 10 people.

- **Make a budget.** Your prom planning committee will need to talk with your school administrators about your prom night budget. Factor in venue, food, décor, entertainment, attire, and any other applicable expenses.

- **Pick your prom's theme.** The prom theme ties all of your event's elements together. Brainstorm fun themes based on current pop culture or trends.

- **Find a venue.** Research venues that fit your budget and theme. Hotels, event venues, or even outdoor spaces can all work beautifully.

- **Handle logistics.** Figure out how students will get tickets and get to/from the venue. From there, plan your prom's decorations, food, and entertainment.

These are the fun details that make your prom a special night.

Your Prom Planning Checklist
To stay on track, use this helpful checklist while planning:

✓ Set a date

✓ Determine a budget

✓ Choose a theme

✓ Select a venue

✓ Hire entertainment (DJ, band, etc.)

✓ Organize ticketing

✓ Plan food and beverages

✓ Develop event schedule/timeline

✓ Arrange transportation

✓ Purchase decorations

✓ Assign subcommittees (décor, entertainment, food, etc.)

✓ Promote the event

✓ Make a photo area for pictures

Delegating Responsibilities
Prom requires too many moving parts for just one person to handle. Delegate these responsibilities to your prom planning subcommittees:

- **Venue:** This committee will research options, make a recommendation, and provide the school administration with details on costs and making a reservation.

- **Entertainment:** This committee is responsible for researching options and providing details on booking a DJ or band.

- **Food:** Committee members make food recommendations and provide details on lining up a caterer or purchasing snacks.

- **Decorations:** This committee will develop ideas based on the prom theme, then purchase or make the decorations.

- **Ticketing:** This committee manages ticket sales and collects money.

- **Transportation:** This committee is responsible for researching and organizing transportation services.

- **Promotion:** Committee members will make posters and social media posts to get the word out about prom night.

- **Photography:** Committee members will make recommendations for hiring a photographer and will set up picture-taking areas.

- **Safety:** This committee will arrange for chaperones and contact the police about providing traffic control.

The more tasks you delegate, the less overwhelmed you'll feel.

Selecting a Prom Venue
One of the biggest decisions you'll be making is where to host your prom. Here are some factors to consider:

- **Budget:** Some venues have minimum spends. Know how much you can spend.

- **Size:** Make sure the venue accommodates your expected number of guests.

- **Availability:** Reserve your venue six to 12 months in advance.

- **Amenities:** Many offer food, décor, a sound system, and more in one package.

- **Atmosphere:** Event venues, outdoor gardens, and historic buildings all have great ambiance.

- **Accessibility:** Ensure that the location you're considering is compliant with the Americans with Disabilities Act.

- **Location:** Consider travel time and transportation logistics.

- **Parking:** The venue should have adequate parking or valet arrangements.

Selecting Entertainment

The entertainment makes or breaks the event. Be sure to:

- Hire a DJ or band that plays current hits. I recommend giving them a do-not-play list, too.

- Check references: What kind of job have they done at other proms?

- See if they provide lighting, such as a disco ball.

- Request songs or genres ahead of time.

- Have a backup playlist just in case.

- Hire an emcee to pump up the crowd if you don't have a host at your venue.

- Consider live entertainment, like magicians or dancers, for the wow factor.

Planning a prom does take effort, but the payoff of giving your classmates a spectacular night will be incredibly rewarding.

CHAPTER 3

Milestones

CREATING A MEMORABLE QUINCEAÑERA

From the *festa de debutantes* of Brazil to the Jewish bat mitzvah, passage from girlhood to adulthood is a cause for celebration in cultures and countries around the world.

For many Latino families, that celebration is the quinceañera, a traditional and often religious rite of passage that takes place when a girl turns 15. The term *quinceañera* also refers to the celebrant herself.

With its showstopping dresses, rollicking parties, and fabulous cakes, in some ways a quinceañera is similar to a wedding reception. However, the quinceañera has its own unique traditions and rituals as well.

Here, we'll take a look at some of those elements and offer tips for successfully organizing a meaningful and memory-making event.

The Elements

- **A Catholic Mass.** Most Catholic churches will be able to accommodate a quinceañera ceremony, but if you have a home church you regularly attend, it might be special to hold your ceremony there if you can.

- **The presentation of the gifts.** We're not talking about the gift-giving that might take place at a wedding or birthday party; this presentation is part of the quinceañera ceremony. The honoree chooses her godparents, an important family member, or another special person in her life to present her with gifts, which often include a Bible, flowers, jewelry, a rosary, or another meaningful religious item.

- **The waltz.** A dance between the young lady and her father, this special moment is an important part of the quinceañera ritual. It symbolizes the girl's transition into adulthood and, once it's concluded, is her first chance to dance with other young men. This dance can also extend to the members of the quinceañera's court, composed of 14 young men and ladies, all friends of the guest of honor.

- **The rose ceremony.** This special element includes three roses that are presented to the quinceañera. Each flower is in a different stage of blooming: a rosebud, a half-opened rose, and one in full bloom. The young lady's mother presents the rosebud to symbolize childhood and innocence. The half-bloom will come from the quinceañera's godmother or grandmother, and it is meant to remind the girl of the importance of discerning right from wrong. The full bloom is presented by an older female relative to symbolize the fleeting beauty of youth and the importance of the soul.

- **The changing of shoes.** This honor is reserved for the young lady's father or another close male relative. He will replace her flat shoes with high heels, another nod to her passage to womanhood.

- **The *brindis.*** This is a toast offered by the guests to the quinceañera, conveying congratulations and well-wishes for the future.

- **The last doll.** This is yet another marker of a young girl's journey to adulthood. The quinceañera is presented with a keepsake doll, often dressed like her. This is to be the last of her childhood things, which she is to leave behind as she enters a new stage of her life. In keeping with tradition, the doll can be passed to a younger sibling.

Tips for Success

- **Budget carefully.** Figure out how much you can spend before you start considering venues, caterers, gifts, photographers, and other expenses. As you're compiling your budget, keep in mind that a quinceañera calls for as many as three dress changes: outfits for the ceremony, for the party, and in some cases, specifically for the dance. And that's not even getting into accessories, including tiaras and sashes.

- **Consider save-the-dates.** In today's busy world, your guests will appreciate as much advance notice as possible. A good rule of thumb is to send a save-the-date card six to nine months in advance.

- **Ask about your rescheduling options.** It's worthwhile to find out if your venue, and any other businesses you'll be working with, will allow you to cancel or reschedule, if necessary, without losing your deposits.

- **Communicate carefully with potential members of the court.** Like members of a wedding party, the friends who comprise the quinceañera court will have specific responsibilities they should be aware of before committing to participate. Court members, in general, attend dance rehearsals, dress formally (often in a ball gown or tuxedo or similarly fancy attire), attend the mass, are available for video shoots and photoshoots, and in some cases, help put together a surprise performance for the guest of honor.

For many teenage girls of Latin American heritage, their quinceañera is one of the most important days of their lives. Steeped in tradition, religion, and a whole lot of fun, a quinceañera marks a major turning point in a girl's life, and your planning should reflect that importance.

12 IDEAS FOR A MEMORABLE RETIREMENT PARTY

When you think of a retirement party, do images of cake and someone receiving a gold watch come to mind?

Not that there's anything wrong with cake and gifts, but a retirement party can be much more than that. It's a chance to celebrate a major life event, a transition from one chapter to another.

These parties also allow people to tell a retiring guest of honor how much he or she means to them. And retirement parties provide a way to spotlight the impact the retiree has made, whether it was through the work they did or by being a source of encouragement for co-workers.

If you're going to be throwing a retirement party soon, I have some suggestions that can help you make your event truly memorable for the person you're honoring and their guests.

1. **Have a theme.** Pick something meaningful to your guest of honor, whether it's a favorite college football team, a passion for the environment, or their plans to restore classic cars during their

retirement years. You could decorate with memorabilia from their career or hobbies, create a playlist featuring their favorite musical artists, or serve food and drinks inspired by their interests. For example, if they love to travel, transform the party space into a tropical destination or a European city they've always wanted to visit, with related décor, music, and cuisine.

2. **Back to that cake...try something creative.** You can work with a cake artist to design something that refers to the retiree's career, like a chalkboard design for a retiring educator. Or go with a cake that looks like a globe to wish the retiree happy travels. You can even have a sandcastle with edible sand to suggest carefree days relaxing at the beach.

3. **Encourage toasts and speeches.** Invite a few special people— close colleagues, managers, family, or anyone else with a positive story to present—to give a prepared speech. Follow up with an invitation for guests to come up and share a special memory or favorite story.

4. **Display photos.** Try to round up photos of the guest of honor from over the years. You don't have to limit yourself to work pictures—shots of them on their own time or even from childhood are great, too. Arrange the photos where guests can see them, or present a video compilation.

5. **Have a video booth.** Ask guests to record video messages with memories, jokes, and well-wishes for the retiree, and have them compiled. A photo booth is another great way to infuse fun and special memories into the party.

6. **Get creative and have a costume party.** Going outside of the traditional retirement party box with something fun, creative, or even silly can make the celebration more enjoyable for the honoree and the guests. One way to accomplish that is a costume party. You can tie costumes in with your overall party theme or with something else that's important to the retiree, maybe a favorite movie, hobby, or music genre.

7. **Play games.** This is, after all, a celebration. Retirely.com suggests such games as Name That Tune or a trivia game. Another possibility is a game called Two Truths and a Lie, in which participants make three statements about themselves, only two of which are true, and players have to guess which is the fib. You can also rent games like cornhole or a giant Connect Four set.

8. **Pass around an autograph book.** Do you remember having people sign your autograph book or yearbook? Why not do something similar for the retiree? The exception here is that they won't have to ask people to sign; you can do that for them. In the end, they'll have a keepsake filled with touching and funny messages.

9. **Have people sign a photo album.** In your invitation, ask guests to bring photos of themselves with the retiree, or their favorite pictures of the guest of honor, to the party. At the celebration, they can add their photo(s) to an album and sign near it.

10. **Create a bucket list.** Ask co-workers to suggest experiences, activities, travel spots, and other ideas for things people can enjoy after retirement—the more creative the better—and present them as a gift at the party.

11. **Make a retirement playlist.** You have a surprisingly large selection of songs to consider. If you'd like to include humorous touches, go with "Work is Overrated" by Chicago Skinny or "Hit the Road Jack" by Ray Charles. You can also weave in songs that point to a relaxing or satisfying retirement, like "Vacation" by the Go-Gos and "Come Sail Away" by Styx.

12. **Make a video of the party.** The retiree and their loved ones will want to return to this day and the moments of appreciation, respect, and affection expressed by guests.

GRADUATION PARTY ETIQUETTE: HOW TO PLAN A MEMORABLE CELEBRATION

Graduation is an exciting milestone that deserves to be celebrated. As a parent of a graduate, you may be planning a party to commemorate this special achievement.

While decisions like the optimum venue, the best food for a graduation party, and who should be on the guest list will shape your event, etiquette has an important role to play in the graduate's special day, too.

Here are some etiquette tips to guide you, along with some overall planning ideas.

Set the Date

First things first: Choose a date for your graduation party and secure your event venue. Late May and June, after diplomas are handed out, are typical graduation party months.

Before you make a final decision on a date, check your graduate's schedule and factor in potential conflicts like final exams, vacations, or siblings' events.

Invitations

Once you've chosen a date, order invitations. Your invites should go out four to eight weeks in advance.

On your invitation, specify whether the celebration starts with dinner or if it's a dessert and drinks format.

I recommend setting an RSVP date that falls two weeks or more before your party.

Invitations can be mailed, emailed, texted, or posted on social media. Have your graduate review the guest list to be sure no friends are overlooked.

Encourage RSVPs

If you send print invitations, consider adding RSVP cards with self-addressed, stamped envelopes for guest responses.

As an alternative to RSVP cards, you can provide an email RSVP address or a phone number to text replies to, or you can use online RSVP tools, which make it easy for guests to select "Yes" or "No" for the party.

Phone calls work for a very small event, but I would avoid asking for verbal RSVPs from dozens of guests; you're likely to forget responses.

Use Social Media and Reminders To Get Responses

Social platforms are ideal for sharing party details. You can create a Facebook event page and invite guests to respond. Post party specifics on your grad's social media accounts, too.

Email and text reminders a week before the RSVP deadline, saying something like this:

"We look forward to seeing you at Maddie's graduation celebration on June 4 at 7 p.m. at The Bell Tower on 34th. Please remember to RSVP by May 28. You can call, text, or email me your reply. Thanks!"

Timely nudges like this increase your RSVP rate so you can finalize food, seating, and plans.

Planning Guidelines

Planning a stress-free graduation party requires organization and strategic decision-making. Here's how you can streamline the process and alleviate unnecessary worries:

- **Set a realistic budget.** Determine your budget early on and stick to it. This will serve as a guiding principle for all your planning endeavors, helping you prioritize expenses and avoid overspending.

- **Start early.** Begin planning well in advance to avoid a last-minute rush and make sure everything falls into place smoothly. Create comprehensive checklists outlining all the essentials, from venue bookings to décor items, and begin your preparations at least one to two months ahead. Ordering early will be important, especially for popular party rentals and services that may get booked quickly.

- **Involve the graduate.** Don't overlook the importance of the graduate's input in shaping the party's ambiance and theme. Solicit their preferences for the menu, music playlist, and decorative elements so their personality shines through on their special day.

- **Make excellent food a priority.** While planning the menu, aim for convenience without compromising on quality. Consider catering options like buffet-style meals or preprepared platters that minimize the need for extensive kitchen work during the party. Ordering a cake or dessert tray from a bakery not only adds a sweet touch to the celebration but also frees you up from spending valuable party time in the kitchen.

- **Delegate responsibilities.** Don't hesitate to enlist friends and family members to help with tasks on the day of the event. That might include setting up decorations, managing the guestbook, replenishing food and beverages, or a wealth of other duties. Sharing the workload not only eases your burden but allows everyone to enjoy the celebration without undue stress.

Etiquette Dos and Don'ts for Graduation Parties

A graduation party brings together family, friends, mentors, and classmates of varied ages. Follow traditional etiquette and use common sense to keep things comfortable for all of your guests.

Do:

- Officially introduce the graduate to each guest.

- Give older relatives reserved chairs with backs.

- Serve nonalcoholic drinks for underage guests.

- Play music suitable for the age range attending.

- Provide options for guests with food allergies and dietary needs, and provide signage to help guests navigate their food options.

Don't:

- Have the graduate open gifts in front of guests (do this privately later).

- Assume all guests know each other; facilitate conversations.

- Serve alcohol to anyone under legal drinking age.

Making Guests Feel Welcome

Ensuring the comfort and inclusivity of your guests is paramount to hosting a successful graduation party. Here are some thoughtful strategies to make everyone feel welcome:

- **Venue accessibility:** Opt for a venue that is easily accessible, particularly for elderly relatives or guests with mobility challenges. Avoid locations with stairs or long walks from parking areas to minimize discomfort for older attendees.

- **Ample seating:** Provide sufficient seating arrangements throughout the party venue to accommodate guests of all ages and preferences. Include high-top cocktail tables for casual mingling and chairs strategically placed around food stations to offer respite for tired feet.

- **Designated zones:** Create designated areas within the venue to cater to varying social dynamics. For instance, a separate space or lounge area would allow shy teens to gather away from the main crowd while still feeling included in the festivities.

- **Personal greetings:** Make sure each guest receives a warm welcome by having the graduate personally greet them upon arrival. This simple gesture helps to alleviate any feelings of awkwardness and sets a friendly tone for the event.

- **Clear signage:** Guide guests through the party space by strategically placing signage directing them to essential areas, including food stations, beverage stations, restrooms, and entertainment zones like photo booths or dance floors.

- **Diverse music selection:** Appeal to a broad range of musical tastes by curating a playlist that encompasses multiple genres and eras. Then guests of all ages will be able to enjoy the music—and they'll be more likely to hit the dance floor.

- **Volume control:** Strike the right balance between setting ambiance and fostering comfortable conversation by maintaining a moderate volume level for background music.

Speeches

Graduation party speeches offer a platform for loved ones to express their heartfelt sentiments and extend well-wishes to the graduate. Here are some etiquette guidelines:

- **Less is more.** Keep guests engaged by limiting speeches to two or three short shares at most. Schedule speeches during dinner or at a designated time to allow guests the freedom to mingle without feeling constrained by prolonged addresses. Along the same lines, encourage speakers to prepare speeches of two to five minutes maximum to maintain audience engagement and prevent monotony.

- **Factor in audibility.** If you're hosting the party in a large venue, provide a microphone so everyone can hear no matter where they're sitting.

- **Consider the audience.** Encourage speakers to tailor their speeches to suit the diverse audience present at the party and to keep their comments family friendly. I would encourage them to safeguard the celebratory nature of the occasion by refraining from delivering lectures on controversial topics.

- **Aim for a moment of special recognition.** If applicable, invite the graduate's mentor, such as a coach or teacher, to deliver a speech. Their words can add a personal and meaningful touch to the celebration.

Thank-You Note Etiquette

Expressing gratitude is always in style. After the party, the graduate should send thank-you notes to those who attended, gave gifts, or helped organize the event.

Printed or handwritten notes should go out within two to four weeks of the party. Emails or text messages can work, too, but formal notes make a lasting impression.

The graduate should mention specific gifts they appreciated or kind acts like giving a speech or baking a cake.

Gracious manners regarding gifts given, time shared, and heartfelt wishes expressed will be remembered long after graduation tassels turn.

6 COOL WAYS TO ADD MAGIC TO YOUR PARENTS' ANNIVERSARY PARTY

Do your parents have a big anniversary coming up? Hosting a party for them is a wonderful way to celebrate their commitment to one another — and express your love and appreciation for them.

And you have all sorts of options for making your parents' celebration meaningful. You can weave in sweet design touches, add elements of nostalgia, or make dramatic, showstopping gestures. Or … you can aim for all of the above.

Here are a few suggestions to get you on your way.

1. Start with a theme.

Selecting a theme gives you a great starting point for cultivating fun party ideas. You can always tie the party in with the number of years your parents have been married. The Spruce, for example, suggests a pearl-themed 30th-anniversary party, incorporating the traditional gift for three decades of marriage.

"It's easy to go elegant with a pearl theme, with opalescent or sea blue linens, seafood, and, of course, oysters," Spruce writer Jackie Burrell points out.

Or, if the party is commemorating 50 years of marriage, you can go gold with décor, invitations (try gold ink, but make sure it's dark enough to be legible—if their guests are old enough to be married 50 years, too, they might have trouble seeing light-colored type), songs ("golden oldies"), gold-foil-wrapped chocolates on the tables, gold-framed photos, and floral arrangements filled with yellow flowers and gold sprays.

You can also consider:

- Spotlighting the year or decade your parents were married with music, images, and videos from that era. Incorporate pop culture references—think 1960s-era tie-dyed shirts or '70s mood rings—into centerpieces.

- Did your parents go somewhere romantic on their honeymoon? Display flowers from the Hawaiian island they visited, or work with your caterer to serve the foods they enjoyed during their first trip as a married couple.

- If your parents have a shared interest they're passionate about, from travel to golf, let that inspire your music, décor, and food choices.

2. Weave in special memories.

Photos are a powerful way to share memories of your parents' romance, their wedding, and the life they created together. Here are just a few ways you can put vintage photos to work:

- Create photo centerpieces or photo walls for your parents and guests to enjoy.

- Assign each table a decade and display photos that help illustrate that time in your parents' lives.

- Invite guests to sign a photo album or book that will be presented to your parents, or have partygoers sign a framed photo of your parents.

- Bring in a photo booth with props that reflect the era when your parents met or married.

- Use a wedding photo of your parents to create a life-sized cardboard cutout for photo ops.

- You can capture special memories by showing home movies, if they're available, playing music from the year your parents married (or songs from their wedding).

- Or create a display of other special items from your parents' wedding day including your mother's gown, wedding and shower invitations, and wedding announcement clips from their local newspaper.

- Another popular option is a chalkboard displaying news; fads; and the average costs of gasoline, rent, and food during the year your parents married.

3. Get the president to send their regards.

If you think your parents would like it, you can arrange to get them an anniversary greeting from the White House. Ideally, you should start this process several months in advance, but no less than six weeks before the anniversary date. And you'll need to follow a few rules:

The honorees must be U.S. citizens, and your request must include the following:

- Name and home address of honoree(s)

- Form of address for the honorees: Mr., Ms., Mrs., Dr., etc.

- Exact date of occasion (month, day, year)

- Number of years of marriage

- Requestor's name and daytime phone number

- Any specific mailing instructions

You have several options for submitting your request. First, you can go through the office of your U.S. representative or one of your U.S. senators. On their website, click on "Constituent Services," or, if you can't find that option, email your lawmaker through their website email form. *Be sure to mention that you want "Presidential Greetings."*

You can also make the request through the White House contact form and follow up by calling the White House "Comments" number at 202–456–1111.

Or mail your request to:
The White House
1600 Pennsylvania Avenue NW
Washington, D.C. 20500

Just remember, while the White House attempts to respond to as many requests as possible, there's no guarantee you'll get your greeting. So if I were you, I'd have more than one anniversary surprise up my sleeve.

4. You can always pay a celebrity to wish them well.

This option is more foolproof than getting a greeting from the president, but there's also a cost involved.

Services like Cameo allow you to pay participating celebrities, from musician Dionne Warwick to actor Brent Spiner, to create a personalized video message. The site provides each participant's cost and how much advance notice they require, along with a form for making your request.

In addition to actors and musicians, you can find athletes, comedians, political leaders, gamers, and more on Cameo.

5. Get them on the news.

If your parents are celebrating a big anniversary, you might be able to get an article or announcement about them, with a photo, in your community newspaper.

In Houston, for example, *The Leader* newspaper shares articles about local residents celebrating anniversaries. Local TV news shows might be willing to help, too, even national shows. And you can always save the coverage and share it at the party. Most venues can accommodate your audiovisual needs.

6. Enlist a creative type.

Few things say romance like poetry. So why not commission a poet to pen something special in honor of your parents' lasting love? You can find writers willing to help on Etsy and on poetry sites.

Be sure to ask the writers you're considering to provide you with examples of their work.

And if poetry isn't your parents' thing, you can hire a quilter, artist, or songwriter to create something special for them.

The general idea is to add personal touches to your parents' party, whether it's displaying a beloved photo, sharing a cool or touching message, or giving them a special something made just for them. Whatever you decide to do, you'll be illustrating your love for your parents in an unforgettable way.

FAMILY REUNIONS: PLANNING TIPS THAT WILL MINIMIZE YOUR STRESS

If you think trying to get 10 or 20 relatives together for the holidays is problematic, how does the idea of wrangling thousands of them sound? Somehow, writer A.J. Jacobs pulled it off.

In June 2015, he managed to bring together more than 3,700 close, distant, and really, really distant relatives for a massive gathering, the Global Family Reunion, at the New York Hall of Science. The theme was "We're all part of one big family."

Jacobs' reunion tied in with an even larger effort: an attempt to build a family tree of the entire human race. He wrote about the project in his book "It's All Relative: Adventures Up and Down the World's Family Tree."

Ultimately, Jacobs succeeded in creating an incredibly cool gathering—Sister Sledge even sang "We Are Family" there—but his take on the day may resonate with many other family reunion organizers.

The reunion, Jacobs told *The Guardian*, like many things involving family, was complicated. He described it as "Horrible. And great. It was the best worst day of my life."

As Jacobs' experience attests, planning a family reunion is equal parts excitement and stress, apprehension and thrill. And those emotions apply regardless of the scale of the event. Even if you're not rounding up thousands of third, fourth, and fifth cousins on genealogy sites like Jacobs did, arranging any family gathering can be formidable. But there are ways to make your role as an organizer a bit easier.

Start the planning process far in advance.

You'll want to give yourself a huge reserve of wiggle room to reach your relatives, let them know you're planning a reunion, and get their feedback on its timing and location. People will need time to figure out when they can get vacation time from work and make sure there aren't other conflicts. And you'll need lots of time to get everyone's input and move the planning forward.

Most event pros and family reunion-organizing veterans say this process should start at least 12 to 18 months in advance.

Also, it's important to keep your expectations in check when it comes to finalizing your date(s): It's very unlikely that you'll find a window of time that works for everyone. Aim for something the majority of your family can work with.

Becca Robins, creator of the "Love Our Crazy Life" blog, wrote that she learned the hard way about the difficulties of getting relatives to agree on a date when she planned a weekend gathering for her parents, all seven of her siblings, and their families. As a result of that stressful experience, she changed her approach to organizing family gatherings.

"The next one I planned, I chose three weekends and asked which ones worked best for others," Becca said. "Rather than stress on finding a weekend when everyone could be there, I chose a weekend most people could be there. It helped a lot."

Create and stick with a budget.

Before you delve into planning, you'll need to know how much money you'll have to work with and who's pitching in to pay for the event. Are family members willing to chip in a set amount so you can rent a venue, hire a caterer, or go on an outing together?

In the case of large events, organizers typically collect contributions early in the planning stages, open a reunion checking account, and assign a "finance director" to maintain the budget and handle expenses.

If you and your family have something expensive in mind, like a cruise or overseas gathering, you can always hold some fundraisers like garage sales or car washes to help cover your expenses.

Select your location strategically.

The same approach for date selection can apply to determining your reunion location: Give your family members three or four options and go with the place that works for the majority. If you and your relatives, like many families today, are spread out across the country, there are online tools available to help you find central locations.

PARTIES AND SPECIAL EVENTS

In any case, developing your location suggestions will require some time, research, and initial input from the family.

A few factors to keep in mind:

- Will the location work for a wide range of budgets? Think travel-related expenses (from airline tickets to car rentals to hotels, campgrounds, or resorts) and the circumstances of those attending. Your single cousin may find it easier to pay for a flight than your brother, sister-in-law, and their three children.

- Are any of the hotels, lodges, resorts, vacation home rentals, or campgrounds in the area willing to provide you with a group discount?

- How about food: Will your relatives have access to restaurants? Will they be able to buy groceries and prepare meals where they stay?

- If you want to rent an event venue for a day or an evening, how many people can it accommodate? Is it conveniently located? Are area restaurants and attractions nearby?

I also encourage you and your relatives to make all of your reservations early, including hotels and your venue. That will prevent the disappointment of anyone being left out or of your having to scramble to come up with alternative plans.

Keep the lines of communication open.

Once the reunion dates and location are settled, get the details to family members as soon as possible.

Aim to mail invitations or save-the-date cards to family members a few months ahead of time. It's also a good idea to send text messages or make phone calls about a month before the reunion to remind attendees it's getting close and make sure they're still planning to be there.

But your communication shouldn't stop there. You should stay in contact with your relatives throughout your planning process and invite their input.

If you're planning a catered meal, ask family members about preferences, allergies, and dietary restrictions.

Before mapping out activities, ask relatives what they and their children would enjoy. Tell them what you've been considering.

Don't be afraid to ask for help.

Depending on the size of your reunion, on your aspirations for games and activities, and on your ability to pull everything together while juggling your usual work and life responsibilities, you may benefit from the help of other family members. Look to individuals or committees to handle activities, supervision, and activities for the children attending; correspondence with family members; food; lodging; décor; administration (keeping track of paperwork and reservations); and even gathering photos and family mementos to display.

You can seek help by emailing a sign-up sheet with key tasks, or, if you feel more comfortable entrusting specific tasks to specific people, contact relatives individually and ask for their assistance.

Be prepared for things to go wrong.

One thing I've learned during my years in the events industry is the importance of preparing for the unexpected. Life happens. At a family gathering, that could range from someone forgetting to bring the family reunion bingo game they promised to technical difficulties interfering with the video you hoped to present.

Some things simply can't be helped, but there are steps you can take to ensure success no matter what happens.

- Expect uncooperative weather. If outdoor games and activities are part of your reunion itinerary, line up a location, possibly a pavilion, where family members can take shelter. Have some board games, crafts, or other activities ready.

- Bring just-in-case items. These could include:
  - One or more first aid kits
  - Extra phone and laptop chargers
  - A backup camera for getting quality pictures or videos
  - Extra bottled water
  - Nonperishable snacks
  - Climate-appropriate supplies, whether that's sunscreen and insect repellent or hand warmers

- Make sure you've got their number. I'm talking about flight numbers, reservation numbers, and phone numbers (relatives and venues).

Don't forget to have fun.

Organizing a large event can get stressful, and yes, family gatherings can get complicated. But they can also be incredibly rewarding. They provide a chance to better understand yourself and your family's history. To connect with people you may not have seen since childhood (or, like Jacobs, ever). To make cherished memories.

So, yes, plan carefully. But please give yourself a chance to be in the moment and relish your time with family.

Hopefully, your reunion will be one of the best times you've ever had.

WANT TO INCLUDE YOUR PET IN YOUR EVENT? IT'S PAWS-IBLE—WITH CAREFUL PLANNING

A dog named Ollie managed to move TikTok viewers to tears as they watched him respond emotionally to a video of his human parents' wedding. Not only was Ollie transfixed by his "mummy and daddy" in the heartwarming clip, but also by footage of himself: He was an honored participant in their nuptials.

A *Newsweek* article about Ollie's TikTok fame noted that it's not at all unusual for dogs to be part of weddings.

"In a 2022 survey of 2,000 dog owners, commissioned by Amazon Handmade and conducted by OnePoll, 60 percent of respondents said they knew someone who had their dog at their wedding while 76 percent believed guests would react positively to having a canine involved."

And if people are finding ways to include their pets in their wedding—with some even welcoming their fur babies into their wedding party or inviting them to walk down the aisle—why not include them in other important celebrations like a milestone anniversary or birthday party?

Having your dog (or even your cat) be a part of a special day can be a fun and memorable way to celebrate. But it does require some extra planning and precautions to make sure it's a positive experience for everyone involved, including your pet.

With that in mind, I've put together a guide on how to safely and smoothly involve your pet in important events, from weddings to large family celebrations.

Reasons to Include Your Pet

People's reasons for including their furry friends in their events can run the gamut from sentimental reasons to the desire to make their special day unique. Here are some reasons why having your pet at your event may be the right fit for you.

- **They're family.** Many people think of their dogs and cats as children. So naturally they want their beloved pet to be present at major life events.

- **In the case of a wedding,** they're part of the love story. Maybe you and your partner got your pet together early in the relationship. Or your pet played matchmaker. Including them in your wedding pays homage to the role they played in your love.

- **You want the photo opportunities.** Pets often make for adorable photos that you'll treasure forever. And they add variety to typical wedding and event shots.

- **You want to honor a deceased fur baby.** You may want to pay tribute to a beloved pet that has passed but was an important part of your life.

Factors to Consider

If you're planning to include your dog or cat in your wedding or big celebration, there are some important things to take into account:

- **Breed and personality:** Consider your pet's breed, age, health, and personality. High-energy dogs or very anxious pets may not be suited for wedding duties or handling all the commotion of a large birthday party.

- **Training:** Untrained animals are risky in large crowds or at important moments. Be sure your pet has mastered basic obedience commands so you can redirect them as needed.

- **Comfort level in crowds and travel:** Make sure your pet is comfortable around lots of people and can handle travel to the event location. If not, they may be better off sitting it out.

- **Needs and schedule:** Be sure to plan for things like potty breaks, feeding schedules, nap time, and walks to keep your pet happy on the big day.

Doggie Dos and Don'ts

If you will have your dog present at your wedding or celebration, follow these dos and don'ts:

Dos: Steps to Create a Positive Experience

- Keep your dog leashed and attended at all times. Don't let it roam loose.

- Bring water, food bowls, and potty supplies. Have what your dog needs so it's comfortable.

- Offer your dog breaks in a quiet area. Give it a place to rest and get away from the noise when necessary.

- Introduce your dog to venues/vendors in advance. Let it get familiar with the setting before the big day.

- Touch base with close friends and family on your guest list (and your wedding party, if applicable) to see if having your fur baby at the event will make them uncomfortable or trigger an allergy reaction.

Don'ts: Pitfalls to Avoid

- Don't leave your dog unattended. Don't tie it up alone or let it get loose.

- Don't let it eat anything that could make it sick. Keep it away from event food, drinks, and floral arrangements.

- Don't tire it out pre-event. You don't want it exhausted. Moderate exercise is better.

PARTIES AND SPECIAL EVENTS

- Don't expect perfect behavior all day. Be prepared for some misbehavior, like jumping or barking.

- Don't dress your dog up unless you know it will tolerate it. Test-run any costumes or accessories.

Including Cats on Your Special Day

If felines are your furry friends of choice, you can still include your cat in your festivities. But cats tend to be a bit less social and tolerant than dogs when it comes to crowds and commotion. Here are some tips for safely involving your kitty:

- Consider your cat's personality. Shy, anxious cats will likely get overwhelmed. Confident, social kitties may enjoy the attention.

- Keep participation short and limited. Have a trusted helper carry your cat down the aisle at your wedding, or arrange a kitty cameo appearance at your party. Avoid long duties or honors.

- Designate a cat handler. Choose someone your cat knows well to oversee its needs during your event.

- Set up a secure side room. Offer your cat a private, quiet space with food, a litterbox, and hiding spots to retreat to.

- Use leashes and carriers. Keep your cat under control and contained when out and about. Decorated cat carriers work well for kitty ring bearers.

- Give breaks often. Make sure your cat has chances to rest calmly and quietly away from guests and noise.

- Avoid costumes. Only dress your cat up if you know it will tolerate it. Test ahead of time.

- Check with the venue and vendors. Notify them that a cat will be present, in case of allergy issues.

- Limit handling. Don't pass your cat around to guests too much if it's easily stressed by strangers.

- Prep backup plans. Be ready to remove your cat or modify duties if it gets overwhelmed or agitated.

- Consider just photos. For some cats, snapping some photos together may be better than actual event inclusion.

How to Include Your Pet Without Its Presence

If your pet isn't suited for attending your event, or you'd rather spare it the commotion, there are countless ways to include your pet in spirit. Here are a few creative ideas to consider:

- **Photos and paintings:** Display framed photos of you and your pets around your venue. Commission a custom pet portrait for your wedding wall.

- **Table place cards:** Have place cards with photos of your pet to represent where people should sit.

- **Signage and décor:** Work your pet into custom signage, such as a "reserved" sign on its designated seat. Have floral arrangements that feature its favorite treats, toys, or colors.

- **Signature cocktails:** During your cocktail hour, offer a signature drink named after your pet or favorite breed.

- **Pet groom's cake/wedding cake:** Have a small pet-themed cake in addition to a traditional cake.

- **Speeches and toasts:** Mention your pet in toasts, thanking those who helped you find love.

- **Donations:** Make a charitable donation to a local animal shelter or pet cause in lieu of favors.

Photos with Pets

Getting great photos with pets takes a bit of extra planning:

- Do a pre-event photoshoot. Get your pet accustomed to the photographers and their equipment beforehand.

- Schedule the pet photos first. Do them before your pet gets tired out, so you can get their best behavior.

- Have treats on hand. Use favorite snacks to capture your pet's attention and happy expressions.

- Use squeakers and toys. Get playful shots by including your pet's favorite fetch toys.

- Pick a suitable location. For the best shots, choose areas without major distractions or room to roam.

- Have your pet primped beforehand. Give it a bath and a brushing close to photo time so it looks its best.

- Include your photographer in the planning. Let them know you want pet shots, so they can make time for it.

- Do posed shots and candids. Get some traditional photos, but also capture your authentic interactions.

- Use child props if needed. If your pet is small enough, hold or place it in a wagon, stroller, or bike basket for cute poses.

- Patience is key. Be prepared to spend time getting the perfect pet photo. Frequent breaks may be needed.

HONORING A LOVED ONE DURING YOUR EVENT

Shortly after Joanna lost her mom at age 22, she made plans to wear her mom's gown at her upcoming wedding. She also thought about wearing a flower crown, just like her mother did on her wedding day. In the end, though, Joanna didn't do any of those things. Her tributes were more reflective of her mom's personality. The wedding car, for instance, was the car her mom drove: a VW Beetle. Looking back, Joanna says she felt surrounded by love at her wedding, through the loved ones who were there and by the gentle reminders of her mom. And that is what matters.

"My advice—there's no right or wrong way to do this," Joanna later wrote for One Fab Day. "For me, time didn't heal, but it helped. If it's still painfully raw, maybe allow things settle in a bit more. It's hard to make decisions in the midst of grief."

Well said, Joanna. If you find yourself in a similar position, if a deceased loved one has been on your heart as you've been planning your wedding or an important family celebration, only you can decide what, if anything, will be the best way to honor that person. You don't have to do anything; you don't have to limit your tribute to one thing; and you can change your mind as many times as you need to as you make your plans.

The point is to do what gives you the most peace and comfort. This is truly one of those times to trust your instincts.

The only exception to this rule, I would say, is to ask yourself if anything you're doing could be difficult for others at your event who are feeling the same loss.

'Thinking of You'

If you would like to do something special to memorialize a loved one at your wedding or major family event, and you're not quite sure what that should be, here are some possibilities for inspiration:

- **Set aside a seat in their honor.** A saved seat can serve as a poignant reminder of the loved one you're thinking of. You can go a step further, if you'd like, by displaying photos, mementos, or a letter written to the one you're thinking of on the chair.

- **Incorporate photography.** Displaying photos on a reserved chair is one of many photography options. If you (and any guests close to your loved one) are emotionally up to seeing images of a late loved one, you can create a special photo table in their honor, add a photo to your bouquet, or work some photos of your loved one into a slide show. I suggest images that capture your favorite memories.

- **Be creative with key elements.** For example, if you will be getting married under the chuppah—a canopy used during Jewish weddings—you can incorporate jewelry, clothing, or other meaningful items into its design. An mlive.com article described a couple that exchanged vows beneath a custom chuppah made from squares of fabric that family members provided. The bride said it felt like she and her husband were married under the love and good wishes of her family, which would have made her late father happy.

- **Keep something special with you.** Carry or wear something meaningful, maybe a piece of jewelry or something your loved one wore when they were married.

- **Bring back one of their favorites.** Another way to feel your loved one's presence is to add a special touch—maybe a song, poem, food, or flowers—to your event that reflects their taste.

You Don't Have to Be a Rock

One other piece of advice to consider as you plan: Don't feel you have to appear to be strong or happy. It's perfectly normal to be dealing with mixed emotions during this time.

Tiffany Ayuda, who lost a cousin to cancer before her wedding, interviewed Dan Wolfson, PsyD, a psychologist specializing in grief, for a feature about loss and major life events for *NBC News Better*.

"Grief never goes away," Wolfson told Ayuda. "It is something we all learn how to adapt to. The intensity of grief changes over time. One of the big things that helps us adapt to loss is to make space for these emotions. This allows you to re-engage with your life and have a vision that's meaningful in the absence of your loved one."

Wolfson also encouraged those planning personal events to practice self-care, whether that takes the form of leaning on friends, journaling, or joining a bereavement group.

Ultimately, honoring a deceased loved one in your event can be a source of healing and a way to make it richer. You shouldn't feel obligated to do this, but if it will give you peace, I encourage you to add a tribute that feels right to you and those closest to you.

A GUIDE TO CREATING A GIFT REGISTRY

Like many things related to event planning, the idea of creating a gift registry can be exciting—and a bit daunting.

That's why I've put together a list of tips to help create a positive experience, both for you and for those who want to give you gifts.

In case you're familiar with the term *registry* but fuzzy on how one works, a registry is a wish list you establish with one or more retailers so that your guests, and those who want to give you a gift at a major life event (wedding, shower, milestone anniversary, etc.), know what you need without trying to guess at your tastes and preferences.

Most registries show shoppers what has already been purchased, and some online registry services allow people to consolidate lists from multiple sources (ranging from brick-and-mortar shops to online retailers) into one convenient list.

So what should you know about setting up your registry? Here are some tips.

Etiquette Tips for Wedding Registries

In the case of a wedding registry, it should be devoted to items that you and your partner will use in your life together. It's not the place to ask for clothing, jewelry, or other things specifically for one of you.

Along the same lines, don't ask for gifts you would like to use at your wedding (like signage to set up at your venue or floral displays). It creates a vibe that you're asking people to help pay for your wedding, and that's not considered good etiquette.

Putting registry information on your invitation is an etiquette no-no. Instead, include a link to your wedding website on your invitations.

Asking for money is frowned upon, but you can set up funds for your honeymoon, saving up for a house, or other goals you share as a couple.

When and How Much?

Create your registry sooner rather than later. Some people will rely on your registry to buy for you more than once, and they would appreciate access to a registry (even if you plan to expand it) two or three weeks after you announce your wedding or big celebration. If that's not practical, you should have a registry ready for guests at least four to six months before your event.

This is one of those times when it's helpful to ask for a lot—or at least to give people lots of options—including gifts that sell for less than $50. It's OK to include some options that are $100 or more.

You probably will be tempted to make your list too short. I suggest adding two or three gifts for everyone on your invitation list—in other words, if you're inviting 100 people, put 200-300 items on your registry list. And remember, you're not going to get everything you ask for.

Check your registry from time to time. While it's unlikely, it's possible it will run out of gifts before all of your guests get a chance to do their shopping.

Stick with two or three stores, possibly a large department store with household goods and maybe a specialty store.

Getting Started

Before you start browsing store inventories or working with a registry guide, create a list of what you'll need. Then you can look at what retailers offer and find specific products that you (or you and your partner, in the case of wedding registries) like.

Research registry sites. Consider the types of items you can register for, ease of use for you and the people who will be relying on your registry to shop, the availability of different price points, refund policies, and perks—some retailers offer registry assistance, loyalty program points, and even gifts.

If it's for your wedding, work on your registry with your partner. You'll be asking for items you'll be using and enjoying together, hopefully. You both should agree on the items you're requesting. Categories can include bedding, bathroom, kitchen and dining, cleaning, home appliances, home décor, home improvement, garden and outdoors, luggage/travel, living room, smart home/electronics, recreation/entertainment, storage/organization, and special funds.

Some people opt to ask people to make donations to charitable causes close to their hearts. This is a great option if you don't necessarily need tangible gifts. Loved ones still get to do something special to honor you. Some registry programs let you include a link to a charity's donation page. Other sites, like The Good Beginning, are designed for charitable giving.

Address Considerations

Another registry tip: Put thought into the shipping address you want to provide. Will someone be there to accept gifts? Is there room to store them?

Some online registries offer a "hold" feature, meaning you'll receive a notification when someone buys an item on your list, but it won't be shipped until you're ready. This helps reduce chaos during your event planning and preparations, and if you realize you've received duplicates of a gift, you can exchange one before it's sent to you.

Overall Advice

Look ahead. Don't limit your list to items you need immediately. If you hope to buy a bigger bed in a couple of years, for example, or to start entertaining, register accordingly.

Register for items you'll actually use; don't limit yourself to high-end items like fancy china for special occasions. You don't have to limit yourself to practical items either, and there's nothing wrong with including some splurges.

HOSTING A BABY SHOWER?
HERE ARE 6 TIPS TO DE-STRESS YOUR MENU PLANNING

Hosting a baby shower can be tons of fun, hugely rewarding, and, depending on what you have in mind, a bit daunting.

As a host, you have so many choices. Should your shower have a theme? Would guests enjoy games or find them embarrassing? Is it best to let the guest of honor open her gifts in front of everyone or wait until later?

Menu planning comes with its own set of challenges. Generally, you'll need a nice selection of foods that accommodate varied tastes (and dietary restrictions), but at the same time, you'll want to keep the needs of mom-to-be front and center in your planning.

While I can't tell you what theme to go with, or whether the Baby Price is Right game is a good fit for your particular event, I can help in the area of food and beverages.

Here are six tips to help with your planning.

1. Ask the mom-to-be for her input.

Keeping the mom-to-be in the loop is key to avoiding disaster. That guideline applies to all of your planning, including food and beverages. The dessert that sounds delicious to you may not sound remotely appealing to her. And she may be finding that certain foods have started disagreeing with her since she became pregnant. Find out what she would enjoy and what dishes or ingredients should be avoided.

Also, don't forget that some foods are off-limits for pregnant women because of health risks; these include pâté, raw or partially cooked eggs, certain cheeses, and raw or undercooked meat and fish.

2. Offer yummy nonalcoholic beverages.

This goes back to remembering the needs and limitations of the mom-to-be. Alcohol is not an option during pregnancy, and you don't want your guest of honor to feel left out.

Safe alternatives (depending on the conversation I recommend in Tip No. 1) could include fruit punches, apple cider, limeade or lemonade, and iced tea.

Another fun option is to offer creative mocktails, from virgin sangria to alcohol-free mojitos.

3. Give your guests variety.

When you're planning a shower, or any kind of event, your guests will likely have a wide range of tastes. And while you won't be able to please everyone, guests will appreciate it if you give them options. I suggest offering at least two choices for each type of food (appetizers, entrées, and desserts).

4. Don't be afraid to venture away from finger foods.

Don't get me wrong: Finger food is a helpful choice for events like showers, especially if guests will be mingling and munching at the same time. Still, if you decide to hold the shower at an event venue or enlist the help of a caterer, you might want to capitalize on the availability of tables and a professional cooking team by offering a wider variety of entrées, side dishes, and desserts. (If you do decide to book a venue, be sure to make your choice and reservation early.)

If you're thinking of a morning shower, brunch selections like bagels and cream cheese, biscuits and gravy, waffles, pancakes, French toast, breakfast meats, breakfast casseroles, or mini omelets could be fun. If you're working with a caterer, ask about brunch food stations.

Lunch entrées could include sandwiches and wraps, fajitas, or mini pizzas.

For supper, how about skewers (veggie and/or meat), barbecue sandwiches, or even a carving station?

If you feel finger foods are the best choice for your event, you have a wealth of options available including finger sandwiches, empanadas, sliders, and quiche bites.

Dessert is another area that lends itself to baby shower creativity, from customized cookies and cupcakes to a candy table.

5. Consider a craving station or table.

For many women, food cravings are part of the pregnancy experience. In fact, about 50-90% of American women have a specific food crav-

PARTIES AND SPECIAL EVENTS

ing during pregnancy, a Healthline article reported. Why not play up that idea and offer foods associated with cravings, from pickles and olives to chocolate and peanut butter? This is another area where input from the mom-to-be will be valuable. If she's been craving something, you'll want to include it.

6. Don't forget dietary restrictions.

Do your best to find out in advance if you'll need to provide vegan selections or gluten-free menu items.

I recommend adding a line to the shower invitation encouraging guests to alert you to food allergies, intolerances, and dietary preferences in their RSVPs.

As an added precaution, you can always display ingredient labels or cards so guests will know what they're eating.

CHAPTER 4

Being Prepared

HIDDEN EVENT FEES YOU SHOULD BE WATCHING FOR

While wedding and event planning can be exciting, it also comes with some less-than-fun aspects.

For many people, one of them is dealing with costs and creating a detailed budget. Few people get excited about this step, but it lays the foundation for nearly every decision you'll be making.

And as you look into expenses for your gathering, from renting affordable venues to lining up photography, you should know that some costs are more apparent than others.

To help you create an event budget breakdown and plan more effectively, I've put together a list of hidden fees that can be lurking out there.

The good news is that knowing what to look for — and how hidden fees could impact your overall budget — can help reduce your stress. And that, in turn, can make your planning process easier.

Hidden Fees Overview

Here are some less-than-obvious expenses to be on the watch for:

Additional Servers

Catering represents a significant portion of total wedding and event costs. And if you're hit with hidden labor fees, your catering costs can consume even more of your budget. I encourage you to ask about labor fees for servers, bussers, attendants, dishwashers, and anyone else who could be on duty.

Catering and Travel Fees

When couples opt to bring in outside caterers for their event food, their expenses can also include travel fees for the team that shows up to feed their friends and family. This cost usually is charged on a per-mile basis. The hidden fees don't stop there: Your catering service may also bill you for off-site catering fees and rental fees. You can avoid these costs by working with a venue that provides catering services. The Bell Tower on 34th offers multiple catering and beverage packages.

Cheap Event Venues

Yes, you read that heading correctly. Sometimes, event venues that appear to be your most affordable option at first glance will be the ones most likely to hit you with a long list of fees. As you consider venues, read their service agreements carefully and ask them to go over all of the fees and additional costs you should be expecting. There's nothing wrong with researching affordable venues; I'm simply warning you to make sure you know exactly what you'll be paying.

Bar Costs

Does the venue you're considering provide a bartender, or will you need to hire one? The amount you'll spend for a bartender for your big day varies quite a bit, depending on the level of service you need (pouring wine versus making your signature cocktail). Rates generally range from $30 to $50 per hour. But if you need to hire a bartender, your guest count will impact your event budget, too.

Unless you're planning something very small, you really should be thinking about hiring a bartending staff. A good general rule is to hire one bartender for every 35 guests. You also should plan to tip your bartenders $10 to $15 per guest. (Make sure they haven't received tips from guests, though.) You may also be expected to lay out some dollars for your bar supplies, including alcohol, glassware, mixers—even security. Not all places will require you to pay these costs, though. The Bell Tower on 34th, for example, offers a variety of inclusive bar packages.

Cake Cutting

Your hidden fees could also include a charge for wedding cake cutting, known as a cakeage fee. What exactly would you be paying for? This fee covers the cost of staff members cutting your cake and serving it to your guests. Costs vary, but they can range from $2 to $5 per guest. Ask about this as you consider your location.

Cancellation Insurance

This is not necessarily one of your hidden fees, but paying for event cancellation and postponement insurance often gets forgotten during event planning and the process of creating a budget. These policies are extremely valuable, though, and can protect you from losing money if you have to cancel or delay your event.

Invitations and Thank-You Cards

You probably are including your save-the-dates and invitations in your wedding budget, but have you thought about the cost of the thank-you cards you'll be sending? Along the same lines, you may be surprised to see how much postage for these items can add to your expenses. Not only that, but stationery with square envelopes, oversized pieces, heavy pieces, and unusual shapes cost more to mail.

Linens: Setup, Teardown, and Delivery

If you decide to rent linens like tablecloths or napkins, your expenses could include more than the rental of the linens themselves. Many rental services charge to deliver linens, and some venues will bill you to set them up and take them down after your event. Ask about this and what your options are. Some venue packages include linens.

Parking

This one may surprise you, but parking is one of the more common hidden fees that event doers encounter. If your venue doesn't have enough parking spaces, they'll charge for providing valet parking or additional parking for your guests. This expense usually runs from $2 to $10 per car.

Ask about parking for every location you consider. The Bell Tower on 34th does not charge extra for valet parking services.

Post-Event Cleanup

This is another area people don't always consider: Some venues and vendors charge cleaning fees. This cost is for putting away décor and rentals, clearing food and plates, and throwing out trash. Find out in advance if the vendors and sites you're considering charge cleanup fees, and if they do, how much they are.

Your outdoor event contingency plan

The supplies you line up to keep your guests dry and comfortable during an outdoor event will plump up your budget. Be sure to factor in the costs that come with renting outdoor heat lamps or tents—and even having a supply of extra umbrellas.

Security

Most people, when they think of event budgets, probably think of food, entertainment, and photography—but security? Yes, event security guards could cost extra, and you may need them. In fact, in recent years, many venues have been requiring security when alcohol is served at an event.

Hiring security officers can cost approximately $150 to $500. But it's not a given that security will be among your hidden fees.

Silverware and Glasses
When you talk with venues about your event's meal tables, ask about what's included in your package. Some locations simply provide space, leaving you responsible for what goes on the table, including your silverware and drinking glasses. Other businesses offer catering packages, but even in those cases, be sure to be clear on what's included. If you need to rent your flatware (silverware), it can range from $200 to $500. The glasses on your tables, from wine and water glasses to cocktail glassware, can run you from $200 to as much as $1,000.

Taxes and Service Charges
Make sure the estimates from prospective locations and vendors are clear about the taxes and service charges they'll be charging you. It's common for businesses to leave these costs out when they provide quotes.

Vendor Meals
Event doers don't always think about this as they create their budgets, but you should plan to provide a meal for every vendor present during your reception or celebration. That list could include your planning team, photographers, videographers, your band or DJ, and other entertainers.

Talk with your caterer and ask how much you can expect to pay for your vendor meals.

By the way, people sometimes forget to include themselves in the head count for event meals. Be sure to add the cost of a plate for each of you to your budget.

Attire Alterations
While you've probably been researching what you'll wear at your celebration, don't forget to consider the possibility you'll need to pay for alterations, which can add a couple of hundred dollars or more to your budget.

PARTIES AND SPECIAL EVENTS

Favors

This isn't necessarily one of the hidden fees people encounter, but favors can add significantly to your expenses. These gifts tend to cost $3 to $8 each. Depending on your guest count, they'll add up quickly.

Wedding Party Gifts

Have you been thinking of offering gifts of appreciation to the members of your wedding party?

This is a lovely way to say thank you, and it will be appreciated, but you should know that the cost of providing these gifts can add up, impacting your overall budget.

Welcome Basket Delivery

If you plan to provide welcome baskets for the guests who travel to attend your event, you could have more hidden fees waiting for you. As you research welcome baskets, look into how they'll be delivered to guests' hotel rooms and how much you'll be charged.

More on Tips

I encourage you to consider tipping as you develop your budget.

Etiquette calls for tipping many of the people who play a role in your event, including your wedding officiant, photographers and videographers, florist, musicians, hairstylist and makeup artist, transportation providers, DJ, waitstaff, and parking attendants.

PLANNING AN EVENT WHEN YOU'RE CRUNCHED FOR TIME

When writer Camille Bautista learned her sister was engaged, it was a bit of a bombshell. Bautista and her family were thrilled about the news, but not so much about the wedding date.

It was less than seven days away.

"Judge away, but they simply didn't want to wait to start their lives together," Bautista later wrote for Bustle. "After basking in the glow of my sister's new bling, reality set in: We had to plan a wedding in a week. ONE WEEK."

While a one-week deadline would be pretty intense, plenty of couples opt for short engagements (less than a year).

It's not unheard of to be asked to plan other big events in a short period of time, either, like showers, anniversary parties, and other family celebrations.

If you find yourself in that situation, don't stress. It is entirely possible to create a wonderful event in a rush. (In fact, Bautista notes in her article that her sister's wedding was beautiful.)

Here are some planning suggestions to get you started.

Effective Planning

Rushed event planning can lead to a frustrating cycle: Less planning time can cause stress; stress can lead to procrastination; procrastination heightens stress. I suggest giving yourself deadlines for individual planning tasks, but don't beat yourself up if you miss some of them.

Think of your deadlines as motivators that can help you keep your planning moving.

Remember, you don't have to do everything on your own. If your budget allows it, a professional planner will be a tremendous resource. See if you can find someone who has successfully organized events in short time frames.

Friends and family can be helpful, too. They can brainstorm ideas with you, and you can always see if some of them are available to take on small to-do items on your behalf, such as a bit of online research. Designate tasks fairly, without putting unreasonable burdens on others, and try to match jobs with volunteers' interests and talents.

Another word of advice: It will be tempting to make quick decisions during your planning so you can move on to the next thing on your list. That's why it will be very important to have a budget in place before you make any decisions.

Inviting Guests

One of the first steps in your planning process should be deciding who you'll invite. If you won't be able to give your guests very much lead time, touch base with people you want at your event about their availability as soon as possible. And because time is of the essence, consider digital save-the-dates and/or invitations instead of mailing print versions.

Selecting a Location

While you're working out who can attend your event and when they can be there, you'll also need to figure out exactly where it will take place. Consider booking a venue on a day other than Saturday, when they're more likely to have openings. As you speak with venues, ask if they can offer advice and resources for streamlining your planning process. They may be able to help with vendor recommendations, too.

The Rest of Your Checklist

Creating a list will be particularly helpful as you attempt to rush through your planning tasks. It will ensure items don't slip through the cracks and give you a sense of accomplishment as you mark tasks complete.

Ongoing Communication

Throughout your planning process, remain in close communication with those helping with planning, along with your caterer and your venue, who likely will need information about your head count, menu choices, vendor choices, and more.

Flexibility Is Your Friend

Be flexible on items that require significant lead time. Instead of ordering an elaborate cake, for example, go with cupcakes.

Be reasonable about your goals. Understand that if you want to add a special element to your event, like a sunset ceremony for your wedding or a vegan menu for your big party, you'll probably need more time for planning and preparation.

Above all, dismiss ideas of perfection. It's not attainable, even if you have years to prepare. Instead of trying to plan a perfect event, aim for a joyful one. Focus on sharing a special day with people you love. If you do that, you will be able to consider your efforts successful.

WHEN CHILDREN ARE ON THE GUEST LIST: PLANNING FOR LITTLE ONES AT YOUR SPECIAL EVENT

If the term "children's table" evokes memories of family Thanksgivings spent sitting in the kitchen eating turkey and mashed potatoes off paper plates, you'll probably be surprised to learn how grown-up things are for kids now, at least in the world of catered events.

No longer are children considered disruptive little beings who have to be corralled (or kept at home). Increasing numbers of brides, grooms, event planners, and other hosts are making them feel like valued guests with child-friendly menus, fun and memorable activities, and imaginative seating arrangements that consign those old kids' tables to the past, where they belong.

Burgers. Fries. Filet Mignon?

Kids may be notoriously picky eaters, but that doesn't mean they only want hot dogs, burgers, pizza, and fries (although you can't go wrong with serving them). As times have changed, so have children's palates. Kids might like lobster, filet mignon, or chicken cordon bleu as much as anyone, although in smaller portions. With some creative adjustments, you can serve similar fare to everyone, adults and children alike.

One option? How about using a picnic basket, bento box, cafeteria tray, or tin camping plate to present a right-sized portion or slightly modified meal? The lobster tail you serve to adults becomes lobster mac-and-cheese for the kids; filet mignon can be cut into smaller bites and presented with vegetables as a kebab, only without the skewer.

Or how about working with your caterer to create a unique meal in a mason jar? Chicken pot pies, burrito bowls, and even chili can be spooned out of a jar. Reluctant to put glass jars in the hands of your smallest guests? Try filling plastic mason jars with warm pizza sauce and cheese for dipping breadsticks made from pizza dough.

Busy Hands, Busy Bodies

Let's be honest: No one under the age of 10 or so is an expert at sitting still for hours on end. (Some adults don't fare much better!)

So how do you keep the little ones engaged at a wedding, reunion, or other event? How about themed coloring books and crayons ... or handheld blackboards and chalk? As an alternative, top the kids' table with butcher paper and hand out crayons or markers so they can draw to their hearts' content.

One Fab Day recommends favor packages with classic games like jacks and hangman, costumes and masks for playing dress-up (especially fun for a photo booth), and candy.

And Martha Stewart suggests setting out cushions so young guests can make pillow forts, or using "interactive" centerpieces at the kids' table—a display of toy dinosaurs, small stuffed animals, or mini Etch A Sketches, for example.

Although there's always the possibility of less-than-ideal behavior, crying, and distractions during key moments, children have a way of adding to the poignancy of your wedding, party, or special event. There's something particularly meaningful about watching your parents enjoy celebrating their 50th anniversary with their great-grandchildren or seeing the groom share a dance with his niece. Little ones can add elements of beauty, whimsy, and wonder to an event, and taking extra steps to ensure smooth (as much as possible) sailing during their time there just might be worth it.

STRESSING OUT ABOUT WHAT-IFS? THESE PLANNING STRATEGIES CAN HELP

In some ways, major life celebrations can seem larger than life. The emotions, the significance of the day, the expenses involved: With so much at stake, it's only natural to want everything to come together perfectly.

Maybe it will ease the pressure to know that these events—no matter how lovely, touching, and momentous they can be—are rarely perfect. Curling irons or the bride's "something borrowed, something blue" items are forgotten. Speeches get muddled or awkward. Weather interferes with your vision.

That said, there are steps you can take to prevent some of the more common wedding and event mishaps—or at least minimize their impact. I hope the strategies you find here will give you the peace of mind to get through your planning without overwhelming anxiety about "what-ifs."

Someone You Were Counting on Cancels

It can feel like a blow if someone close to you, someone you were counting on or looking forward to sharing your big day with, backs out. It feels even worse if the cancellation comes at the last minute.

My advice is to try to step back from the moment, give yourself time to cool off, and respond with patience and understanding. Ultimately, extending grace will be better for your mental and emotional well-being and for the health of your long-term relationship with the person who's canceling.

In the case of a wedding, if it was a bridesmaid or groomsman who canceled, the simplest, least stressful solution could be to simply move forward without scrambling to find a replacement. And if you end up with someone walking down the aisle alone or grouping people in threes, no one, most likely, will give it a second thought.

Now, if a maid of honor or best man backs out, you may want to line someone up to take their place, or delegate some of their responsibilities. This takes a bit of thought; you don't want to make someone feel like you only see them as a second-choice substitute. MyWedding.com suggests asking a relative in your wedding party to help you if possible. Whoever you ask, though, be honest with them about what happened and explain how much you would value their help. After the wedding, be sure to send a handwritten note of appreciation or a thank-you gift.

Beyond wedding party considerations, you'll have a few more to-dos if someone, including a guest, cancels at the last minute. Here's a short checklist:

- Alert your venue.

- Update your seating chart.

- Notify appropriate vendors and service providers, such as your caterer.

If you have a well-organized friend or family member, or a wedding planner, consider delegating some or all of these calls to them. You'll save yourself some time and aggravation.

You Forgot Something

Forgetting items, from clothing to personal supplies, is a common mishap. That's why my venue maintains an "event cabinet" stocked with the items customers most commonly forget, including bobby pins, tampons, buttons, bra strap clips, reading glasses, toothbrushes, hairbrushes, and more.

The tendency for brides and grooms to forget things is also the inspiration behind the many checklists and packing lists found online. You can even purchase ready-to-print lists on sites like Etsy.

I suggest taking advantage of these resources and building on them with weddings in mind. The lists usually include the following:

- Attire for the bride and groom

- Ceremony items (including rings, your marriage license, and, if applicable, the vows you wrote)

- Guest favors

- Overnight supplies

- Personal items and toiletries

- Photo IDs

- Signs

- Travel supplies

- Your emergency kit (included later in this chapter)

Pull together as much as possible in advance. If you're really worried, recruit someone to remind you to double-check what you've packed or even go through your checklist with you.

Someone Crashes Your Wedding

Most wedding experts recommend asking a person you trust to step in for you if you realize there's someone at your wedding who wasn't invited. Your designated representative would be the one to speak to the crasher and ask them to leave immediately. This allows you to continue enjoying yourself without getting caught up in a potentially unpleasant confrontation. If you feel strongly that you should be the one to confront your unexpected company, it's still a good idea to ask for help.

If the crasher refuses to leave, you have the option of asking a venue manager or security officer to step in or calling the police. If you do call in law enforcement, ask a few people to watch for the police and speak with them discreetly, so guests don't get alarmed.

The Weather Doesn't Cooperate

This is another common occurrence. Weather is one of the most unpredictable elements of an event. So if some or all of your big day will be taking place outdoors, I strongly recommend having some contingency plans in place.

If you're going to use a tent to protect your guests from the elements, for example, look at options with sidewalls that will help not only during a drizzle, but even if it's pouring.

In an interview with *Brides* magazine, wedding professional Skylar Caitlin suggested going a step further.

"See if the venue will allow your tenting company to set up the structure a few days before the wedding, so it can protect the ground a bit and avoid an overly soggy ground day-of," Caitlin said.

It's also a good idea to talk with your venue in advance about the option of moving everything indoors if necessary. Know exactly what you can expect and whether additional charges are involved.

If there's a chance of rain, you can also offer a few comforts to make your guests' lives easier, from setting up containers with umbrellas and flip-flops to placing large, absorbent towels in the bathrooms.

Another word on weather: If the conditions on your event day go beyond rain and wind to a weather emergency like a hurricane or tornado, you'll be glad you had event cancellation and postponement insurance in place to protect you. A policy purchased in advance can cover you in cases of extreme weather, along with such disasters as medical emergencies and even ruined attire.

Consider an Emergency Kit

One of the most proactive problem-solving steps you can take for your wedding is to create a personalized emergency kit. This is a small bag filled with supplies that can help you address potential mishaps, like popped buttons, headaches, or stained clothing. Depending on how many items you want to add, you can put them in a makeup bag, tote, or small travel bag.

I recommend customizing your emergency kit based on your needs and preferences, but this list might serve as a good starting place:

- Bandages
- Bobby pins
- Brush or comb
- Contact lenses (spares)
- Deodorant
- Eyelash glue
- Fashion tape
- Dental floss
- Hairspray
- Ibuprofen and any other needed medication
- Jewelry backups, including extra earring backs
- Lip balm

- Lint roller
- Makeup backups
- Makeup wipes
- Mouthwash
- Nail polish (for chips)
- Pepto-Bismol/antacid
- Phone charger
- Sewing kit
- Snacks
- Static Guard
- Super Glue
- Tide To Go pen
- Tissues
- Tweezers

Pack your kit several weeks before your wedding date, and ask a reliable friend or relative, or your planner, to hold on to the kit for you on the big day.

Ultimately, the wisest approach to event planning is to prepare as best you can for mishaps. From there, let go and enjoy the beauty, warmth, and yes, even the imperfections of your special day.

CHAPTER 5

Etiquette and Stationery

YOUR GUIDE TO THANK-YOU NOTES

Even in today's era of email, texting, and social media, there's something to be said for messages written on real paper. This is particularly true when it comes to thank-you notes, which not only brighten the recipient's day but also do some good for those who write them.

The benefits of handwritten thank-you letters actually was the subject of a psychological study led by assistant professor of marketing Amit Kumar at the McCombs School of Business at The University of Texas in Austin, in collaboration with professor of behavioral science Nicholas Epley at The University of Chicago Booth School of Business.

"Saying thanks can improve somebody's own happiness, and it can improve the well-being of another person as well—even more than we anticipate, in fact," Kumar said. "[Writers] think about things like, 'Am I going to get the words just right and am I going to be articulate?' That might be a barrier to actually sitting down and writing the thing. But when you're the recipient of something like a gratitude letter, you tend to evaluate things on the basis of warmth and prosocial intent. As long as somebody's expression is sincere and warm and friendly, recipients are often going to have a very positive reaction to that."

I hope the knowledge that both writing and receiving notes of appreciation are beneficial will give you comfort as you look ahead to working on your wedding, shower, or party thank-yous.

(By the way, thank-you card etiquette calls for a separate note for your wedding shower gifts and the gifts you receive at your wedding. It's not a good idea to combine them.)

In case you're still a bit apprehensive about your note-writing marathon or wondering what you should say, I have some basic guidelines and tips for you.

A Simple Structure

Elaine Swann, founder of The Swann School of Protocol, told *Brides* magazine that all a thank-you note requires are a few simple elements between the opening (Dear Aunt Sandy) and the sign-off (Love, Olivia).

Thank the recipient for what you're grateful for, whether it's a gift, a guest's presence at your event, words of encouragement, someone who lent a hand, or all of the above.

Say something about what you're grateful for, possibly why you're excited about the luxurious towels you received or how much it meant to you that the person you're writing to helped you mail invitations or create centerpieces.

Of course, you can add more thoughts if you like, but ultimately, being sincere will be more important than being lengthy.

One of the best ways to make people feel appreciated is to work details in your notes. Avoid generic statements like "Thank you for your generous gift."

An exception to this guideline: thanking people for their cash gifts.

"Whether they gave you a $20 gift or a $200 gift, all should be treated equally, and you should never ever, ever mention the amount (ever) within your message," online bridesmaid dress shop Kennedy Blue wrote in a recent blog post.

Pro tip: If you know one of your guests gave you something, but there's some confusion about which gift it was, write a note thanking them for attending your wedding or event. Tell them how much you appreciate them for celebrating your special day with you.

Thank the Ones Who Helped Make the Day Successful

This is not mandatory, but if you appreciate the businesses that helped make your big day unforgettable, go ahead and thank them, too.

I recommend a short note that highlights how they stood out, whether you appreciated the thoughtful service that your caterer provided or the photographer who went the extra mile to ensure amazing images.

You can also express your gratitude by writing positive customer reviews using the same approach. Comment on what made your experience wonderful.

Organizational Tips

One way to make your note-writing more manageable is to develop a system for keeping track of who gave (or did) what and who you've written to so far.

This strategy should begin with how you open your gifts. Have a volunteer take notes on each gift as you open it. It also helps to have someone take a photo of each gift as you open it to help you write about it more specifically in your note.

Better Late Than Never — It's True

If life gets in the way of sending prompt thank-you notes, don't panic. And don't assume it's too late to send them, even if a year or more has passed since your wedding or celebration.

That said, I know that the more time that passes after your event, the more daunting the note-writing becomes.

A blog post by Postable recommends a multi-pronged strategy:

- Make a mental commitment to getting the notes written.

- Choose your note cards or stationery.

- Block off writing times in your calendar ... and

- Get those notes written.

If your notes are late, Postable added, add an apology between initial words of thanks and your sentence(s) about the gift (and/or action) you're writing about.

Remember: You're Sharing Joy

I know writing large volumes of thank-you notes is time-consuming, but this act of kindness will be remembered and appreciated long after you're done.

And, as I mentioned, you'll probably experience some warm fuzzies yourself.

OPTIONS FOR ENVIRONMENTALLY FRIENDLY INVITATIONS

If you're planning a celebration for someone who's passionate about protecting the environment—whether that's you and your partner, a family member, or a dear friend—what better way to honor that commitment than by selecting invitations that are kind to the planet?

Here we'll explore the world of eco-friendly invitations and discover how you can make a stylish and sustainable statement right from the start.

Save the Date — and the Planet

Increasing numbers of invitation providers are offering creative, environmentally friendly save-the-date and invitation options.

For example, you can find plantable save-the-date invitations printed on paper embedded with seeds, usually wildflowers or herbs. After the recipients receive them and (hopefully) add your event to their calendar, they can plant them and grow something beautiful.

Along the same lines, some people are sending save-the-dates that can serve as mementos of the event honorees—including mugs, small framed photos, and refrigerator magnets—so recipients can save them well into the future.

Whether you choose plantable or a different option, you can avoid waste by sending your save-the-dates to households instead of individuals. A good rule of thumb is to order save-the-dates for half the number of people on your guest list, possibly throwing in two or three extras for last-minute plan changes and a souvenir for yourself.

Another save-the-date trend gaining traction is skipping the paper altogether and creating a digital message. E-invitations are a popular, user-friendly option, or you can take a more personal approach and send a video with your event location, date, and (if applicable) event website.

Going Green with Your Invitations

While the ideas above aren't necessarily limited to save-the-dates, you also have eco-friendly options geared specifically for your invitations. Some companies, for example, provide invitations on 100% post-consumer recycled paper, plant a tree for each order, or donate a percentage of your purchase to an environmental cause. You can also find invitations that are printed sustainably, possibly with soy or vegetable ink.

If you don't find a recycled paper option that speaks to you, explore papers made from sustainably grown materials, such as bamboo or hemp.

Here are a few more ideas to consider:

- Send postcards, which save paper, and refer people to your event website for more details.

- Another twist on this is to create a save-the-date that does double duty and encourages people to follow your website for wedding information.

PARTIES AND SPECIAL EVENTS

- Consider paying a professional calligrapher, which bypass-es the chemicals and energy expenditures associated with printing. You'll also have the benefit of gorgeous, elegant invitations.

- You can choose a printing service that offers carbon offset-ting. This means it balances the activities involved in creat-ing your final product, from paper milling and printing to shipping your invitations, with environmentally beneficial activities such as tree plantings.

Taking a few extra measures to send eco-friendly invitations is definitely manageable, and if protecting the earth is a goal close to your heart, it will make your event preparations all the more satisfying.

THE INS AND OUTS OF PLACE CARDS

One of the decisions you have to make when you plan a large cele-bration is how guests will find their way to their seats.

Most people go with one of several options: seating charts, place cards, or escort cards.

Here, we're taking a closer look at place cards, what they are, and some of the benefits of using them.

Place Card Basics

Place cards display a guest's full name and are meant to be waiting at that person's place setting. Typically, guests will find their place cards by referring to a seating chart displayed near the event's entrance or by being guided by event staff or volunteers to their assigned table.

Cards can be flat, much like a business card, or tented — meaning they're folded in half and can stand alone. You can lay flat cards on place settings, lean them on something, or display them in a place card holder. It all depends on the look you want.

Weave in Some Personality

With a little creativity, place cards can be functional while also pro-viding some decorative flair to meal tables.

Take inspiration from the celebration's theme, setting, colors, or honorees' personalities to make place cards that wow. Here are some ideas to inspire you:

- **Use photos.** Print a small photo of each guest on their place card. It's a cute, personalized touch. Or print photos of the event honorees on each one.

- **Make them 3D.** Have cardstock folded into creative shapes like hearts, houses, or flowers, and print the table number and name on each one. It adds some whimsy.

- **Theme them.** Match place cards to your event's theme or colors. Try rustic wood slice cards for a barn wedding, seashells for a beach-themed retirement party, or superhero logos for a fun comic book birthday party.

- **Use food.** If it's edible, you can display names on it. Possibilities include cookies, chocolates, macarons, or mini meringues.

- **Double them as favors.** Attach small gifts or favors like a lottery ticket, a small bottle of liquor, a candle, or a donation to charity in the guest's name.

What About Escort Cards?

Escort cards are a less formal version of place cards. They guide guests, too, but only to their tables. From there, guests can select their own seats.

If you have place cards, you'll display one name on each card. With escort cards, you can display one name and a table number, or you can create larger cards, one for each table, listing the names assigned to that table.

Place cards are displayed at place settings. Escort cards are displayed somewhere easy to spot, usually near the entrance to the event area.

There is no "right" choice when it comes to place cards versus escort cards; it's a matter of taste and preference.

Benefits of Place Cards

Place cards are not a must. For that matter, you don't have to go with table or seating assignments either, depending on the formality of your event and your planned approach to the meal.

PARTIES AND SPECIAL EVENTS

But in many cases, assigned seats and place cards will make life easier for your guests.

Here are a few benefits of using place cards (and, by association, having assigned seats):

- Place cards prevent confusion; they help people quickly and easily find their seats.

- You free guests from potentially awkward moments related to selecting a seat.

- You free guests from even more awkward moments of forgetting someone's name.

- You avoid empty seats.

- If you're serving plated meals, your catering staff will rely on place cards to ensure the right dishes go to the right people. This is particularly important if anyone has made a special request or if a guest has food allergies.

- Place cards can add to the visual appeal of your place settings.

- Place cards can reflect your event theme and personality. They can add a sense of fun to your décor or enhance your event's sense of formality and elegance.

KICK OFF YOUR EVENT COUNTDOWN WITH SAVE-THE-DATE CARDS

One of the most helpful things you can do for the friends and family you plan to invite to a wedding or major celebration is to send them save-the-dates.

The primary save-the-date purpose is to notify guests when and where your event will be in advance so they can keep their calendars open on that date and, depending on their location, begin making travel arrangements.

Not only that but sending save-the-dates provides an excellent way to be creative and set the tone for the celebration.

Do I Need Save-the-Dates?

Save-the-date notices are highly recommended if:

- Your event is on a holiday weekend. People tend to plan for holiday events far in advance.

- You'll have quite a few out-of-town guests. Give them time to request paid time off and make travel arrangements.

- You're having a destination wedding. Guests need extra time to book flights and hotels for weddings in another city or country.

- Your event date might change. If your venue or details are not yet finalized, save-the-dates provide flexibility if you need to change the date later.

- Your guest list is very long. Give guests advance notice that a formal invitation is coming. This is thoughtful if you plan to invite more than 100 guests.

- Save-the-dates are optional if your event is local with under 100 guests on a normal weekend. Informal word-of-mouth notice may suffice.

When Should I Send the Save-the-Dates?

I've found that guidelines for save-the-date timing vary, but a good rule of thumb is to send them six to eight months in advance of your event date.

As soon as you've nailed the when and where of your event—and who you want to invite—try to make sending your save-the-dates a high priority.

One word of caution: There is a fine line between giving your guests ample time to get your event on their calendars and sending save-the-dates too early—say, more than a year in advance. When you do that, there's a risk that your notification could get lost, and your event could slip through the cracks.

What Should the Save-the-Dates Say?

When it's time to create your save-the-dates, you don't have to include a lot of information, but you should include the basics:

- Names: Bride and groom, bar mitzvah boy, anniversary couple

- When: Event date, including the year

- Where: Event location (If you don't have a venue lined up, provide the city/region and some kind of statement that makes it clear that you're sending a save-the-date, not your invitation. You can accomplish this by simply stating, "Invitation to Follow.")

If you have one, it would be helpful to include a link to your event website, where your guests can get more details and registration information.

You do not have to include the time of your event, attire guidelines, or details about food.

Also, you should not include RSVP cards. They go in your invitations.

Should Everyone on the Guest List Receive Save-the-Dates?

Yes. If you plan to invite someone, they should receive a save-the-date. Even if you've spoken, texted, or emailed about your event plans with some people, don't leave anybody out.

Do I Need To Send a Paper Save-the-Date?

There are pros and cons to both paper and digital save-the-date notifications.

Sending paper save-the-date cards is the traditional way to go, but you will not be breaking any etiquette rules by emailing your save-the-date or sending it by text. You can always take a look at a save-the-date site or two to see what you think. (You can also opt to use a save-the-date app to help you manage responses. Technology can be your friend when you're juggling multiple planning tasks.)

As long as you get your save-the-date to guests in time for them to make unrushed plans, and it has your date and location information, you're in good shape.

Pros and Cons of Postcards

This is another area where there is no correct answer.

Some people prefer enclosing their save-the-dates in envelopes to keep the details of their event private and to help prevent folding or smudging.

On the other hand, save-the-date postcards can be more affordable. They save you not only time, but money on postage.

The Save-the-Date Booklet

In addition to traditional postcards, a fun option for save-the-dates is a booklet. Save-the-date booklets allow you to include more details and photos. You can have pages with information about the event venue, accommodation details, weekend timeline, travel information, things to do in the area, and more. It can be designed with different artistic touches like a ribbon closure or a sticker seal. Booklets are a great way to get guests excited about the upcoming festivities.

What If I Want More Formal or Traditional Save-the-Dates?

If you prefer save-the-dates that resemble wedding invitations, stationery is definitely an option. You can find a number of elegant, luxurious choices in a wide range of materials and designs.

You can also opt for premium cards, specialty cards, and other creative possibilities to suit your taste.

What Can You Tell Me About Etiquette for Save-the-Dates?

One common question I hear about save-the-dates for weddings is how to approach names.

The traditional approach is to list the bride's name before the groom's name. You also have the option of listing the names in alphabetical order.

Another etiquette point to keep in mind, for both save-the-dates and invitations, is to leave off your gift registry information. Instead, include your event's website address.

Is It OK To Incorporate Humor into Save-the-Dates?

Absolutely! Save-the-dates are a fantastic way to showcase personalities and give guests a sense of your upcoming event's vibe. If laughter and fun are important to you or the honoree, why not choose save-the-dates that reflect that?

You can weave in a play on words or shop around for a funny save-the-date template.

Save-the-Date Via Text

Sending save-the-date announcements via text message is a quick, convenient option. Here are some tips for doing save-the-dates by text:

PARTIES AND SPECIAL EVENTS

- Design a customized graphic with the same details you would include on paper save-the-dates.

- Limit the text to key details: "Save the date! John & Jane– May 27, 2024–Hawaii"

- Provide a link to your wedding website in the text for more info.

- Be sure you have current mobile numbers for all guests.

INVITATION OPTIONS: FINDING THE PERFECT FIT

Invitations do more than convey information; they give guests a glimpse into the style and formality of your celebration. No pressure, right?

I know that, like many of the decisions you make when you're an event doer, choosing wedding invitations can feel overwhelming. This guide will walk you through some of the available options and their benefits.

Classic Invitations

Traditional paper invitations remain the most popular choice for weddings and major celebrations. Printed on high-quality card stock or paper, they convey a sense of elegance and formality.

While they're more expensive than digital options, their beauty lies in the tactile experience for the invited guest as they hold the weighty paper and run their fingers along the raised lettering or embellishments.

Traditional invitations come in three main formats:

- **Flat/single card:** A simple invitation printed on one card.

- **Folded:** The invitation components (host card, RSVP card, accommodation info, etc.) are printed separately and assembled in a folded jacket. This multipiece style is suitable for formal invitations.

- **Booklet/multi-page:** All invitation content is bound together like a miniature book using wax seals, ribbons, or enclosures.

Pros: Timeless aesthetic, luxurious feel, tangible keepsake, can display calligraphy/printing methods

Cons: Most expensive option, requires more lead time, can't update details after printing

Digital Invitations

In our digital age, many event doers opt for online invites delivered via email or posted on a website. These allow you to easily update details and avoid the environmental impact and costs of printed materials. Here are some popular formats for digital wedding invites:

- **Email attachment:** The full invitation design is sent as a PDF or image file attachment.

- **Online RSVP form:** Guests visit a personalized website or app to view details and RSVP.

- **Video invitation:** Guests are treated to a multimedia experience with motion graphics and video greetings.

Pros: Eco-friendly, affordable, easy to update, instant delivery, integrated RSVP tracking

Cons: Lack of tangible keepsake value, tech challenges for older guests, less formal aesthetic

Hybrid Invitations

The best of both worlds: Hybrid invitations combine printed and digital elements.

A prime example is sending printed host invitations for the tangible experience while directing guests online to RSVP and view additional details via an event website. Other hybrid options:

- Digital wedding invites with printed keepsake cards
- Video invites with printed host cards

Pros: Convenient digital RSVP tracking, keepsake printed pieces, eco-friendly

Cons: Higher costs than fully digital, tech challenges for some guests

Stationery Choices

The stationery you select for your invitations plays a major role in the overall aesthetic. Here are some of the most popular paper options.

- **Premium cotton paper:** This option is considered the gold standard for formal event invitations. Cotton paper has a luxurious, textured feel and a weighty thickness. It handles decorative printing and embellishments beautifully.

- **Kraft/recycled paper:** For an earthy, natural look, kraft paper's fibrous brown texture evokes a rustic or bohemian vibe that's perfect for outdoor celebrations. Recycled/eco papers are another sustainable choice.

- **Vellum paper:** This translucent style offers an ethereal, dreamy aesthetic for invitations. It's often used as an overlay or jacket enclosing other invitation pieces.

- **Velvet paper:** With its soft, flocked finish, velvet paper has an upscale vintage look and a luxurious hand-feel. This distinctive texture is perfect for glamorous or vintage-inspired designs.

- **Metallic paper:** Add a touch of shimmer and luxury with paper infused with metallic foils, like genuine silver and gold. Metallic paper ranges from subtly glittering to boldly shining finishes.

Printing Options

In terms of printing methods, here are the main options:

- **Thermography:** Raised ink provides an engraved, elegant look for invitations.

- **Letterpress:** Uses thick paper for vintage charm.

- **Foil stamping:** Uses a metallic foil to create a shiny, reflective design on paper.

- **Engraving:** This is a formal option with recessed lettering.

- **Digital printing:** Modern inkjet/laser allows photo printing and affordable color.

The Invitation Suite

An *invitation suite* refers to all the separate printed components included alongside the main host invitation card, such as:

- **Enclosure cards:** Additional inserts provide relevant information not displayed on the host card, including:

  - Directions/map card
  - Accommodation information card
  - Event website URL card

- **Response cards:** RSVP cards often double as the reply vehicle if no digital RSVP option exists. Some people also use cards for the following:

  - Reception response card (if hosting two separate events)
  - Song request card
  - Meal preference card

- **Envelopes:** Two envelopes are typically provided: an outer envelope for posting/guest addressing and an inner envelope that holds all interior invitation components.

- **Envelope embellishments:** Your invitations can also feature the following:

  - Custom stamps: A commissioned design printed on the envelopes
  - Envelope liners: A coordinating printed pattern or color on the inner envelope
  - Envelope printing: Guest addressing printed directly onto envelopes
  - Wax seals: An antique wax-sealed closure for a classic look

Working with Invitation Providers

Most stationery retailers offer several options for customizing your invites.

- **Ordering samples:** Before committing, order a sample pack of the invitations you're considering. This lets you experience the stationery's look, feel, and print quality firsthand and, ultimately, receive a final product you absolutely love. Samples are extremely helpful since digital swatches can differ from real life. Most retailers apply the sample cost toward the final purchase.

- **In-house design services:** Many invitation companies employ in-house designers who can customize premade templates by changing colors, fonts, and motifs, or designing suites from scratch. This service is ideal if you want a pro's assistance but don't have printer-ready art files for your invites.

- **Print-ready design upload:** If you're hiring a graphic designer to create a custom invitation design, you'll need artwork files that are ready for printing. Most printers accept vector formats, such as AI, EPS, or PDFs with embedded fonts and trim lines. Vector formats are scalable without losing quality, ensuring a crisp and professional print. Be sure to double-check your printer's specific file requirements before submitting.

- **Rush printing options:** Ideally, you should order your invitations at least two to three months before the mailing date, but many retailers expedite invitation orders for an added fee.

- **Assembly and addressing services:** Full-service printers can assemble a multipiece invitation suite, address outer envelopes with calligraphy or printed fonts, and stamp the enclosures with custom designs. These add-ons save time but increase costs.

Tips for Affordable Invitations

It is possible to cut invitations' costs sensibly while avoiding cheaply made invites. Here are ways to trim expenses:

- **Print digitally:** Digital printing provides photo-quality images and text at low cost compared to engraving, thermography, and similar options. Consider flat or folded styles rather than bulky multilayer assemblies.

- **Order samples:** Before ordering full suites, sample the weight, stock, and colors to avoid reprint costs due to something being off.

- **Limit enclosure cards:** Only include cards with absolutely essential information to cut back on printing/assembly expenses. Display other event details on your website instead.

- **Use digital addressing:** Having invitation envelopes digitally printed with guest addresses costs less than commissioning traditional calligraphy or handwritten styles.

- **Consolidate and downsize:** Reduce portioning costs and excess paper waste by selecting a single-card invitation format instead of multipiece suites. Use smaller, simplified designs printed on lighter card stock.

- **Forgo accessories:** Opt out of decorative finishes like envelope liners/belly bands/ribbons/foil/wax seals. These embellishments make invites feel luxurious but add costs quickly.

PARTIES AND SPECIAL EVENTS

CHAPTER 6

Celebration Food and Bar

Courtesy of Luke and Cat Photography

WORKING WITH YOUR CATERER: HOW TO MAKE THE MOST OF YOUR MENU TASTING TO ENSURE YOU AND YOUR GUESTS ENJOY EVERY LAST BITE

When you're planning a major celebration or special event, a skilled caterer can transform your vision into a culinary reality. When you work together, your guests are not just fed, they're delighted. But how do you find the right caterer for your celebration, and how do you collaborate to create a menu that reflects the vibe you're aiming for?

Here, I'll guide you through the steps of working with a caterer, from tastings to final decisions, so you can confidently curate a memorable dining experience for your celebration.

Tips for Your Tasting

During a food tasting with a caterer, you get to sample menu items before making your final choices. Here are some strategies to make the most of this time:

- **Come prepared.** Before you sit down with your caterer, you should have a good idea of your dining concept—buffet, stations, plated—and main food choices. The tasting is the time for you to sample what your guests will be eating and to help you choose between a few options you've preselected. It's not productive to go into the tasting with no idea of what you want. Also, too many choices can easily overwhelm you; streamline your sampling choices ahead of the tasting so you can have a focused session and make good decisions.

- **Be sensitive to your guests' special dietary needs.** If you know some of your guests are gluten- or dairy-free eaters, vegan, vegetarian, or have food allergies, it's up to you to make sure they will have ample options. Talk this over with your caterer while making preliminary choices and planning your tasting.

- **Ask about specialty foods.** If the chef has a special dish that's a known crowd-pleaser, it may be a good idea to include it in your tasting selections.

- **Don't eat too much beforehand.** While you'll only be taking a few bites of each dish, you'll still be doing a lot of eating during your tasting. It's important to have room in your belly to try out a little bit of everything.

- **Limit your party.** Speaking of being overwhelmed with too many choices, too many opinions can produce the same effect. To avoid that, ask only two or three people to tag along to offer their thoughts on the spread.

- **Be aware of what drinks will be served.** The tasting isn't just about sampling food; it's also about sampling the drinks that will be served along with it. If this includes alcohol, it goes without saying that you should only sip to avoid becoming tipsy or drunk. It's not a small task for a caterer to put together a tasting, so you should respect their time by keeping a clear head with which to make important decisions.

- **Give honest feedback and ask lots of questions.** The chef wants their food to be a success as much as you do, so don't be shy about inquiring about how the food will be cooked, presented, and served. If there is anything you don't like, tell your caterer; there's a good chance a few tweaks can solve the problem.

Questions to Ask During Your Tasting

- How many appetizers will be passed out per tray?
- What's on the children's menu?
- Are there options for late-night snacks?
- Can you make any changes to the menu?
- What type of wine and/or cocktail options do you recommend?
- Will the event food be prepared as it is for the tasting?

Like other aspects of your planning, the tasting can be fun, and you can make it a mini-event for you and the lucky few who get to tag along. Still, it's an important part of the process for your chef, so respect their work in putting the tasting together, and honor that work with thoughtful questions and honest feedback. It'll all add up to a dining experience you and your guests won't forget.

CREATING A MENU THAT WILL DELIGHT YOUR GUESTS

Ask people to tell you about a celebration they attended, and chances are good that one of the things they'll mention—in addition to the emotional impact of the day—will be what they thought of the food.

Food helps shape memories. It influences our mood.

I'm not saying this to stress you out about your celebration's menu choices. Instead, try to think of food as an opportunity, a powerful tool for enhancing your guests' experience, not to mention your own.

To help, I've compiled a collection of ideas for celebration meals, along with some planning tips to keep in mind.

How to Choose Your Celebration's Menu

Keep the following suggestions in mind as you begin the process of planning your menu.

Give yourself plenty of time.

In other words, put your menu planning high on your list of planning to-dos. Do your research, and if you're working with a caterer, schedule your tastings. I'd also suggest trying to book your caterer at least a year in advance. If your event will take place during their busy wedding season, late spring through early fall, you might even need to book earlier.

Make a decision: sit-down dinner, food stations, or buffet?

Don't worry: There's no wrong answer here. Select the approach that best fits the vibe you're trying to create. Or look at the food options for these approaches and see what speaks to you. Maybe you'll love the idea of a macaroni and cheese station, or you'll want your guests to enjoy filet mignon being served to them at their table. You may gravitate toward traditional fare, or you may be looking for a chance to try something a little different. Ask prospective caterers about your options, top food station ideas, and menu examples.

Plan to offer plenty of choices.

While you won't be able to provide every guest with their favorite foods, try to create a menu with variety. You might want to, for instance, offer one or two meat entrées and a plant-based dish for your vegan guests. Or you can select American comfort food along with something more spicy or exotic.

Be ready to accommodate special requests.
Ask potential caterers how they handle special requests like gluten-free or kosher options. I also recommend including a place on your invitations where people can note food allergies and dietary restrictions that you and your caterer can consider when selecting food items.

Pick appetizers, main dishes, and sides.
Another reason to give yourself plenty of time to make your menu decisions is that you will be selecting more than main courses. You'll be mulling over your options for all of the food provided.

Do you want dessert options?
This is another consideration: Do you plan to have a cake (birthday, anniversary, etc.) for dessert, offer an alternative, or include desserts in addition to your cake?

Your Food Ideas
Here are a few possibilities to help you create a feast that is absolutely delicious.

Buffets
Buffets create an informal environment where guests can mingle while serving themselves.

Generally, a typical party or event buffet might include a chicken entrée, beef, pasta, multiple side dish options, salad, and dinner rolls, along with choices for vegan guests and those with dietary restrictions.

You can also tweak the buffet options to include the honoree's favorite dish, from seafood to lamb. Or you can include foods that tie in with your theme, like fried chicken or barbecue for a rustic celebration.

Sliders
Sliders have been growing in popularity at parties and special events. They're delicious but not too filling. They're not messy, and they lend themselves to a lot of creative options.

Paella

Served in a pan, paella is a big crowd-pleaser as an appetizer or main dish. Guests are drawn to the aroma of the rice, vegetables, and meat, along with the sound of sizzling food and the colorful, delicious ingredients.

Grazing Tables

When it comes to cool food ideas, one fun option is the grazing table: a generous, colorful, family-style food presentation. Grazing tables often feature a large charcuterie or a display of meats, cheeses, olives, pickles, and loaves of bread, along with fresh fruits, dips, crackers, and nuts.

These tables encourage mingling and relaxed conversations as guests help themselves to the food.

Food Tower Ideas

With food, presentation plays a major role in creating appeal. And at parties and special events, one popular mode of presentation is a dramatic, showstopping tower.

You can talk with your venue or caterer about a cookie tower, a champagne tower, or a cheese tower — the possibilities are practically endless.

Skewers

Grilled kebabs are tender and flavorful. You can offer creative combinations of meats, cheeses, and vegetables.

Braised Meats

Braised dishes (chicken, pork, or lamb) are an excellent choice for celebrations and special events. They're flavorful and juicy, and they pair with a wealth of side dishes. They also offer great visual appeal.

Fish Options

If you're thinking about including fish on your menu, salmon is a popular choice because it holds its shape well and makes for a beautiful presentation in a plated meal.

Other excellent fish and seafood choices for your entrée include sea bass, red snapper, and shrimp.

Add a tasty sauce to enhance flavor.

Pizza

If you're looking to infuse a sense of casual charm and universal appeal into your menu, consider the timeless option of pizza. Here are some pizza varieties to consider:

- **Traditional Margherita:** Classic and simple, featuring tomato sauce, fresh mozzarella, basil, and a drizzle of olive oil.

- **Meat lovers' delight:** Packed with savory goodness, including pepperoni, sausage, bacon, and other meaty delights.

- **Veggie extravaganza:** A garden-fresh option with an array of colorful vegetables, from bell peppers to cherry tomatoes.

- **Custom creations:** Allow guests to craft their own personalized pizzas with a variety of toppings, ensuring everyone gets exactly what they crave.

Luxury Menu Ideas

For those of you looking to add an extra touch of elegance and sophistication to your menu, here are some luxurious options to consider:

- **Caviar station:** A caviar bar with blinis, crème fraîche, chopped onions, and other savory accompaniments can make for an indulgent and memorable cocktail hour.

- **Oyster bar:** Fresh-shucked oysters on the half shell with mignonette sauce and lemon wedges create a refined and upscale vibe.

- **Lobster tails:** Serve decadent lobster tails as a main course or in individual cocktail-sized portions.

- **Beef Wellington:** This classic dish of tender beef wrapped in flaky puff pastry exudes elegance and luxury.

- **Foie gras:** Consider offering foie gras, the fatty liver of a duck or goose, as an appetizer, possibly paired with a sweet fruit compote or reduction.

- **Champagne tower:** A towering display of champagne flutes creates a celebratory and opulent focal point.

- **Dessert bar:** Offer an array of petit fours, macarons, chocolate truffles, and other delicate gourmet sweets.

Brunch Dishes

Looking for some unique food ideas? Serve breakfast for dinner.

Brunch foods are huge crowd-pleasers. You can offer a crepe station or serve up pancakes, smoked salmon, crab cakes, fruit kebabs, and deviled eggs. Other fun choices include mini quiches, donuts, and Belgian waffles.

Nontraditional Food Ideas

Looking for menu ideas that are anything but ordinary? Explore these creative, nontraditional food options:

- Try tasty Asian dishes like chicken and broccoli, fried rice, or hoisin beef.

- Instead of chicken, offer roasted duck or lamb.

- Go with popular regional dishes like Texas barbecue, chicken fajitas, or blackened chicken with crawfish étouffée sauce.

- Another fun option is to offer late-night snacks on your menu. Burgers, slider sandwiches, tacos, fries, or milkshakes provided late into the night are great for soaking up cocktails and satisfying hunger after dancing up an appetite.

Refreshments

In addition to food, you should be prepared to offer a wide variety of liquid refreshments including water, iced tea, juices, and sodas.

You could also offer punch, mocktails, fruit-infused water, lemonade, coffee, cold-brew tea, or hot chocolate.

Menu Sign Ideas

Displaying your menu is a great way to let guests know what delicious foods will be served. Menu signs also double as attractive décor elements. Here are some creative approaches to inspire you:

- Chalkboard signs

- Framed paper signs

- Signs on easels

- Individual table menus

- Flower menu boards (Arrange a menu on a board surrounded by flowers.)

- Mirrored signs

- Signs on wood slices

Ask the Experts

These suggestions are only a few of many, many options available. I encourage you to talk with your venue or caterer and ask for their thoughts and menu ideas based on your event's season and theme. They can offer suggestions for fresh, locally grown foods and give you ideas for pairing entrées and catering side dishes.

EXPECTING GLUTEN-INTOLERANT GUESTS AT YOUR EVENT? TRY THESE TIPS

Could something as seemingly innocuous as a crouton make a guest at your next event ill?

It could if they are sensitive to gluten, a protein found in wheat, barley, and rye (and many other grains), or if they have celiac disease, which is a serious autoimmune disorder triggered by eating gluten that can damage the small intestine.

After all, croutons are little more than tiny, tasty bread cubes—and conventional bread is full of gluten. Even though most people who have celiac disease or gluten sensitivity are extremely careful about what they eat, a crouton tossed into a salad can pose a hidden danger. (It's important to know that gluten isn't the only concern for people with celiac disease; they may also have trouble digesting alcohol, excessive sugar, dairy, and eggs.)

That said, hosting guests with gluten sensitivities or celiac doesn't have to be stressful—it just takes some thought and planning. More and more chefs today are whipping up marvelous gluten-free meals, and most caterers are happy to help you create a delicious menu with options that meet the dietary needs of all of your guests.

I've put together some tips to help you and your caterer ensure everything served at your gathering will be scrumptious and safe.

Talk with Your Caterer

Your first step is to ask whether your caterer can provide gluten-free options for guests who prefer it. If your venue doesn't have a specific gluten-free menu, is the chef willing to make some adjustments to accommodate guests with special dietary needs?

Remember, Gluten Can Be Sneaky

In addition to croutons and other more obvious sources like dinner rolls and sandwich bread, gluten can show up in sauces, salad dressings, soups, and even puddings, usually as a thickener. Arrowroot and cornstarch are excellent substitutes that chefs are typically willing to use.

Here are a few more things to discuss with your caterer if you're expecting guests with celiac disease or gluten sensitivities:

- Soy sauce contains wheat and should be avoided. So do dumpling wrappers. And imitation crabmeat.

- Ask your caterer if it's possible to use nut crumbs, coconut flakes, rice flour, or almond flour in place of more typical breading.

- What about desserts? Is it possible to bake a pie without wheat flour? Of course! Sweet rice flour makes a flaky, delectable crust.

- Serving fish may seem like a safe idea, but remember: Some chefs dust fish with flour before cooking. If you would like to include a fish option, grilled is probably better than baked.

Smart Practices

Being mindful of ingredients is important, but there are additional steps your caterer can and should take if gluten is a concern for some of your guests.

One of the biggest issues is something a person without the illness might never consider: cross-contact on preparation and cooking surfaces. If a cutting board, grill, griddle, or deep fryer has been used for prepping or cooking a wheat product like pancakes or a breaded food like French fries or fried chicken, unless it's cleaned thoroughly, it may harbor enough gluten to trigger a severe reaction. Talk with your caterer about the importance of preventing this.

Here are a few more tips to keep in mind at your event:

For events with both gluten-free and "regular" meals, using different-colored plates will help distinguish one from another and make sure there's no mix-up during serving.

As a general rule, a sit-down meal with plated food is safer than a buffet. Although labeling buffet items can help guests make appropriate choices, serving utensils can get mixed up when many people are using them.

Giving your caterer a seating chart that indicates where people with gluten sensitivities or celiac disease will be is a great help to servers. Color-coded place cards are useful, too.

Another possible (and unexpected) gluten source? The oil in the deep fryer. Most of the time, fryer oil is changed a couple of times a week. Ask your caterer if they'll change the oil specifically to prepare gluten-free foods.

And one more source you might not have thought of? Pastry chefs often dust baking pans with flour to prevent sticking. There are many gluten-free flours they can use instead, including almond, coconut, and rice flour.

Menus for All

Is it possible to plan a menu that will please everyone? Absolutely. It just requires a little creativity. For example, beef fajitas with corn tortillas are a tasty and safe choice. Add beans and rice on the side, and you've got a great Mexican-inspired meal.

Grilled salmon with grilled vegetables makes a satisfying lunch or dinner, too, as long as the grill was cleaned to prevent cross-contamination.

Does prime rib with mashed potatoes and mixed vegetables sound good? Just make sure the mashed potatoes aren't from a mix that contains gluten.

Remember, your caterer can suggest ideas, too. Together, you'll develop a menu that will not only satisfy the robust bread- and pasta-eaters on your guest list but also those avoiding gluten.

FOOD STATIONS: A CROWD-PLEASING ALTERNATIVE TO BUFFETS AND SIT-DOWN DINNERS

At an event, food does so much more than provide sustenance. It enhances guests' experience. It makes events more memorable.

And it's a catalyst for connections. This is especially true at big celebrations with food stations, because they contribute to an interactive and social atmosphere. Food stations encourage guests to mingle, explore, and share their culinary discoveries.

If the idea of sparking conversations and encouraging lasting memories appeals to you, this look at event food stations will serve as your guide.

Customizable Cuisine

"Accommodating" is likely the best word to describe food stations and the reason they've become so popular. Guests always appreciate options, and food stations (also known as food bars) make more options possible. A sit-down dinner or buffet can offer some options, but food stations are the culinary equivalent of a guest-centric free-for-all—they're completely customizable. Vegetarians or vegans among your guests? No need to consign them to a vegetable platter while everyone else dines on chicken or steak—set up a food station just for them.

And what about people with celiac disease or gluten intolerance? A food station full of carefully selected gluten-free options can eliminate worries. Guests can enjoy themselves without having to poke around their plates for an errant breadcrumb.

Creativity on Display

Food stations also provide an opportunity for you to amp up your creativity.

There's nothing wrong with offering customary event fare, but consider how much more interesting it would be to have food stations that reflect your family's heritage or a station filled with the dishes that were served where the anniversary couple became engaged or got married. Your caterer will be able to help develop menus that best reflect your preferences—and that are suited to your budget. An event with multiple food stations, for example, could offer such eclectic offerings as seafood enchiladas, tamales, and build-your-own tacos, or possibly sushi and other Asian fare in Chinese take-out containers.

By the way, those take-out containers are another example of how food stations let your style shine through. Unique presentations—think a donut wall instead of (or in addition to) a three-tiered cake or a build-your-own mac-and-cheese bar—double as entertainment in addition to being delicious. Decorating each station adds "flavor" as well.

No wonder Julie Savage Parekh of Strawberry Milk Events told MarthaStewart.com, "Food stations are the new buffet—a little bit trendier and more modern way to do it."

Additional food station ideas:

- Crudités and fruits with dips.

- Charcuterie boards—a great way to accommodate guests who keep kosher or only eat halal meats, for example. Just make sure any cheese is separate

- A build-your-own waffle bar with all the toppings is perfect for a brunch event.

- Made-to-order pizzas.

- An omelet station where guests pick the fillings, from veggies to meats.

- A fast-food bar. Not just for children, this can include wings and sliders or more gourmet choices such as mini lobster corn dogs or butterscotch popcorn served in paper cups that match your theme.

- A fondue station. Yes, that throwback delight is popular again. After all, who can resist the allure of melted cheese?

A Different Dynamic

Varied menus that appeal to a variety of guests aren't the only benefits of food stations. Let's take a look at some of the other advantages:

- There is less chance of congestion or long, slow-moving lines like you might find at a buffet.

- Because food stations don't require the same number of servers as a sit-down dinner, you may save money. However, if you have cook-to-order food stations, you might need more chefs.

- Cook-to-order stations mean guests will get to enjoy their food prepared exactly as they prefer.

- Guests get to eat when they want to, whether that's as soon as they arrive at the celebration or after they've had a chance to visit with others and maybe even hit the dance floor. That said, you can leave your food stations open for the entire event or for just a couple of hours. Either way, they provide more flexibility than a buffet or sit-down dinner.

Working with Your Caterer

To ensure your food stations are a hit with guests, your caterer will need to know:

- How many guests you expect

- Any special diets you need to consider

- What kind of atmosphere you want to create

- Your budget

With those factors in mind, together you can create a memorable event that scores big with everyone.

DESSERT IDEAS FOR YOUR CELEBRATION

When it comes to celebrations and special events, the dessert table is more than just a sweet ending—it's a reflection of the overall vibe you're creating and another opportunity to cement the day into your guests' memories.

You might be picturing an elegant cake adorned with delicate flowers, or maybe whimsical cupcakes or decadent macarons are more your style. Maybe you want all of the above: to have your cake and eat it, too, so to speak. Well, that's doable. The world of event desserts is vast and delightful.

In this section, we'll explore a delectable array of sweet treats that cater to every taste, budget, and guest list.

Cake and Dessert Table Combo

Have a special cake for your event, along with a separate dessert table. This allows you to offer cake slices for those who want them, plus an array of other sweets like pastries, fruit tarts, candies, cookies, and bite-sized treats. Guests can pick and choose their favorite desserts along with a slice of cake.

Passed Dessert Trays
Another option is to have servers pass trays of desserts like mini cupcakes, petits fours, and other small bites, while also giving guests the chance to visit the cake table.

Dessert Bars
If you're skipping the cake, think about a dessert bar. This popular option offers endless variety. Imagine a decadent selection of mini cheesecakes, colorful macarons, or gourmet cupcakes.

Cake Pops
These adorable little handheld treats offer all the deliciousness of cake in a portable form. You can have cake pops made to coordinate with your event's colors and designs. Display them on an attractive stand or tree for a modern dessert table showstopper.

Ice Cream Sundaes
What could be more fun than building your own ice cream sundae? Set up a fully stocked ice cream sundae bar with multiple ice cream flavors, a variety of sauces, sprinkles, whipped cream, cherries, and other toppings.

Candy Stations
Reminiscent of childhood candy stores and bake shops, candy stations are an undeniably nostalgic event trend and pure heaven for anyone with a sweet tooth. Set up stations with glass jars or apothecary dispensers filled with favorites like jelly beans, gummies, chocolates, and other candies. You can intersperse baked goods like cookies, brownies, rice crispy treats, and more for variety.

S'mores Bar
Add a cozy campfire feel to your dessert course with a s'mores bar. Provide all the fixings for guests to roast their own marshmallows and build ooey-gooey s'mores sandwiches. Safe Sternos,

long skewers or roasting forks, graham crackers, chocolate, and of course plenty of marshmallows are all you need for this fun, interactive station.

Cupcakes

You can get creative with cupcake flavors, fillings, frostings, and decorations. Plus, their built-in portability is perfect for allowing guests to satisfy their sweet tooth while mingling.

Arrange cupcakes on tiered stands for a pretty display.

Desserts To Fit Your Theme

Your desserts are also an opportunity to reinforce your celebration's theme or vibe. For example, for a rustic outdoor event theme, feature naked cakes with rustic wood accents, along with mason jars of pudding, cobblers, and pies with whipped cream.

Seasonal Desserts

The time of year can also help guide your dessert selections. For summer events, frozen treats like ice cream, sorbets, and frozen yogurt are refreshing choices. You could even have an ice cream truck.

Winter celebrations provide cozy dessert opportunities like hot chocolate and warm cookies, pies, or cobblers. If your celebration will take place during the Christmas season, offer gingerbread cookies, peppermint bark, and candy canes. Additional options include eggnog, mini fruit cakes, or yule log cakes.

For spring, you could go with lemony desserts like individual fruit tarts, zesty cupcakes, or a refreshing lemon meringue pie. Or offer strawberry treats like shortcakes, cheesecakes, or macarons bursting with sweet berry flavors.

Fall is perfect for warm spiced apple desserts like classic pies, crumbles, or cider donuts; pumpkin delights ranging from spiced cakes to mini pumpkin cheesecakes; or pear-based treats with hints of cinnamon or cardamom for a sophisticated touch.

Regional Dessert Ideas

Drawing inspiration from your event's location can also lend delicious local flavor to your desserts. Where we are, in Texas, creative dessert options could include the following:

- **Fancified takes on state fair treats:** You could offer gourmet versions of things like funnel cakes, fried Oreos, candied apples, or kettle corn.

- **Tex-Mex desserts:** Churros, tres leches cakes, margarita pie shooters, and more.

- **Down-home classics:** Pecan pies, cobblers, bread puddings, and Blue Bell ice cream.

- **Dr. Pepper cupcakes with a cream cheese frosting:** This playful twist uses an iconic Texas drink for a unique and slightly nostalgic flavor.

- **Pecan pralines dipped in dark chocolate:** A classic Texas treat, this decadent dessert can be presented in small boxes as favors or arranged beautifully on your dessert table.

- **Miniaturized Texas sheet cakes:** Adorned with tiny Texas flags, these bite-sized treats will deliver that classic rich chocolate flavor everyone will love.

Creating an Appealing Dessert Display

No matter what desserts you choose, the presentation can be just as enticing as the treats themselves. Use varied heights, levels, platters, and serving pieces to create an elegant, overflowing dessert table. Pretty linens, flowers, greenery, and candles can help dress up the display. Personalized dessert menu signs are also a nice touch. Get creative with your sweets layout for an Instagrammable spread.

Don't be afraid to have fun and make your desserts an interactive, thematic part of your celebration. Your guests will sweetly remember the decadent final course.

EVENT BAR IDEAS

A bar can be a key part of providing a fun, relaxed vibe for the guests at your event. Thirsty for inspiration? Planning a major celebration is hard work, but working on the bar experience doesn't have to be. Here, you'll find some information and tips to get you started, along with fun ideas that will have everyone talking.

Bar Types

Before you dive into your bar plans, you should know what your options are. Here's a general guide to event bars:

- **Open bar:** With an open bar, your guests can order any type of alcoholic or nonalcoholic beverage they want throughout the event, all hosted on your tab. This is the most guest-friendly option but also the most expensive.

- **Limited open bar:** To reduce costs, some hosts opt for a limited open bar that offers beer, wine, champagne, and select basic liquors, plus nonalcoholic drinks. Signature cocktails can be an add-on option.

- **Hosted beer and wine bar:** Covering beer, wine, champagne, and nonalcoholic beverages keeps the focus on lighter drinks. This scaled-back bar is appropriate for more casual events.

- **Consumption or cash bar:** Your guests pay for their own drinks at these bars. Consumption bars allow guests to put drinks on their tab; cash bars require cash payments. These options save you money but may receive mixed reviews from guests.

- **Dry bar/mocktail bar:** Nonalcoholic cocktails, fancy sodas, juices, and sparkling waters create a dry yet festive bar.

When selecting your bar format, factor in your overall budget, the vibe you want, and your guest list makeup. Your venue's offerings and bar staffing fees will also impact your decision.

Bar Packages

Most venues offer bar packages that include various combinations of beer, wine, liquor, and nonalcoholic beverages along with bartending services. Event sites may also suggest specific drink menus or signature cocktails.

Be sure to inquire about bar package pricing before booking your venue. Things that add to the costs include specialized glassware, extra hours of service, additional staffing needs, top-shelf liquors, elaborate cocktails, and high-end mixers and garnishes.

When weighing bar costs, keep your overall vision in mind. Splurging in this area can be worth it if you want to create a luxurious, celebratory vibe.

Affordable Bar Ideas

If your venue's bar packages don't fit your budget, get creative to provide alcohol at an affordable price point.

- **Offer beer and wine only.** Good-quality domestic and imported beer combined with a modest wine pour gets you solid drink options without the high cost of liquor.

- **Serve punches, sangria, and champagne.** Pitchers of premixed punches with a base spirit, fruit juices, and club soda or ginger ale make a tasty cocktail for a crowd at low cost. Fruity red or white sangrias and champagne toasts also please guests.

- **Set up an eclectic self-serve bar.** Offer a couple of signature cocktails premixed in dispensers with fun straws and garnishes, plus beer, wine, and nonalcoholic beverages. Let guests mix and mingle.

- **Provide bar tickets.** To control quantity and cost, give each guest two or three drink tickets for beer, wine, or a specific cocktail.

- **Set an hourly limit.** With this option, you'd have an open bar for the first one or two hours of your event, then switch to wine, beer, and nonalcoholic drinks.

- **Serve mimosas or Bloody Marys at your brunch event.** A basic Bloody Mary mix or mimosas made with inexpensive sparkling wine or juice hit the right note for daytime gatherings.

With smart strategies, you can create a full guest experience without going overboard on the bar tab.

Signature Cocktails

Serving up a signature cocktail is a fun way to offer guests a taste unique to your event. If you're a wine aficionado, a specially labeled red or white blend could be your signature sip. Or maybe a favorite spirit represents your personality (or the personality of the event honoree).

When dreaming up your signature drinks, consider elements meaningful to the honoree(s), family (for a reunion event), location, or theme. Then partner with your bartender to make it come to life.

PARTIES AND SPECIAL EVENTS

Here are some signature cocktail ideas:

- Feature local flavors like peach bourbon lemonade in Georgia or cucumber maple vodka sodas in Vermont.

- Infuse cultural traditions with tropical rum punch for a beach party or sangria bars for a Spanish villa celebration.

- Play off your event palette with vibrant lavender prosecco cocktails or saffron gin and tonics matching your colors.

- For literary nerds, name cocktails after your favorite book or fictional characters, like a Bridget Jones Chardonnay Spritzer.

Creative Bar Décor

Your bar should match the style and vibe of your event. Use décor details to integrate your bar into the ambiance. Here are a few ideas to get the ball rolling:

- Set out votive candles, lanterns, or string lights lining the bar for an inviting glow.

- Use chalkboard menus for rustic flair. Or frame ornate printed bar menus.

- For outdoor bars, string bistro bulb lights overhead and use reclaimed wood surfaces.

- Lay down a patterned runner or area rug under the bar if space allows.

- Create custom signs with fun drink names, quotes, or even the names of the couple or person being celebrated.

- Set up a DIY cocktail garnish station where guests can personalize their drinks.

- Have drinks served in interesting glasses, vintage coupes, mason jars, or even copper mugs to add a touch of personality.

- Instead of plain ice buckets, use galvanized tubs, vintage coolers, or even hollowed-out watermelons to keep drinks chilled.

- Customize cocktail napkins and stirrers with the event's logo, date, or a special message.

- Enhance the drinks with beautiful and delicious garnishes like fresh herbs, citrus twists, berries, or edible flowers.

- Adapt your décor ideas to the size and style of your venue. A minimalist approach might be best for a small bar area, while a larger space allows for more elaborate decorations.

- The area behind the bar is a prime opportunity for décor. Use a tapestry, a photo collage, or even a greenery wall to create a visually appealing backdrop.

- Avoid overcrowding the bar top with too many decorations; this can make it difficult for bartenders to work efficiently.

Outdoor Bars

A bar instantly livens up an outdoor event. Consider these tips:

- Create a shaded area with a tent, trees, or an umbrella. Direct sun exposure will overheat drinks.

- Select level ground and provide a sturdy surface, such as a wood platform, if needed.

- Check electrical access or have a generator to power coolers, lighting, and music.

- Use durable surfaces like reclaimed wood tops and stone counters that can withstand minor spills and drips.

- Secure tablecloths on bar tables with weights in case of windy weather.

- Use outdoor-friendly glassware, such as acrylic or heavy-duty plastic. Avoid delicate stemware.

- Embed or securely anchor bar stations so they don't shift or blow over.

- If no glassware washing will be available, provide biodegradable or disposable cups.

- Offer cooling stations with buckets of ice, water bottles, and chilled towels for overheated guests.

- Have plenty of water and soft drinks on hand.

DECIDING WHETHER TO OFFER ALCOHOL AT YOUR CELEBRATION

One question you will need to tackle early when planning a large celebration or special event is whether you'll be offering guests alcohol.

In some cases, the answer will be a no-brainer. Maybe, because of your personal convictions, serving alcohol simply wouldn't feel right to you.

Or maybe the answer is a resounding "Of course we will."

If you're somewhere in the middle, though, and are on the fence about offering alcohol at your event, I can help. Here are some pluses of offering your guests alcohol—and of skipping it.

Plus Sides of Offering Alcohol

To be blunt, if you're planning an evening affair, many of your guests will be expecting alcohol.

And there's a reason people serve alcohol at celebrations: It can contribute to a more festive event, a greater sense of fun. Guests who've had a drink or two are more likely to mingle and get on the dance floor. You could say that offering drinks is a way of showing your guests you appreciate them. It goes hand in hand with serving excellent food.

Alcohol also comes in handy when it's time for toasts. Yes, they can be done with sparkling cider or juice instead of champagne, but some may find that nonalcoholic substitutes fall flat.

Serving alcohol can be a significant expense, but you do have options for reining in your costs. If your venue offers beverage packages, you can select the one that works best for your budget, possibly one with more affordable liquors instead of premium liquor brands. Another option is to offer complimentary beer and wine and skip the liquor—or limit the liquor to one or two signature cocktails.

You can also offer a cash bar instead of an open bar, meaning guests will be expected to pay for their own drinks. A compromise would be to serve complimentary glasses of wine or champagne to welcome guests, or for your toasts, in addition to the cash bar.

Benefits of Skipping Alcohol

For one thing, drinking and serving alcohol may conflict with your personal or religious beliefs. If that's how you feel, your friends and family will respect that.

And, as I mentioned, alcohol can be costly. Depending on the size of your event, offering a full open bar (allowing guests their choice of drinks at no cost to them) costs an average of $2,000 to $4,000. Skipping the alcohol saves you money and allows you to spend more on other areas that are important to you, from high-end entertainment to videography.

Other benefits of a dry event:

- If you know that someone on your guest list has struggled with alcohol, or is struggling with it now, a dry event will allow them to relax and enjoy the celebration without the tug of temptation.

- You minimize the risk of alcohol-induced uncomfortable moments, from a tipsy toast-giver to less-than-appropriate behavior.

What's more, you may not be going for a party feel; you may simply want the celebration you're planning to be a time for close friends and loved ones to enjoy time together. You absolutely can do that without alcohol. And, if you're concerned about disappointing guests, you can always hold a brunch event, when they'll be more interested in coffee.

If you go with the no-alcohol option, be sure to offer your guests other beverage choices including sodas, juices, iced tea, lemonade, and water. Fruit garnishes are a nice touch.

Also, you can always offer a signature mocktail, from the Virgin Mojito (lime juice, lime wedges, simple syrup, mint leaves, soda water) to the No Tequila Sunrise (orange juice and grenadine). Or you can come up with something creative and unique to your event.

Ultimately, go with what feels right to you and your event honoree(s). Yes, making guests feel happy and appreciated at your event is important, but you have many options for accomplishing those goals.

SECTION 2

<u>WEDDINGS</u>

CHAPTER 7

Wedding Planning

Courtesy of Blanca Duran Photography

14 TIPS FOR PLANNING A SECOND WEDDING

If you're getting married for a second time, I suggest keeping two general rules in mind during your planning process.

First, be considerate of others as you announce and plan your wedding.

Second, there are no other rules. You don't have to deny yourself the wedding you want or consider any traditions off-limits simply because you've been married in the past.

As Alyssa Brown wrote for *Martha Stewart Weddings*, "If you're under the impression that a second wedding should be tiny, that you can't have a wedding shower, that you can't wear white, or that you shouldn't have a bridal party, think again. It may be your second, but it's still your wedding. These etiquette rules no longer have much standing, and your guests certainly won't be thinking about them when they see how happy you are on your wedding day."

I agree and have put together some tips and guidelines to help you and your spouse-to-be create the wedding you both want.

1. **Consider your children's feelings.** Whether they're little ones or full-grown, they should be the first to learn you're planning to remarry. Do as much as you can to involve them in your planning and the wedding itself. If you're planning to change your name after marriage, include that in your discussion.

2. **After talking with your children, share the news with your parents, immediate family, and friends**. Your former spouse probably will appreciate receiving the news from you as well.

3. **Think carefully before inviting former spouses or their family members.** Yes, sharing the news of your engagement is a thoughtful step, but it's not necessarily a good idea to invite your ex-husband or former mother-in-law to the wedding. Even if you're on friendly terms with them, their presence can create tension and discomfort that no one needs.

4. **Do what it takes to keep you and your partner on the same page.** Discuss everything: goals, budget, priorities, guests—you name it. It could be that you have very different ideas about the scope

of your celebration. Try to identify what's most important to both of you and work out a compromise.

5. **You can have a bridal shower and bachelor/bachelorette parties.** Maybe these are experiences you missed out on the first time around; maybe you want new housewares to kick off your new life; or perhaps these pre-wedding events are something you've been looking forward to. A wedding after-party is great, too. If you want to enjoy these events, plan them.

6. **You can have a religious ceremony—probably.** Some religions object to people having a religious ceremony when they're remarrying. Talk with your house of worship or clergy about what you're hoping to do.

7. **Find fitting roles for your children.** You don't have to limit your children's involvement to traditional roles like flower girl or ring bearer. Your children can walk you down the aisle, be part of the wedding party, present a reading... anything that you and your children feel comfortable with. That said, don't saddle your children with roles they don't want. Your wedding should be a positive experience for them, too.

8. **A wedding registry is perfectly acceptable.** Some worry that registering for gifts is a bit tacky when you're remarrying, but that's just not true. Your loved ones will still want to give you gifts, and a registry will be helpful to them. Create a registry for the items you want or set up a honeymoon fund.

9. **Size doesn't matter.** When it comes to your wedding, go as big or as little as you'd like. If you want to keep your celebration simple and small or hold a reception after a private ceremony, that's perfectly OK, but an all-out wedding bash with gorgeous décor is your prerogative, too.

10. **Your invitation wording is up to you.** It may feel strange to use the last name associated with your ex-spouse, but that may be the name most people know you by. In the end, go with the name you feel comfortable with.

WEDDINGS

11. **Select a dress that you love.** Look for a dress that matches the venue you'll be married in, the season, and the overall ambiance you're going for. Something that flatters you. Want a white dress? Go for it! You also can choose pastels, neutral shades, metallics, multicolor patterns, or floral prints. Again, the goal here is to make choices that bring you happiness.

12. **If you'd like, honor late loved ones.** If you or your partner want to celebrate the memory of a late spouse—and you both feel comfortable with it—you can find ways to honor them. Possible ideas include reading a favorite poem or Bible verse, displaying photos, or asking someone close to you to say a few words.

13. **Make the day uniquely yours.** If you and your spouse feel comfortable with it, write personalized vows that celebrate your commitment and the new life you'll be building together. Maybe you'd like a theme: Pick something meaningful to both of you, maybe a shared interest, something you aspire to do together, or something that ties in with a meaningful memory, like the movie you watched on your first date.

14. **Set this wedding apart from the last one(s).** Don't be afraid to be untraditional. Try a brunch wedding. Skip the dancing. Select a gorgeous venue that makes you feel special. Or…go all out with over-the-top entertainment. Create memories you and your guests will treasure.

Ultimately, I recommend planning with the goal of creating an unforgettable event, no matter how many times you've been married up to now. You are embarking on a new journey with the one you love. Celebrate in a way that brings you both joy.

HOW TO INVOLVE YOUR PARTNER IN YOUR WEDDING PLANNING

When you see the term "wedding planning," do you picture images of a bride-to-be doing research, calling vendors, and scheduling time to visit the venues she's considering?

It's not uncommon for brides to assume a large portion of wedding planning duties, but saddling one person with most of the work is not necessarily ideal.

As joyful as it is to plan a wedding, it's stressful, too. And if one partner feels as if their soon-to-be spouse is letting them carry most of the load, it can create tension in their relationship. That's the last thing a couple needs while they're preparing to begin a life together.

Besides, there are plenty of upsides to planning your wedding together. It keeps you and your partner on the same page about preferences and goals so you can make sure the resulting wedding reflects the two of you as a couple. And it encourages communication about spending decisions, meaning you're more likely to stay within your budget.

So here are some steps you can take to help ensure that you and your partner are, well, partners, throughout the process of planning your big day.

- **Talk about what you both have in mind.** Be open about what your expectations are for your wedding and for one another. If one of you envisions something small and intimate, and the other wants to go all out, you'll need to work together to find a solution that works for both of you. As for planning responsibilities, one partner may be assuming that the other wants to take control of the planning. Keep in mind that there are some tasks the two of you really should do together, like selecting your wedding bands.

- **Break down the to-dos.** Planning a wedding can sound like one massive, overwhelming job, but in reality, it's made up of many smaller tasks. Make a list of them together and talk about who's willing to do what.

- **Be sure to talk about money.** As you work out what you want for your wedding, you'll need to know if your goals are financially doable. If you decide to let one element go to free up funding for something more important to the two of you, that will shape your planning process.

- **Find tasks that match your partner's talents and interests.** Is the groom-to-be a music fan? Maybe they can be in charge of researching entertainment. Or maybe their way with words would make them a natural choice for writing invitations and your wedding website content. Someone with an artistic flair would be a great choice for finding, or creating, unique décor for your reception.

- **Be flexible.** If your partner really, really doesn't want a specific task—or differs from you on how a certain aspect of your wedding should be approached—don't let it become a major conflict. Maybe if you agree to be the one to handle a to-do your groom doesn't want, you can find something else he can do instead. As for differing ideas about elements of your wedding, if it's something that has great meaning to you, explain your feelings. Otherwise, pick your battles strategically.

- **Be there for one another.** Another benefit of planning your wedding together is that it gives you an experience to share, something that's uniquely yours. That's a way to strengthen your relationship. And both of you now have an empathetic source of encouragement and support when your planning duties become frustrating or exhausting. Remember, the two of you are in this together.

Overcoming Disagreements

Even with the best intentions, you and your partner may hit some bumps when planning. Disagreements can happen over finances, the guest list, or a wedding vision. But avoiding or prolonging conflict won't help. Here are tips on overcoming common planning disputes:

- **Listen first.** If tensions rise, avoid snapping back. Listen first to understand your partner's viewpoint. Maybe, for example, certain traditions hold personal meaning for them that you weren't aware of.

- **Compromise.** You won't see eye to eye on everything. Be prepared to meet halfway sometimes. Compromise shows you respect each other's opinions.

- **Focus on what matters.** Minor details like invitation fonts can seem huge in the moment. But in retrospect, they likely won't matter. Redirect talks to your big-picture vision.

- **Give yourselves a break.** Planning stress can make small issues blow up. Step back, regroup, grab some water, and wait an hour or so before returning to planning.

- **Bring in a mediator.** When you've reached an impasse and can't get past it together, ask a neutral third party (like your officiant) to help you see each other's perspectives and guide you toward resolution.

The goal is to focus on your marriage, not just your wedding day. Disagreements are normal, but overcoming them respectfully strengthens your foundation as a couple. Compromise when needed without abandoning what matters most in your wedding vision.

TWICE THE LOVE: PLANNING A DOUBLE WEDDING

For couples with close friends or siblings who are also engaged, a double wedding offers a unique opportunity: a chance to embark on the journey toward married life side by side.

If you and your partner have decided to take this exciting path with another couple you cherish, I have some tips that can help you plan an unforgettable double wedding.

Why Have a Double Wedding?

There are many potential reasons why couples choose to have a dual wedding:

- **Cost savings:** By combining resources and sharing expenses, both couples can significantly reduce the overall costs associated with a traditional solo wedding.

- **Simplicity:** Planning one grand event instead of two separate weddings can streamline the entire process and ease some of the stress for everyone involved.

- **Twice the excitement:** Having another couple to share the buildup and energy with will double the thrill and anticipation in the months and weeks leading up to the big day.

WEDDINGS

A Fair Planning Process

Even when just one couple is involved, wedding planning tends to be a challenging (albeit rewarding) process. If you're taking on the endeavor of planning a joint wedding together, open communication and an equal division of responsibilities will be critical from the beginning.

Each couple should have an equal voice in every aspect of the celebration. Begin with laying out a comprehensive planning timeline, complete with a checklist of tasks that can be divided equitably among both couples.

Make a point of meeting regularly to discuss ideas and updates and to resolve any differences. During these discussions, remember the value of flexibility and the beauty found in blending visions.

It's unlikely that every decision will align perfectly with everyone's initial vision, but compromise and mutual respect can lead to innovative solutions that enhance the celebration for everyone involved.

Setting a Budget

Speaking of costs, it's wise for each couple to determine their individual budget up front and then sit down together to discuss total funds and how they'd like to distribute expenses. Below are some common joint wedding costs to allocate:

- Venues for your wedding ceremony and reception

- Catering/bar services

- The save-the-date and wedding invitation

- Photography/videography

- Attire

- Décor and florals

- Entertainment

- Wedding favors

- Transportation

Splitting shared costs 50/50 or according to each couple's total budget amount are two potential approaches.

I also suggest setting aside a contingency fund. Unexpected expenses can arise, especially in a double-wedding scenario. Along the same lines, consider getting wedding cancellation and postponement insurance. I recommend it for all couples, and when two couples are sharing their wedding day, the risk of "life happening" only increases.

Choosing Your Venue and Vendors

When it comes to key vendors like your venue, caterers, photographers, and florists, it's important that both couples are equally satisfied with the selections. Here are some ideas that can facilitate a cohesive double wedding experience:

- Select venues that can accommodate your ceremony and reception in one location.

- Hire vendors with experience in handling double weddings.

- Work with a planner experienced in double weddings who can streamline the planning process.

- Communicate the overall visions both couples have for the shared celebration.

Reflecting Your Unique Styles

While a double wedding involves combining some elements, it should still feel true to the unique personalities and preferences of each couple.

Work together to establish unified details like an overall color palette, florals, and décor, but make sure everyone gets a chance to put their own spin on special touches. This could include anything from your wedding party's outfits to personalized vows, special dances, toasts, and more.

The wedding ceremony itself can involve individual sections that are customized for each couple amid the shared traditions.

Avoiding Double Trouble: Potential Challenges and Solutions

Planning a double wedding comes with unique challenges. Overcoming them requires thoughtful preparation and clear communication. Here are some issues you might encounter and strategies to address them:

Combined Guest Lists
Challenge: Merging two guest lists without exceeding venue capacity or budget

Suggestions: Prioritize immediate family and closest friends for the ceremony. You can always hold a larger, separate reception to include extended family and friends. Use digital RSVP platforms for efficient tracking and to easily update guests on changes.

Different Wedding Traditions
Challenge: Integrating diverse cultural, religious, or family traditions in a way that honors both couples

Suggestions: Host a "traditions workshop" with both families to learn and decide which customs to include. This can be facilitated by a cultural consultant or wedding planner experienced in multi-traditional ceremonies. Also, creating a mixed traditions ceremony script can symbolize the union of both backgrounds.

Families' Strong Opinions
Challenge: Navigating vocal opinions and wishes of family members

Suggestions: Establish a wedding planning committee comprising members with ties to both couples and possibly a neutral arbitrator. Invite group members to weigh in on major decisions, so all voices are heard. Note: While family members' input should be respectfully considered, ultimately, the couples getting married should have the final say on wedding decisions.

Dividing Attention
Challenge: Preventing one bride or groom from feeling left out; avoiding feelings of competition or neglect

Suggestions: Allocate individual moments for each couple during the ceremony and reception. For instance, separate vows, dances, or toasts can highlight each couple's unique bond, even as they share the wedding day. Throughout wedding planning, schedule planning check-ins with your co-couple to maintain open lines of communication and ensure both parties feel involved and valued.

Guest List and Invitations

An important early step is deciding as a group who you'll invite to your special day. There may be some differences in number and some overlap, but aim to create a cohesive list that makes sure no one feels left out.

As for invitations, you can combine details and wording from both couples into one invitation suite or create separate pieces that coordinate through design and wording choices. You have similar options with your wedding website(s).

Reception Seating and Traditions

For a double wedding reception, you have several options when it comes to sweetheart/couple tables:

- One long sweetheart table for both couples at the front

- Two smaller sweetheart tables, still situated at the head area

- One longer table with both couples seated with members of their wedding parties

No matter the seating setup, be sure each couple has a chance to take part in all the special reception traditions, which may involve any of the following:

- Doing a joint grand entrance or grand exit

- Each couple having their own first dance

- Allowing both sets of parents and wedding parties to give toasts

HOSTING A RECEPTION FOLLOWING A PRIVATE WEDDING CEREMONY

Typically, when people imagine their dream wedding, they envision a ceremony where they say their vows, surrounded by their wedding party, and then float happily down the aisle amid beaming family and friends to the sound of wedding bells. Immediately afterward, it's off to the reception, with the promise of food, drink, festivities, and fun.

It's a pretty safe bet to assume this traditional wedding day combo is here to stay, but, as with many time-honored traditions, there are

WEDDINGS

always those who like to shake things up. For those folks, throwing a reception-only wedding celebration is an option worth considering.

But before I launch into the hows of pulling off a delayed reception to celebrate your marriage, here are a few reasons why having guests at a marriage celebration instead of a wedding may be right for you and your partner:

- You're looking to elope but want to celebrate with friends and family later.

- You need/want to get married in a hurry.

- You desire an intimate wedding ceremony but want an unforgettable night with a rollicking, large-scale celebration.

- You're hosting a destination wedding reception for guests but want to be married in your local church/mosque/synagogue or other house of worship.

- You married during the height of the COVID-19 pandemic with no bridal party and few or no guests, and now you want to celebrate on a larger scale.

- You want to invite children to the reception but fear they will disrupt a solemn ceremony.

When you opt for a reception-only celebration, the focus is on creating an unforgettable evening of festivities without the formalities of a traditional ceremony. Plus, reception-only celebrations can give you the flexibility to tailor your event to your preferences and budget. You can prioritize elements like food, entertainment, and décor to create a memorable experience for your guests without the constraints of a traditional wedding timeline.

How To Plan a Reception

Just like a traditional wedding, a reception-only event calls for careful planning and consideration. Here are a few items to consider as you figure out how to host a wedding reception:

- **Budget.** The first item on your to-do list is to set your budget. A good rule of thumb is to keep your venue and food costs to approximately 18%-20% of your budget while allotting 10%-15% to photos and/or video and perhaps 10%-12% for vendors and service providers, from your florist to a professional planner. You'll also need to budget for invitations, wedding cake, and other reception essentials. Remember to include 5% for those extras that will inevitably pop up.

- **Find your location early in the planning process.** Narrow your search to places that can accommodate your budget and the number of guests you have in mind. Ask each potential reception venue about fees, its contract requirements, and how it can support your vision for your wedding reception. Consider locations convenient to your out-of-town guests.

- **Set a date and make a guest list.** While making these decisions, consider the schedules of your most important guests, like parents, grandparents, and best friends.

- **Decide what you and your honey will wear.** Re-wearing your ceremony attire is fine, but the choice is up to you.

- **If you're planning a reception-only event,** you will need to give careful thought to invitations. Everyone you ask to join you for your ceremony should be invited to your reception. But you'll also need a list of additional people you'd like at your reception.

Be clear that the invitation is for a reception, not a ceremony. One way to word it is "You are invited to a reception in celebration of the marriage of …" Another option is "Mr. and Mrs. Michael Smith and Mr. and Mrs. James Castle invite you to a reception celebrating the marriage of their children, Elizabeth Ann and Thomas Paul, on …"

I also advise making invitees aware of the dress code, as they may be unsure.

Send out invitations in a timely manner. Two months before your event is a good timetable to keep to.

- **Price, select, and book your vendors.** While sticking to your budget is the first consideration when choosing whom to work

WEDDINGS

with on your reception, make sure to view or sample prospective vendors' work. And ask for and follow up with referrals. Word of mouth is often the best judge of quality service. Be sure to get quotes from at least two or three vendors for each needed service.

- **Decide whether to accept gifts.** Some people may fret that it's rude to expect guests to bring a gift if they're only invited to the reception, but these fears may be baseless. After all, presents to celebrate a marriage can be given at any time, and, considering you're likely treating your guests to a meal, drinks, and entertainment, it's not outside the bounds of etiquette to share your registry. However, if you still aren't sure, leave that information off the invitations and simply tell people if they ask.

Managing Expectations with Clear Communication

Once you've made up your mind to hold the wedding ceremony and the reception separately, it's important to let people know, particularly if they will be invited only to the reception. Explain why you're making your decision and that you're thrilled to celebrate with them when the time for the big bash comes.

If someone seems a bit hurt that they're not invited to both events, stand your ground and reiterate your reasons and why it's best for everyone involved, then move on. Loved ones will understand, and you'll be making it up to them with a great party!

HOW TO PLAN A MEMORABLE MICRO WEDDING

The year 2020 will forever be associated with, among other things, certain terms and figures of speech. As the COVID-19 pandemic began changing nearly every aspect of daily life, references to "working remotely" and "Zoom meetings" became commonplace. So did "social distancing," "flattening the curve" (the ability to manage the number of COVID-19 cases without overwhelming hospitals), and "panic shopping."

The wedding industry gained its share of newly popular terms, too, mostly resulting from the creative approaches people took to getting married as safely as possible during a pandemic. One of those words is "minimony," a small wedding ceremony held with the intention of following up with a larger celebration later. Another term we started hearing quite a bit in 2020 was "micro wedding," which describes an intimate wedding with no more than 50 guests (some definitions use even smaller numbers). Unlike a minimony, a micro wedding is the main event, not a precursor to a more elaborate ceremony or reception to come.

Many in the wedding industry believe the micro wedding is a term, and an option, that's here to stay.

"Micro weddings aren't only romantic and intimate. They have multi-fold benefits, such as savings on cost and smaller amounts of planning," a Taylor & Hart blog post explained. "As people discover the charm and character of a more stripped-back wedding, it's a format for celebration that will only be perfected over time."

With that in mind, I've put together some guidelines to help you achieve micro wedding success.

First, let's take a closer look at what micro weddings have to offer.

Small Events, Big Benefits

Micro weddings became a trend to meet a practical need: They made holding weddings in the COVID-19 era more doable. The small number of guests at micro weddings made it easier to keep couples and guests at a safe distance from one another, reducing the risk of spreading illness.

But micro weddings have other benefits, too. These small-scale events allow participants to spend time with loved ones and share a meaningful experience. Micro weddings have cost-cutting potential as well. With a smaller guest list, you need less food and beverages, which often represent a major portion of wedding expenditures. (That said, depending on your food, vendor, and location choices, a micro wedding, like any other event, can get quite expensive.)

Making the Most of Your Micro Wedding

If the benefits of a micro wedding appeal to you, these suggestions can help you capitalize on them.

- **Put careful thought into whom to invite.** Trimming down your guest list is tricky but important. Be sure to include your immediate family: parents, siblings, and grandparents.

- **Don't forget your oldest and dearest friends.** Another possibility could be mentors: coaches, teachers, and others who have had a significant impact on your life. Be prepared to accept the fact that some friends, extended family, and colleagues simply won't make it onto a pared-down small-wedding guest list.

- **Play with your food.** A micro wedding is a perfect opportunity to incorporate fun or creative touches into your wedding menu, from comfort food stations to a special entrée.

- **Include personal touches.** Incorporate elements with special meaning into your day. That might mean creating your own vows, writing out invitations, or picking sentimental items to keep with you.

- **Capture the day.** No matter how small your wedding is, it still will be a hugely important day. You'll want to hire a photographer and/or a videographer. Talk with your vendor about creating a special package of shots that meets your needs.

Should You Hire a Planner?

When planning a tiny wedding, you may be on the fence about whether you need to hire a professional planner. Here are some factors to consider when making this decision:

Pros of a Wedding Planner

- Handles logistics you may overlook when new to planning

- Helps design floor plan, order rentals, manage vendors, and other tasks

- Provides guidance on etiquette questions

- Keeps you on track with timelines and budget

- Diffuses family differences of opinion and personality conflicts

- Allows you to relax and enjoy your special day

- Can provide proven small wedding ideas

Cons of a Professional Planner

- Costs a portion of your budget you may prefer to save

- Requires that you give up control over certain decisions

- May not be necessary to hire an "expert" when you have a small guest list

In general, hiring a wedding planner, even just for day-of coordination, can be worth the investment to reduce stress. But couples comfortable doing their own planning can pull off a micro wedding seamlessly on their own.

Talk to trusted vendors and married friends to decide what's right for you. The choice comes down to your budget, planning style, and priorities.

Infusing Creativity into Your Celebration

One advantage of a micro wedding is the ability to get creative and personalize all aspects of your day. Here are some romantic ideas for you to consider:

- **Purposeful décor:** Use décor representative of special memories, such as vacation souvenirs and ticket stubs.

- **Bespoke menu:** Work with chefs to plan a customized multi-course menu for your wedding filled with your favorite foods.

- **Sentimental music:** Have a playlist of songs that are particularly meaningful to you.

- **Personalized vows:** Pen your own vows to share rather than using traditional scripted vows.

- **Specialty entertainment:** Consider something special, whether it's a band that specializes in cover tunes for your favorite group or a specialty entertainer like a magician or stand-up comedian. Or invite a close friend or family member to sing or perform in some way during your ceremony or reception.

- **Guest involvement:** You can ask loved ones to do readings or share memories during your ceremony.

In a way, a micro wedding is less about size and more about customization. It's your chance to celebrate your new life together with the people you love most, doing what you most enjoy.

PROTECTING YOURSELF FROM WEDDING SCAMS

A North Texas wedding photographer recently made headlines for all the wrong reasons. The Better Business Bureau (BBB) issued a warning about the vendor after receiving 18 complaints from couples claiming she failed to show up at their weddings or engagement shoots. To make matters worse, the photographer accepted deposits ranging from $300 to $800 for each event.

"This particular situation is very sad given the bride-to-be not only is out the deposit money paid, but they do not have pictures of their special day," BBB spokesperson Monica Horton told photography publication PetaPixel. "Every wedding planning season we warn about these types of scams that can ruin a special day."

Busy couples can easily fall prey to con artists and scams like this as they attempt to juggle wedding planning with their other day-to-day responsibilities.

The good news is that there are reasonable steps you can work into your wedding planning process to make yourselves less vulnerable to fraud. These precautions may require a little more time from you now, but they can save you considerable time and aggravation down the road.

Too-Good-To-Be-True Gowns

One common problem is the prevalence of websites that offer surprisingly low rates for designer dresses. In most cases, they're selling cheap counterfeit versions.

Many of these sites even post designers' photos to convince brides they've stumbled across an amazing deal.

According to the consumer advocacy organization Consumer Notice, signs that a site could be selling fake gowns include the following:

- Its "designer dresses" are priced at $200 or less.

- The site has no U.S. address or phone number in the "Contact Us" section.

- Its sales agreement has terms or conditions that can make getting a refund difficult.

I also suggest making sure any retail site you're considering has a lot of customer reviews and looking it up on independent sites to check for consumer complaints.

Something Doesn't Ring True

Just like dresses, the promise of a seemingly great deal on a spectacular engagement ring or wedding band can leave couples vulnerable to markups, buying fake diamonds, and other rip-offs.

If at all possible, have a professional ring appraiser take a look at the ring(s) you're considering.

Pretend Planners

Couples should select wedding planners carefully as well. Con artists have been known to pose as planners, accept large fees from couples, and disappear. Here are some signs of a fraudulent planner:

- No business card

- No business location

- Large deposit requirement (more than 50%)

- No website; using a free email service

Venues, Vendors, and Broken Promises

Of course, pretend planners aren't the only ones eager to help themselves to your money.

It's not uncommon for con artists promising spectacular venues, products, or services to let couples down.

In most of these cases, the fraudulent venue or vendor accepts payment for something, from a reservation to get married at their scenic facility to photography services, and never delivers.

Some photographers do show up, Consumer Notice warns, but they refuse to provide the photos they shot unless the couple pays more money.

Some of the best ways to protect yourself from one of these nightmare scenarios are to read reviews, check references, and look up your potential venue or vendor on independent consumer sites. Are they the subject of complaints with the Better Business Bureau?

Even after taking those steps, it's wise to insist on a written service agreement, with signatures, that clearly outlines the products and services the venue or vendor will provide.

Honeymoon Scams

A honeymoon is supposed to be a romantic, memory-filled vacation after a couple gets married. Unfortunately, scammers sometimes target newlyweds to try to swindle them out of their hard-earned money. Here are some honeymoon scams for couples to watch out for:

- **Fake travel agencies:** Couples should be wary of booking their honeymoon through unfamiliar or questionable travel sites. Scam sites pretend to offer luxury all-inclusive packages at unbelievable prices, but they take payment without actually booking anything. Double-check reviews and do research before booking.

- **Nonrefundable deposits:** Some crooked vendors request substantial nonrefundable deposits up front, then disappear or never fulfill the booked services. Ask about refund policies and read the fine print before paying anything.

- **Upselling tactics:** Unethical vendors use high-pressure tactics to keep selling additional upgrades, insurance policies, etc., which may not be needed. Know exactly what is included so you don't get tricked into excessive purchases.

- **Fake prizes/vouchers:** Scammers pretend to offer free or discounted honeymoon packages if couples attend a timeshare presentation or sign up for a membership trial. Read the fine print carefully on any vouchers.

Fraudulent Registries

A wedding registry allows couples to select gifts they'd like to receive for their new home. But dishonest people sometimes create fake registries to try to scam unsuspecting gift givers. Here's a closer look:

- **Fake store registries:** Scammers set up sham registry accounts with made-up store names at fake websites. After guests purchase gifts, no items are ever shipped. Only register with established, reputable retailers.

- **Fake charity registries:** Couples sometimes create registries where gifts go toward a certain cause. Scammers make up fake charities to pocket these donations. Vet any unfamiliar charities before donating.

- **Hacked accounts:** Criminals may hack into a couple's real registry account and change details to redirect gifts and payments. Use unique, complex passwords and alert retailers if you suspect someone has accessed your account.

Wedding Crashing

Predators have been known to slip into weddings uninvited to take advantage of the festivities. Be vigilant for the following:

- **Gift theft:** Crashers sometimes sneak off with envelope gifts or steal from the gift/card table. Assign someone to watch gifts carefully.

- **Food theft:** This is when uninvited guests take advantage of buffets, drink stations, and refreshments. Tighten catering counts and check for extra guests.

- **Property theft:** Crashers scope out and then steal unattended personal property, such as purses and phones. Don't leave valuables unattended.

More Measures of Protection

The Better Business Bureau has put together additional tips to help you bypass wedding scams:

- Consider high-pressure sales tactics a red flag.

- Get everything in writing, including cancellation policies, prices, fees, dates, services, and products.

- Try to pay with credit cards instead of checks or cash. Credit cards offer more protection against fraud.

- Watch your credit card accounts carefully after your event, and report questionable charges to your credit card company right away.

12 ETIQUETTE TIPS FOR WEDDING PLANNING

In the 1920s and '30s, a popular resource for brides-to-be was "The Bride's Portfolio Advice and Etiquette Booklet," a 12-page publication produced by Good Housekeeping.

The many topics in the guide ranged from formal invitations to getting the new relationship between the bride and her soon-to-be in-laws off to a good start.

"To establish cordial and congenial relations with her husband's family is one of the real tasks to confront the bride," the guide stated. "It will be hard for her to sometimes realize that his family knows him, perhaps even better than she does, and the meeting with them, as well as the relationship to be established socially with them, present a very real opportunity for her to prove herself equal to her new position of wife and hostess in her own home."

While wedding considerations have changed considerably since then, some of the same goals that inspired etiquette rules a century

Courtesy of Epic Photography

ago still apply today. Etiquette helps people create a memorable occasion — one worthy of a major life event — while considering the feelings of the people who will be there.

By the way, some of the guidelines in place in the '20s, like thanking guests for gifts as quickly as possible, still make sense in the 2020s. That's one of the topics I cover in your 12 etiquette tips below.

1. Make sure you tell your close family and friends you're engaged before you post about your exciting news. As strong as the temptation may be to share a photo of your engagement ring or your partner's romantic proposal right away, you want your loved ones to know they come before your other social media friends and followers.

2. Don't include your wedding registry info on your invitations. The main purpose of invitations is to graciously invite guests to share in your marriage celebration, not to tell them you expect gifts. Instead, share registry details on your wedding website or through word of mouth. This allows you to provide the information to those who ask for it, without appearing gift grabby.

   If you feel you must mention registries, do so subtly. At the bottom of the invitation, write "Registries available upon request," and be prepared to share links privately when asked.

   On your wedding website, devote a page to accommodation info for out-of-town guests before detailing registry information on a secondary page.

   When asked about registries in conversation, casually mention store names but don't share direct links or product details unless asked.

3. Don't invite someone to one of your wedding-related events, like your bridal shower, unless they'll be invited to your wedding too. You don't want to suggest that you want someone's gift, but not their company, on your wedding day.

4. As for shower etiquette, these events can be hosted by anyone who steps forward. The exception is the bride, since the party is

being held in her honor. If there will be more than one shower, invite different people to each event so no one feels pressured to buy multiple gifts.

5. Be considerate of wedding party members' needs, along with the time and expense of being there for you. Keep communication open and be sure to express your appreciation verbally, with a thank-you note, and, if your budget allows, with gifts. It's also a good idea to check in regularly as the wedding approaches to see if they need anything.

6. A few more suggestions for taking good care of your wedding party:

   • Delegate thoughtfully. If you're feeling overwhelmed with your planning to-dos, it's OK to ask a bridesmaid for some help—within reason. But take care not to make bridesmaids feel like your personal servants.

   • If you give gifts, don't make them souvenirs of your wedding with your names or monogram. Aim for personalized gifts that reflect wedding party members' interests and passions—or at least pick something they can use.

   • Consider covering some of their expenses, whether that's paying for bridesmaids to have their hair and makeup done or buying wedding party members a meal to eat during wedding-day preparations. This shows your appreciation for their time and commitment.

7. Plan with your guests' comfort in mind. If you'll be having a morning ceremony, for example, make coffee available to guests before the ceremony starts. Planning an evening event? Avoid an excessive gap in time between your ceremony and the cocktail hour or reception. Be sure to provide appetizers, and even entertainment, if there will be a significant wait.

8. Other ways to keep guests comfy:

   • Work with your venue to make sure it's not too hot or cold.

- Provide just-in-case accessories for outdoor weddings, from sunglasses to umbrellas.

- Space seating so guests aren't crammed together.

- Keep entertainment volumes at reasonable levels.

9. While not everyone agrees on this topic, many feel that having a cash bar — asking your guests to pay for their drinks — is in poor taste. Yes, bar bills can be sizeable, but there are workarounds, including limiting drinks to beer and wine and, possibly, one signature drink.

10. Not only should you plan to make guests comfortable, but you also should consider the needs of the people who will be spending their day helping you achieve the wedding you want: your vendors. So be sure to provide meals and beverages for your photography and videography teams, bands, DJs and their assistants, and your wedding planner.

11. Try to greet each of your guests during your wedding. The time you spend with them, even if it's limited, will be appreciated. If you do miss someone, be sure to add a few extra lines to your thank-you note to tell them how happy you are that they supported you on your important day.

12. Back to the subject of thank-you notes: Don't put these off. Ideally, you should send them no later than two or three months after your wedding. Otherwise, you'll find yourself working in awkward apologies for being late and working twice as hard to convince people you love their gifts.

HOW TO WORD YOUR WEDDING INVITATION

At first glance, coming up with wedding invitation wording seems fairly straightforward. All you need to include is the who, what, when, and where, right?

That's essentially true, but now that it's time to work on your invitation, you may have questions.

Should we mention each of our parents? What if they're divorced? How formal do we need to be?

I have answered those questions, along with a few others I commonly hear, in the section below.

Open With the Hosts

As a general rule of thumb, your invitation will open with the names of the hosts, which usually are the bride's parents.

A few examples:

Mr. and Mrs. John Paul Brown (This highly formal option includes a middle name.)

Mr. and Mrs. John Brown (still formal)

Mr. and Mrs. John and Cynthia Brown (still formal with both first names)

Cynthia and John Brown (not so formal)

If a parent is deceased, try starting with the couple's names.

Elizabeth Cohen, daughter of Mr. Mark Cohen and the late Judy Cohen, and Brandon Adams, son of Mr. and Mrs. Douglas and Susan Adams

If parents are divorced, put each parent on a separate line. Put stepparents on the same line as their spouses.

Mr. and Mrs. Randall and Ann Thompson

Mr. and Mrs. James and Greta Smith

The same rule of thumb applies to hosts who are not married: Put them on separate lines.

If you and your partner are paying for your own wedding, you do have the option of skipping the host line of your invitation.

Or, if you're receiving financial contributions from parents on both sides of the family, you can list all of the parents' names. Or start with the names of you and your partner and add a phrase such as "Together with their parents" or "Together with our families."

Ask Your Guests To Attend...

Next, the invitation should have a request line that essentially says, "please come."

The way you put this will vary, depending on how formal you'd like to be. Here are a few options:

request the honor of your presence

would love for you to join them

invite you to celebrate with them

Your Wedding

And then tell people exactly what you want them to attend. You might write:

at the marriage of their daughter

at the marriage of

as our children tie the knot

as we exchange vows

Add the Bride's and Groom's Names

Now, if you haven't mentioned them yet, it's time for the names of you and your partner. You can put your names in a size that's larger than the rest of the text or use a different font, if you'd like, to make them stand out.

If you're taking a formal approach, start with the bride, with her first and middle name, followed by the groom's full name and, if appropriate, title. You might write:

Elizabeth Anne Parker
and
William Robert Evans, M.D.

You also can list names in alphabetical order, or for a more casual approach, stick with first names.

Tell Guests When To Arrive and Where They Should Show Up

Now list that all-important date and time, which will be spelled out on a formal invitation. Be sure to include the day of the week, especially if you're planning a Friday or Sunday wedding.

Saturday, the twentieth of June, two thousand twenty-two, at half after five in the afternoon.

If you would like a more casual invitation, numerals are fine.

Follow with the location, complete with the city and state. For a destination wedding, you should include the country.

Invitations usually don't include addresses and zip codes of wedding venues, but you should add them for a private residence.

Move On to Reception Information

End with information about the reception: Will it be at the same location as your ceremony? If so, you can write, "Reception to follow."

If not, include full details: reception start time, location name, city, and state.

If space allows, or if you're including an insert card, include the dress code.

Reservations

A formal invitation most likely will include a separate response card. Or you can ask guests to RSVP on your wedding website.

State Decisions Clearly

If there's a detail that could cause confusion or awkwardness, try to be very clear and open about it in your wording.

For example, maybe you're planning an adults-only wedding. State that clearly on the invitation:

We kindly request that this be an adult-only wedding.

Adults-only affair.

If you don't plan to serve dinner, make that clear as well. For example:

Hors d'oeuvres and cocktail celebration to follow the ceremony.

A Few More Thoughts

Your invitations aren't meant to be a depository for all of your wedding details. Provide your registry information on your website.

Whether you're opting for formal or casual invitations, be concise.

Also, aim for clarity. Read what you've written and ask yourself, could anything here confuse a reader?

Proofread. Proofread again. Ask friends and family to take a look, too. Double-check the spelling of all proper names, from your venue to your future in-laws.

If you're asking yourself if you'd prefer formal wording, that decision is entirely up to you. One factor to consider is the formality of your event. Do you plan to go with a black-tie evening event or a more casual brunch wedding? Your invitation will give guests a feel for what they can expect.

WEDDINGS

CHAPTER 8

Celebrations Before and After the Wedding

Courtesy of Blanca Duran Photography

HOW TO PLAN AN AMAZING BRIDAL SHOWER

If you've agreed to host a bridal shower, you may be wondering how to get started. While showers are an important part of a bride-to-be's experience, don't be intimidated or worry about reaching shower perfection.

To help with your planning, I've put together some bridal shower basics and ideas to consider.

Bridal Shower Basics

A bridal shower generally is a chance for friends and family of the bride to "shower" her with gifts she can use and enjoy once she's married. The celebration includes food, beverages, games, or activities — if the bride wants them — and time for the bride to open her gifts.

A bridal shower, by the way, is not exactly the same thing as a wedding shower. The first is all about the bride-to-be, while the other is a coed event for the bride and groom. This section will focus on bridal showers, but a lot of the advice here would work with either approach.

A word about shower hosts: Generally, these celebrations are organized by the maid of honor, close friends, bridesmaids, or the bridal party, but really, anyone can be the host.

Know What You Can Spend

Start the planning process by developing a budget. Categories can include the following:

- Venue
- Food and drinks
- Vendors
- Décor
- Rentals
- Favors

Bridal showers range in price from about $10 per person to more than $100 per person. You have the option of sharing this responsibility with others.

Delegation: Always a Wise Strategy

You also can enlist help with planning and event preparations, a step that I highly recommend. Multiple planners will ease the load you're carrying and contribute to more creative ideas. Go ahead and find helpers to take on tasks that match their strengths and interests.

More Planning Considerations

Here are some of the other factors you should consider as you plan:

- **Timing:** Aim to hold the shower two to six months before the wedding.

- **Location:** If you need venue ideas, you can find a wealth of ideas online. Once you have a list of possibilities, do a deeper dive: Review customer reviews and contact potential venues for price policies and details on their event packages.

- **The guest list:** While planning the shower is something you do to help the bride, she should still have input on her shower, especially when it comes to who's invited. You don't want to miss someone the bride hoped to include or put her in the uncomfortable position of welcoming someone she didn't want there.

- **Distributing invitations:** Aim to put your invitations in the mail (or send your digital ones) about four to six weeks before the shower. If possible, ask guests to inform you about dietary restrictions and food allergies when they return their RSVPs so you can plan accordingly.

- **Dress:** Your invitations should provide guidance on how formal the event will be.

- **Bridal shower gifts:** Refer guests to the wedding website where they can access the wedding registry and find bridal shower gift ideas. You'll also want to remind the bride to complete the registry in plenty of time and to include a variety of practical, fun, and unique bridal shower ideas. Most registries allow brides to incorporate ideas from more than one business.

  Plan to keep track of who gives which bridal gift during the shower so the bride can write thank-you notes. (She will repeat this process after receiving wedding gifts. Even if she thanked people for her bridal shower gifts, she'll need to send a thank-you for each wedding gift.)

A note about bridal shower gifts for older brides: Mature brides, especially those marrying for the second time, may not necessarily need the practical household items a first-time bride will. Consider fun and luxurious gifts, such as personalized keepsakes, honeymoon funds, or date-night packages for the newlyweds.

- **Food and beverages:** Here's a tip that's easy to forget as you get caught up in your planning: Be sure to select food and cake that the bride actually likes. Wondering what to offer? Finger foods, beverages, and desserts are safe bets, but you can, of course, serve a meal. Depending on your budget and the size of the shower, consider enlisting a caterer's help.

- **Music:** You can create a playlist that includes some of the bride's favorite tunes.

- **The groom:** He won't attend a bridal shower, but he can contribute ideas or put together a video message for the guests. Some grooms opt to make an appearance near the end of the shower, with flowers for the bride.

- **A theme:** This is optional. If you want to go this route and need ideas, draw inspiration from the bride and her passions, tastes, and interests. If she's a chocoholic, for example, you'll find a wealth of ideas for throwing a fabulous chocolate-themed shower. Your activities (see more below) could even include making your own chocolate candy for bridal shower favors.

- **Décor:** This is another area that should reflect the bride's interests and personality. She may already have some thoughts on the décor she would like. If she doesn't, consider showing her a few options for colors, flowers, signage, and other decorative elements to select from.

Beyond the Gifts: Shower Activity Ideas

Do you need inspiration for things to do at a bridal shower? More and more showers feature activities that guests might enjoy trying in their spare time, like yoga sessions, DIY crafts, or a bit of pampering.

You'd be surprised at the variety of specialty businesses willing to come to you when you host a shower. You can, for example, line up a wine specialist for tastings and food pairings, a calligraphy instructor, a choreographer who can teach the bride and guests a special dance, a chef to teach a specific recipe, a mixologist who can go over making a signature cocktail, a massage therapist, or a manicurist.

That said, there is nothing wrong with offering bridal shower games, and the bride may have been looking forward to them. You can go with traditional games, like pin the veil on the bride, or create toilet-paper wedding dresses.

Additional game possibilities include purse scavenger hunt, newlywed trivia, and pen a poem, where a guest writes one line of a romantic poem for the couple, folds the paper over to hide their words, and passes it along to the next guest to do the same, until everyone has had a turn. And these are only a few of the many game activities you can find online.

Just remember, the activities, food, and décor you plan will all contribute to the day, but there's no need to stress over the details. If you plan with the overall goal of creating sweet memories for the bride and her guests—and making the bride feel special—the shower you host will be a tremendous success.

HOW TO PLAN AN AMAZING BACHELORETTE PARTY

It can easily be argued that, apart from the actual wedding day, the bachelorette party is one of the most anticipated events of the entire nuptial experience, not only for the bride but for her group of best girls as well.

With so much riding on a great shindig and proper single-life send-off for the bride-to-be, it's important to get it right. From the planning to the location to the guest list and the entertainment, details matter. Here are a few guidelines to help you cover all your bases when planning and executing a great send-off for the guest of honor.

- **Decide who's hosting, how decisions will be made, and how costs will be divided.** The bride should be kept in the loop as you plan, but don't saddle her with the details, especially when she's immersed in working out the details of her wedding. Let her decide when and where she wants to hold the event, especially if it's going to be an overnight or weekend getaway. And, of course, she determines the guest list. Also, find out what she definitely doesn't want or if she has something very particular in mind. However, when it comes to scheduling activities or booking dinner reservations and hotels, don't bother her. This is where delegated tasks among the planners come in.

- **Start planning early.** It may take some time before you can firm up all of the details, but I encourage you to start developing ideas and doing your research well in advance. As soon as the bride and groom determine their wedding date and location, you can start figuring out when the bachelorette party will take place. Assume that most of the attendees have busy schedules and give yourself time to find a date that everyone can agree on.

- **Don't ask for or expect gifts.** In fact, it's a good idea to let it be known that no guests or hostesses are to buy a present for the bride. This should go without saying, but it's best to err on the side of caution and let everyone know the deal up front.

- **You can forgo formal invitations.** Because the bachelorette party is an intimate affair between close friends, email invites will do. After all, the cost would only add to the final tally and eat into a budget better spent on fun activities—like a group spa session!

- **Get your swag ready,** but don't forget the essentials. If you're planning a hotel party, a pub crawl, or even a long weekend at a cabin, it's fun to have party cups, banners, balloons, and bachelorette-themed novelties for the bride and her squad to wear and take photos with. If you're thinking of matching shirts, agree on the design, gather everyone's size, and put in your order well ahead of the party.

Also, remember to designate one or two ladies to stock up on groceries and alcohol for your rental, making sure to allow for any special dietary needs. It's a good idea to have food for a few meals as well as snacks. You might want to have headache medication, one or two board games, and hygiene items on hand, too.

- **Plan activities,** including scheduled downtime. While the bachelorette party or weekend is supposed to be a fun and casual affair, things can stall if there is no rhyme or reason for the festivities. Know ahead of time where you'll be going and how you're going to get there. If eating is involved, make sure you have reservations made or ingredients to prepare something yourself. If you're heading out of town and don't want to dine out or cook every meal, be familiar with nearby restaurants that can deliver. If you'd like someone to make a toast, be sure to give them plenty of advance notice.

A bachelorette party is one of the bride-to-be's last flings as a singleton, so no pressure with the planning, right? Just kidding! A great hen night is all about friends, fun, and making memories. A bit of creativity, organization, and smart planning will allow those things to happen organically.

YOUR GUIDE TO THROWING AN ENGAGEMENT PARTY

An engagement party is a wonderful way to celebrate the exciting journey toward marriage. It's also an opportunity to bring family and your closest friends together to share in your joy.

If you're considering hosting an engagement party, this guide will walk you through the essential elements to ensure it's a memorable occasion for everyone involved.

Is an Engagement Party Right for You?

There are good reasons to host an engagement party, but also a few drawbacks to keep in mind.

Some of the upsides of engagement parties:

- They allow friends and family to join in the celebration of your love and upcoming marriage.

- The celebration provides an opportunity for a more intimate gathering before the larger wedding event.

- An engagement function gives couples a chance to formally introduce families and friends who may not have met before.

Engagement party downsides include the following:

- Another event means added expenses, so consider your budget before committing to and planning an engagement party.

- Planning multiple events may be challenging, especially if you have a short engagement period.

Party Timing

Typically, engagement parties are held one to three months after the proposal. This gives you time to announce your big news before sending formal wedding invitations. Consider your personal, work, and wedding planning responsibilities as you look at potential party dates.

Selecting a Venue

Choose a venue that aligns with the atmosphere you want. It could be a cozy backyard gathering, a private room at an elegant restaurant, or an event venue. Factor in the number of guests and the overall vibe you want to create as you narrow down choices.

The Party Hosts

While you can host your own engagement party, traditionally, the bride's parents host this event. Friends or other family members handle the event planning, too.

Budgeting and Expenses

Establish a budget early on to guide your planning process. Consider expenses such as venue rental, catering, decorations, and entertainment.

Your Party Dress Code

Provide dress code details on your engagement party invitations so guests can plan their attire. Casual, cocktail attire, or black-tie optional are common options.

Party Food and Drinks

Offer an assortment of passed hors d'oeuvres, or display them in an appetizing spread. Popular options include the following:

- Meatballs

- Stuffed mushrooms

- Bruschetta

- Mini quiches

- Cheese and fruit skewers

- Shrimp cocktail

- Pinwheels or tea sandwiches

- Chicken satay

- Bacon-wrapped dates

- Mini crab cakes

If you're offering a seated dinner, opt for crowd-pleasing entrées like pasta, chicken, salmon, or steak. Or you can offer a buffet or food stations so guests can easily serve themselves. Here are some full meal ideas:

- Pasta bar with various sauces and toppings

- Taco/nacho bar with all the fixings

- Slider or mini sandwich bar

- Salad bar with protein additions like chicken or shrimp

- Interactive stations with made-to-order menus

Don't forget desserts: Sweet treats like cupcakes, a cake or pie bar, or an ice cream sundae station make fun additions.

Your Party Décor

Engagement party décor doesn't have to be over-the-top. Décor possibilities include string lights, balloons, flower arrangements, a photo backdrop, engagement photo displays, and fabric drapery. Use colors and props that tie into your theme.

Game Possibilities

Engagement parties are all about bringing people together to celebrate the couple. Adding some interactive games can encourage guests to mingle and get to know one another. Some ideas for fun engagement party games include the following:

- **The Newlywed Game:** The bride-to-be and future groom are asked questions about each other, and the party guests guess the answers.

- **Wedding Trivia:** This game tests guests' knowledge of wedding traditions.

- **Find the Guest:** Clues are handed out describing each guest, and people must mingle to figure out who their clue is referencing.

- **Wedding Advice Cards:** Note cards are supplied on which guests write down marriage tips for the newly engaged couple. The funniest bits of advice are shared with the group.

Toasts

Designate time for toasts to express gratitude and share anecdotes. Make sure that key people, such as parents and close friends, have an opportunity to speak.

More Tips and Ideas

- It's a good idea to hire a photographer or designate someone to capture moments throughout the party.

- While gifts are not mandatory, some guests may bring them. Be prepared with a designated area for gifts.

- Most importantly, relax and enjoy the celebration. It's a time for joy and anticipation, so savor every moment.

WHAT YOU SHOULD KNOW ABOUT REHEARSAL DINNERS

When we think about heartwarming toasts to the bride and groom, family and friends enjoying each other's company, good food, and touching moments, we're usually picturing a wedding reception.

But in many cases, those elements can be part of a rehearsal dinner, too. This pre-wedding meal traditionally is a time for the bride and groom to spend time with close friends and family and get the celebrating officially underway. It's a chance to make special memories and show wedding participants they're appreciated.

Will you be organizing a rehearsal dinner soon? Here are some guidelines and suggestions that can help.

What Will Be Happening at the Rehearsal Dinner?

The rehearsal dinner, in most cases, will follow the wedding rehearsal, when the bride, groom, and wedding party go over the ceremony procession, seating, readings, and recession.

Basically, like a dress rehearsal for a play, rehearsing the day before the wedding is a way to make sure everyone knows what they'll be doing when it's time for the main event.

The dinner that follows gives the rehearsal participants a chance to unwind and get in celebration mode. And it allows wedding party members to get to know each other better.

Aside from eating, what happens during a rehearsal dinner is up to you. You can make it a relaxed gathering focused on good food and conversation, or you can go for a more structured event. You can even have entertainment or fun activities like a photo booth.

If you'd like to put some extra thought and planning into your rehearsal dinner, here are some possibilities:

- **Toasts:** The rehearsal dinner is a nice time for the dinner host to say a few words. Other potential speakers could be the bride or groom (or both) and members of the wedding party. (A few words about speeches: Wedding rehearsal speeches tend to be less formal than speeches made at a wedding, but I do encourage speech-givers to put some time into planning and rehearsing what they'll be saying. Aim for something short and heartfelt.)

- **Gift giving:** The flexibility of the rehearsal dinner makes it a convenient time for the bride to distribute gifts to the wedding party.

- **Announcements:** Do you have any information for the wedding party about policies, dressing rooms, or parking at your wedding venue? This is the time to share it.

Who's Responsible for the Rehearsal Dinner?

Rehearsal dinners traditionally have been formal events hosted by the groom's parents. In more recent years, the dinners have become more casual, and in many instances, the couples have taken over as hosts.

Really, you can take any approach you'd like. The important thing here is clear communication. The bride and groom should speak with the groom's family before planning begins, so everyone is on the same page.

Who Should Be Invited?

Generally, the guest list for the rehearsal dinner should include immediate family, the wedding party and their plus-ones, and out-of-town guests. Some families also invite those who will do a special reading during the ceremony, ushers, the ring bearer, the flower girl, and — if they're close to the family — the officiant and their spouse.

Rehearsal Dinner Invitations

You don't need to send formal printed invitations for your rehearsal dinner. You can reach out to the people you want there with online invitations, emails, or a phone call.

Aim to invite people about four to six weeks before the dinner. Be sure to include details about dress and whether children can attend.

What Kind of Food Should Be Offered?

It's considerate to offer a menu that accommodates dietary restrictions and food allergies, but beyond that, serve anything you'd like. If you're looking for inspiration, consider the foods your town is known for. In Houston, for example, maybe you'd want to include barbecue or Tex-Mex dishes. Or maybe you'd like to work in a dish that ties in with family tradition, like the macaroni and cheese the groom loved as a child or the dump cake the bride's grandmother makes. (Just be sure to check with your venue to make sure it's OK to bring in food.)

A Few Tips for You

Here are a few more considerations to smooth your planning process:

- **Set a budget.** The average cost of American rehearsal dinners is about $1,400. If you need to trim costs, some options include going with breakfast, lunch, or brunch instead of dinner;

sticking with appetizers and/or dessert; or limiting the guest list to parents and the bridal party.

- **Keep commutes short.** If possible, aim for a location reasonably close to your guests' homes or hotels and the location of your wedding venue. You also can look into the possibility of holding the rehearsal dinner at your venue.

- **Consider entertainment.** If you'd like to make the dinner an all-out party, you can always hire live performers, from a band to dancers.

- **Double-check.** Don't forget to confirm your reservations with your venue, caterer, photographer, entertainer, and anyone else you've lined up for the party.

- **Personalize the party.** Consider creating a video presentation or a photo display of the bride and groom (baby and childhood pictures are always a hit). Or tie the dinner to a special theme, possibly something related to the food you're serving, your location, or the theme of your wedding. If your wedding celebrates Hollywood, for example, maybe you'll want your rehearsal dinner to zero in on your favorite science fiction flicks or romantic comedies.

- **Don't forget photography.** Designate someone to take photos, whether you hire a photographer or enlist your cousin. The dinner, most likely, will include special moments you'll want to capture.

- **Don't let the evening stretch out too long.** Aim for wrapping up after about three hours. Depending on when they arrived, your out-of-town guests may be running out of steam, and guests who worked that day may be tired, too. Plus, all of you have a big day coming up.

- **Have fun!** Above all, that's the goal of your rehearsal dinner.

WHEN YOU DON'T WANT THE FUN TO END: PLANNING A WEDDING AFTER-PARTY

When you picture your future wedding day, what's the first thing that comes to mind? Do you envision a beautiful, moving ceremony? The iconic first dance and cake-cutting that takes place during the wedding reception? Or … does your idea of the perfect wedding include partying the night away with your partner, wedding party, and friends?

If the third option is what you envision, a wedding after-party may be a perfect fit for you.

What Is an After-Party?

Wedding after-parties are a huge trend these days. They are parties that begin after the wedding reception ends.

Your approach to the wedding after-party is all about personal preference. Your post-wedding celebration can be as simple as casually inviting your wedding guests to join you for more fun at a pub or friend's house after your wedding.

Or you can plan a showstopping bash with amazing food, beverages, décor, and dazzling entertainment.

Selecting a Party Location

Once you decide you do want to hold an after-party, you'll have some decisions to make. Here are a few guidelines and questions to ask yourself to help get your planning started.

First, you'll need to select your after-party venue. Depending on your wedding venue's policies and hours, you may be able to keep the party going at the same venue where you hold your reception. You can change the music, the lighting—even your clothes—at your wedding venue to signal that you're phasing into wedding after-party mode. Keep in mind, your reception venue may have to comply with community noise restrictions. Ask if you'll be able to continue playing loud music. Also, some wedding venues have liquor-licensing-related time restrictions.

You also have the option of moving your after-wedding party somewhere else: You can have a house party or line up hotel rooms, a hotel bar, a karaoke bar, a nightclub, or any other option that can accommodate you and your guests during the time window you need it.

Whether you are staying at your wedding venue or moving, I recommend booking the spot early in your wedding planning process.

Figure Out the Timing

You'll also need to figure out when you want your after-party to start and how long you want it to last.

In many cases, couples base the timing on their band—assuming they want their band to play during their wedding after-party. They book the band for four hours, which may include two hours during the wedding reception and two hours during their after-party. (Of course, you can always hire a DJ to save money. Either way, if you're lining up music entertainment, let them know if you have any special requests.)

Back to the length of your after-party: The typical length is two hours, but that's not a rule.

If you're holding a destination wedding, for example, you may want the celebration to continue throughout the night.

Keep Your Guests in the Loop

Be sure to let your bridal party and your guests know if you're planning a post-wedding bash, and provide details about the time and location. That said, some couples opt to make their after-party a surprise. If that's the case, you can always share your after-party information on your wedding day, possibly during the reception.

Make a Food and Drink Plan

If the party is going to continue after the reception, you should plan to offer guests something to eat. This is also a great way to offset the effects of alcohol. You can go with late-night favorites like pizza, sandwiches, sliders, and chicken fingers or something more budget-friendly, like chips and dip.

As for serving more alcohol, that will be up to you. If you don't intend to cover your guests' after-party drinks, let them know in advance.

Wedding After-Party Decorations

Having décor specifically for your after-party is another personal preference. Some people like to change the look of their reception venue to create a party atmosphere. If that idea appeals to you, you can always choose new décor that ties in with your wedding theme—or that is completely different.

Think About Taking Photos

A wedding after-party is a continuation of the fun, affection, and sheer joy of your wedding celebration. If you'd like your photographer or videographer to be there to capture it, ask them about additional costs. If that isn't practical, other options include renting a photo booth or giving guests disposable cameras to snap shots of what they observe during the party.

After-Party Etiquette: Frequently Asked Questions

While there isn't an extensive list of etiquette rules for post-wedding parties, there are a few key things for you to consider to make your guests feel valued. Here are a few of the more common wedding after-party etiquette questions I hear, along with my answers:

- **Who should we invite to our after-party?** Invite everyone on your wedding reception guest list. Granted, some people, especially those with children, may choose not to attend. But don't leave anyone out because you assume they won't want to — or won't be able to — be part of your after-party.

- **How should we handle the guest list and invitations?** You don't have to send a formal invitation, but you should provide details on the time and location. One way to do that is to include a note on your wedding website. You also can send emails or texts.

- **Who hosts the wedding after-party?** Whoever is hosting your wedding will be the after-party host. Generally, that person will pay for the after-party, too, but that's not written in stone. If a family member or your parents are helping with your wedding costs and don't necessarily want to pay for a post-wedding party, you and your partner can cover the costs.

- **Should we provide transportation?** While providing transportation is not a requirement, it's a thoughtful gesture. Consider arranging shuttle services or rideshare options to ensure the safety and convenience of your guests. If transportation logistics are not feasible, you can include information about local transportation options or rideshare services on your wedding website or provide recommendations for reputable taxi companies in the area. Ultimately, the goal is to make attending the after-party as seamless and enjoyable as possible for your guests.

Party Ideas

Here are a few after-party tips to help you make your bash memorable:

- **Plan activities.** While most people associate wedding after-parties with drinking, hitting the dance floor, snacking, and socializing well into the early hours of the next morning, some guests may appreciate something different to do. Activities could include bringing in a pop-up karaoke booth or casino games.

- **Make it a late-night movie screening.** If you need a less rowdy party possibility, arrange to watch a movie with your guests. This is an especially fitting choice if you had a movie theme at your wedding reception.

- **Create a silent disco.** This is another fun way to keep the party going if sound ordinances are a consideration. You and your guests wear headsets with different channels and select the type of music you want to dance to. Ask your wedding venue about this approach. Provide glow sticks, party beads, and other favors to help enhance your disco theme.

- **Line up unique entertainment.** In addition to music, you can always line up something special for your after-party entertainment. Depending on the vibe you're going for, you can hire a stand-up comedian, a magician, a dance act—even a fire eater.

- **Have a house party.** If your wedding after-party is going to be small, you can move the celebration to a house. Provide plenty of food, and keep the evening casual. We do recommend talking with your neighbors in advance and trying not to overdo the loud music.

- **Have you considered a post-wedding brunch?** A late-night party is not for everyone. But maybe you want a prolonged celebration so you can spend more time with your closest family members afterward. With a brunch, you come to the party rested. Or maybe you want an event where children will be welcome. In any case, a post-wedding brunch could be the perfect alternative to a late-night wedding after-party. Generally, this event, also known as a farewell brunch, has a

WEDDINGS

laid-back, relaxed vibe that will be reflected in your décor (if you have one), dress code, and food choices.

- **Or...hold a day-after wedding party.** A brunch fits into this category, but additional party ideas include a pizza party, a pool party, a barbecue, a spa day, a picnic with outdoor games, or an outing in the community.

CHAPTER 9

The Bride and the Groom

Courtesy of Ashlen Sydney Photography

WEDDING BOUQUETS: CREATIVE FLOWER CHOICES, TIPS, AND MORE

When you picture a bridal bouquet, does your mental image include roses, peonies, or baby's breath?

It would make sense if it did, since those blooms are among the all-time most popular flower choices for weddings. (Other top choices include anemone, dahlia, calla lily, hydrangea, jasmine, lilac, orchid, ranunculus, sweet pea, and tulip.)

There are reasons why these blooms are selected so frequently — from the symbolism of roses to the beauty of orchids — but there's nothing wrong with going in a different direction. Maybe you'd like to add something that holds special meaning for you or to work in something a bit out of the ordinary.

Need a few seeds of inspiration? I can help.

- **Irises:** These delicate blooms are a great way to add touches of dramatic color to your bouquet. Most people picture irises in a shade of purple, but you can opt for shades of apricot and peach, brown, pink, white, yellow, dark cherry, and more.

- **Delphinium:** Tall and striking, delphinium (also known as larkspur) is an extremely popular wedding bouquet choice, especially in the summer. This bloom is available in a wide range of colors, though the two most popular choices are white and baby blue. Carry it solo, in one or more colors, for a stunning bouquet.

- **Red Ginger:** Roses aren't the only flowers with special symbolism. Ginger plants symbolize strength and prosperity, and red ginger, in particular, represents fiery passion — all of which bode well for a happy marriage. These vivid flowers are ideal if you have a tropical theme, or if you simply want to add some pizzazz to your bouquet.

- **Herbs:** Herbs can contribute delicate scents and unique visuals to a bouquet. And while herbs are making a comeback today, including them in bouquets is a tradition that goes back centuries. Herbs that lend themselves well to bouquets include eucalyptus, lavender, mint, rosemary, and sage. An added bonus: Many of these herbs have calming properties, perfect for those moments just before you begin your walk down the aisle.

- **Protea:** Interest has also been building in the protea, or sugar-bushes, of South Africa. Varieties include the big king protea, the pincushion protea, and the blushing bride protea (sounds like a perfect wedding day choice).

- **Butterfly Ranunculus:** These flowers are known for their "dainty, iridescent petals" and lend themselves especially well to bouquets. "The ranunculus butterfly is a lovely option as a secondary bloom for a more organic or garden-style bouquet, since it features multiple flowers on each stem," writes Roots Floral Designs.

- **Carnations:** This underrated flower is just starting to gain traction as a wedding bouquet choice. "There are many antiquated opinions about carnations; some people believe they are cheap flowers. They are cost-effective, but not cheap looking," florist Teresa Eoff told *Brides* magazine. Carnations are durable and can add an element of lushness to a bouquet.

- **Cosmos:** These five-petaled flowers can give your bouquet a romantic flair. In addition to white and pink cosmos, you can opt for the dramatic appearance of brownish-red chocolate cosmos.

- **Go Texas:** Our Houston-based venue frequently serves clients who are proud of their Texas ties. If that describes you, maybe you'll want to add plants native to the Lone Star State to your bouquet. Texas is especially well known for its gorgeous wildflowers, the bluebonnet in particular. A few additional choices include daffodils, hyacinth, vivid Indian paintbrush, and purple coneflowers.

Struggling with Decision-Making?

If you're not quite sure what you want your bouquet to look like — or if you even want one — keep these tips in mind:

Know What You Can Spend

As with most wedding-planning decisions, I strongly recommend that you have a budget in place for all of your flower expenditures, from bouquets to corsages, backdrop arrangements to reception table centerpieces. And keep in mind, flowers are not required—deciding if and how to use them is up to you.

First Things First

If you do opt for a bouquet, don't rush your selection. While some preliminary research can be helpful, planning experts suggest waiting until you've chosen your dress before you move on to flowers.

"The design of your bouquet is completely dependent on the style, shape and detail of your dress," UK-based floral designer Emma Lappin told Bridal Musings. "I think the key to bouquet design is that it doesn't drown you, hide the silhouette of the dress or unbalance the line."

Seasonal Choices

Keep in mind as you start considering the flowers that will go into your bouquet that some options will not be available if they're not in season. Your florist can guide you and suggest alternatives if you have something specific in mind.

A Guide to Shapes

One of the factors you'll be considering is the shape of your bridal bouquet, which can help influence the overall look and vibe you want to achieve for your wedding.

Some of your options include the following:

- **Asymmetrical:** A more modern statement, this bouquet may be higher on one side than the other or feature an accent on one side that doesn't appear on the other. Asymmetrical bouquets can also feature different flower types on each side. This allows you to mix colors and textures in an artistic way.

- **Cascading:** These bouquets feature a dramatic waterfall effect of flowers and greenery that trail toward the floor. Cascading bouquets are popular choices for whimsical and classic weddings.

- **Composite:** Composite bouquets made of a single bloom type, such as roses or peonies, can mimic the look of one giant, lush flower.

- **Hand-tied:** The stems are tied with a ribbon. These bouquets lend themselves well to weddings with a rustic or romantic vibe.

- **Pageant bouquet:** These bouquets have long stems that lie on the bride's arm and tend to make a dramatic statement. Pageant bouquets are a great choice for contemporary weddings.

- **Posy bouquet:** This is a small, round arrangement that can be held in one hand. They usually go light on greenery and feature blooms in similar colors. Posy bouquets are popular for bridesmaids and flower girls, but they're a lovely choice for brides, too. Their smaller size also makes them budget friendly.

- **Round:** This is a classic bouquet tightly arranged in a dome shape, typically with blooms and no foliage. These bouquets often have a single type of flower or different types of flowers that are the same color — though you absolutely can go with a variety of colors.

WEDDINGS

BRIDAL PORTRAIT PROS AND CONS

Who says your wedding day has to be your only moment in the spotlight?

For many, bridal portrait photo sessions are a chance to enjoy a day of dressing up, complete with hair, makeup, and wedding dress, months before their wedding day.

According to Dallas-based Sami Kathryn Photography, bridal portrait sessions got their start in Europe and are especially popular in the American South.

If you're wondering whether you should have bridal portraits taken, this list of pros and cons may help with your decision. I've also included some tips for you to keep in mind.

Bridal Portrait Pros

For many, taking bridal portraits is a positive experience, and the benefits aren't limited to beautiful photos. (Of course, having gorgeous photos that mark an important chapter in your life is a pretty big plus.)

Here are some of the biggest pros:

- You'll have more time on your wedding day to focus on shots with your new spouse and loved ones.

- Your photo shoot gives you a "practice session," so to speak, to help you adjust to being photographed.

- Having bridal portraits made in advance allows for a more relaxed photo shoot, while day-of-wedding shots may be a bit rushed. It is also easier during your bridal portrait session to get creative or add a bit of whimsy to some of your shots.

- Bridal portraits make wonderful gifts. You can give your partner, parents, and other loved ones a framed print.

- Have I mentioned that these photo sessions can be fun, especially if you enjoy getting your hair and makeup done and dressing up?

Bridal Portrait Cons

Of course, bridal portraits are not a requirement, and for some, the disadvantages outweigh the advantages. Here are some potential negatives:

- Bridal portraits will increase your wedding expenditures and add more to-dos to your list.

  (You can get solo portrait shots taken at your wedding. Just talk with your photographer and let them know it's a priority.)

- You will have to select your dress, and have the alterations done, earlier than you might have otherwise.

- The number of poses you can do alone, instead of with your partner, is limited.

- You'll need to take great care to keep your dress spotless during your portrait session.

Tips For You

If you do want bridal portraits, I have some strategies for making the most of them. A few ideas:

- Don't limit yourself to your wedding dress. Take some shots in another outfit that you feel flatters you.

- Do a bit of multitasking. When you pose for the portraits, try out the hair and makeup styles you have in mind for your wedding. After you see the portraits, you can decide if you want to make any tweaks, from a different hairdo to a different shade of eye shadow. You also can give your wedding shoes a trial run and break them in a bit.

- Communicate with your venue and vendors. Give your seamstress a heads-up about your portrait session date so they can make sure your dress is ready and that you'll look fabulous in it. You'll also want to finalize the session details far in advance with your photographer, and with your venue if you want your session held there. Will other vendors or businesses be involved? Maybe you'll want your florist to create a small bouquet for you; talk with them in advance, too.

- Ask someone to join you for your session. If you enlist the help of a close relative or friend, they can help you and your dress look their best. Be sure to follow up with a note of thanks.

- Give your location careful thought. The "where" for your portrait session is up to you. You can choose a scenic outdoor location (have a backup indoor location in mind), or maybe you'd prefer a place with sentimental value. You also can arrange to do the shoot at your wedding venue.

- Make sure you get enough sleep before your portrait date. Being well-rested does make a difference.

- Make your portrait part of your wedding décor. Display your favorite bridal portrait during the reception.

WEDDINGS

If you decide to have bridal portraits made, I hope you embrace the experience. The months leading up to your wedding can be a blur. This is a chance to capture some of the sweetness of that time and enjoy a bit of pampering while you're at it.

WORKING WITH A MAKEUP ARTIST FOR YOUR WEDDING

Have you been wondering if you should invest in a professional makeup artist for your big day?

Paying someone else to make up your face may sound more like a luxury than a necessity, but many brides find that working with a professional makeup artist minimizes stress and enhances their day.

Here are some pros and cons of working with a makeup artist, along with some tips for success.

Why Hire a Makeup Artist?

To start with, a professional will have the skills, knowledge, and products necessary to produce the results you want. In most cases, it takes a professional to keep makeup holding strong for an all-day event—especially an emotionally packed one.

What's more, makeup artists are fast, meaning that instead of spending a big chunk of time painstakingly attempting to achieve makeup perfection yourself, you can leave that job to your artist and focus on other things, thus minimizing your stress.

Makeup artists also can help you look amazing in your wedding pictures. They know how much makeup is optimal for photos and how to avoid overdoing it or accentuating fine lines. If you want to have a fresh look on your wedding day, your makeup artist can provide touch-ups before you go to the ceremony.

Downsides To Be Aware Of

Hiring a makeup artist can be expensive. The costs depend on your location, the artist's experience, and how many people are being made up. You can expect additional charges if you have a trial session, and some makeup artists charge travel fees outside of a set radius.

Also, if you don't wear makeup often, being fully made-up may make you feel awkward and not quite yourself. If you would feel more comfortable with your own approach, there is nothing wrong with that.

Tips

If you do decide to work with a professional makeup artist, these suggestions can help you get the results you want.

- Take the time to do a bit of research, from wedding blogs to magazine images, to get a feel for the look you want. If you see some looks you love, share the image(s) with your makeup artist before your trial. If you don't, you can at least provide input on colors you find flattering or makeup trends you'd rather avoid.

- A makeup trial is one of the best ways to prevent unwanted results. If you opt to do this, you can get a preview of your wedding day face, and you and your artist can make some adjustments. The trial also gives you a feel for the artist's approach and skills so you can make sure they're the best choice for you. It also gives the makeup artist a chance to see your skin and determine what products will produce the best results for you.

- If you do opt for a trial, try to schedule it early in the day, and leave the makeup on to see how it holds up as your day progresses, including during mealtime.

- Don't experiment with new products on your wedding day. The last thing you need is to break out in a rash. If you don't do a makeup trial, be sure to try the products that you intend to wear on your wedding day a few weeks in advance.

- Be assertive. If you aren't a big makeup wearer, you may not want your makeup artist to get overly creative with your look. If you want something flattering but subtle, be clear about that.

- Along the same lines, be wary of makeup trends. There is a difference between doing something special for your wedding day and getting so adventurous that your makeup doesn't reflect the real you.

GROOM'S GUIDE: YOUR WEDDING PLANNING CHECKLIST AND TIPS

Congratulations on your engagement! While your bride-to-be is likely in full wedding planning mode, you as the groom also have important responsibilities leading up to the big day.

Courtesy of Always Us Photography

Instead of sitting back and letting your fiancée handle everything herself, make sure you take an active role in getting ready for your wedding. Use this groom wedding planning checklist and tips to support your future wife, enjoy the wedding preparations, and pull off an amazing wedding day.

Sharing To-Dos and Decisions

Traditionally, brides take a major role in wedding preparations, from selecting a wedding venue to picking the color theme. You should be helping and providing input as she goes through her planning to-dos and makes key decisions about your wedding.

Here's a more specific look at steps you should be taking to help prepare for your wedding day and related events:

- **Share budgeting responsibilities.** Discuss your personal finances and agree on a wedding budget with your bride. Look for ways to save money, such as finding affordable vendors, minimizing guests, or cutting back on certain details.

- **Help with the timeline.** Collaborate with your bride to create a detailed wedding day timeline. Make sure it includes transportation, photos, venue setup, vendor arrival/departure, wedding party prep, reception events, and more. Having a structured schedule will help ensure everything runs smoothly.

- **Attend meetings and appointments.** Your bride-to-be likely will schedule meetings with wedding vendors, like your prospective wedding photographer, caterer, and florist. Try to attend as many of these as possible — your input matters!

- **Give your opinion.** Look over your bride-to-be's wedding day Pinterest boards, wedding magazines, and other resources. Make sure she knows you care about the wedding-planning process and that you're excited about getting married. Share your ideas and hopes for your wedding day in order to blend your styles and preferences.

- **Choose the tuxes/suits.** Select the style, color, and fit for your own tux or suit first. Then help pick the groomsmen's apparel to complement yours.

- **Book the honeymoon.** Take the lead on researching destinations, travel dates, transportation, and hotels for an unforgettable post-wedding trip.

- **Build the wedding website.** Create your shared wedding website and link your registries, travel information, wedding party bios, and more.

- **Purchase your rings.** Shop for your bride's engagement ring with her style and taste in mind. Get input from those closest to her. (If your partner wants to be part of this decision, shop together or have her pick several options.) When it's time to select wedding bands, conduct the research and shop for the rings with your bride-to-be.

- **Share the bachelor party planning.** Work with the best man to organize a celebration that fits your personality and interests.

WEDDINGS

- **Review contracts and make payments.** Look over contracts from prospective vendors and pay deposits or payments when they're due. This is a responsibility that you should share with the bride. Make sure to keep communication open about contracts, your budget, and expenditures.

- **Rehearse the ceremony.** Attend the wedding rehearsal to practice the walk down the aisle, cues, vows, and any special elements you have planned for your ceremony. You'll also need to attend the rehearsal dinner, where you can give a toast thanking your wedding party.

Supporting Your Bride From Engagement to 'I Do'

Your partner might sometimes feel overwhelmed by the wedding planning process. Make sure you provide emotional and practical support along the way:

- Listen to her ideas and share your honest opinions.

- Give encouragement through the stressful times.

- Help research vendors and wedding details when needed.

- Provide a second opinion when she's deciding between options.

- Attend tastings and show your enthusiasm about menu choices.

- Give reassurance if conflict with family members or drama arises.

- Accommodate requests, like communicating with guests and helping with rehearsal dinner plans.

- Express your excitement as the wedding day gets closer!

By supporting your bride every step of the way, you'll lay a strong foundation for your marriage.

Picking Your Wedding Party: Groomsmen and Best Man

One of your first tasks is selecting the important people who will stand by your side on your wedding day. Here are some tips for choosing groomsmen and your best man:

Selecting Groomsmen

Generally, you should aim for three to eight groomsmen, but those numbers are not set in stone. Brainstorm a preliminary list of friends, brothers, and cousins. From there, consider including college friends, work colleagues, teammates, or other significant people in your life.

You'll want to choose reliable, supportive friends who you know will attend events and fulfill their duties. If possible, try to mix personality types—close friends, life-of-the-party types, sentimental friends, and others.

Inform them that they're selected with a phone call, creative gift, or invitation. Just ask—most will be thrilled to take part!

Your Best Man

Typically, you'll pick your closest friend, brother, or cousin for this honored spot.

Make sure he is someone responsible, comfortable with the role, and who won't flake on best man duties. Consider who keeps you balanced, shares your values, and will give a heartfelt, meaningful speech.

Ask in person if possible, and explain why he's so important to you. You might want to provide a small gift, such as engraved cuff links.

Take time to get him up to speed on your goals, and make sure you're both on the same page when it comes to best man responsibilities.

Once your wedding party is set, work with the best man to choose suits and plan a killer bachelor party.

Groom Wedding Day Tips

After months of planning, your wedding day will be here before you know it. Follow these tips so you can enjoy a smooth, stress-free day:

- Make sure you get a good night's rest leading up to your wedding day.

- Don't forget to eat. Even if you're nervous, you'll need a good breakfast to get energy for the long day.

- Allow plenty of time for getting ready with your groomsmen.

WEDDINGS

- If you have personalized vows, read them out loud multiple times to practice.

- Bring essentials like vows, rings, the marriage license, your outfit, and accessories.

- Stay focused and avoid seeing your bride before the ceremony if you're doing a first look.

- Make sure you and the groomsmen put on boutonnieres.

- Maintain your emotional composure during the ceremony, and smile at your bride walking down the aisle!

- Hold hands affectionately, make eye contact, and speak clearly during your vow exchange.

- Give hugs and thanks to parents, the wedding party, and guests at the reception.

- Prepare a toast thanking your bride and important loved ones. Keep it personal and heartfelt.

- Don't get drunk at the reception—pace yourself and hydrate.

- Soak in every moment with your new spouse on the dance floor and during wedding events.

Groom Wedding Etiquette Tips

Brush up on some basic wedding etiquette to ensure you make a polite impression on guests:

- Arrive early or on time for the ceremony and reception.

- Stand to greet wedding guests at the reception line.

- Thank parents and in-laws for their support and contributions.

- Write heartfelt thank-you notes to your groomsmen.

Planning a wedding may feel overwhelming initially. Make sure you break tasks down step-by-step, ask for help when you need it, and remember what the big day is really all about—celebrating the love that you and your bride share.

DAPPER GROOM: A GUIDE TO WEDDING-DAY STYLE

While all eyes may be on your bride's gorgeous gown on your wedding day, as the groom, your attire will play a big role in setting the tone and style for your celebration, too.

You have quite a few factors to consider when it comes to nailing your wedding day look. To help, I've compiled some guidelines on selecting groom wedding apparel, including tips on fabrics, colors, accessories, and the latest trends, to help you look and feel your best on your big day.

Suit Versus Tuxedo: Pros and Cons

One of the first decisions you'll need to make is whether to wear a suit or a tuxedo. Both have their advantages and drawbacks, so weigh your options carefully.

Suit Pros

- Suits are more versatile and can be worn for other formal occasions.
- They're generally more affordable than a tuxedo.
- You'll have a wider range of colors and styles available.

Suit Cons

- A suit may not be as formal as a tuxedo for an evening wedding.
- Your outfit will require more coordination with your groomsmen's attire.

Tuxedo Pros

- Tuxedos create a classic and formal look, perfect for evening weddings.
- They're easier to coordinate with groomsmen's attire.
- You can't deny their timeless and sophisticated style.

Tuxedo Cons

- Generally, a tuxedo will be more expensive than a suit.
- It's less versatile for future use.
- A tuxedo is considered formal attire; it may not be an ideal choice for a casual or daytime wedding.

Day Versus Night Weddings

The time of day you're getting married also plays a role in determining the appropriate level of formality for your wedding attire.

For daytime weddings, suits in lighter colors or breathable fabrics like linen or cotton are popular choices.

Dark suits or tuxedos are usually reserved for evening affairs. They have a more formal and elegant feel.

Formal Wedding Considerations

If you're having a traditional, formal wedding, a tuxedo is often the way to go.

Choose a classic black or midnight blue tuxedo with a crisp white dress shirt and a bow tie or necktie.

Add a stylish cummerbund or vest to complete the look.

For a touch of sophistication, consider a peaked lapel or a double-breasted jacket.

Outdoor Wedding Considerations

Outdoor events present their own set of challenges when it comes to choosing the right wedding attire.

This is particularly true for a summer wedding, when you'll want an outfit that keeps you cool and comfortable while still looking sharp. Linen suits in light colors like tan, ivory, or pale blue are a classic choice. Pair them with a crisp white dress shirt and a lightweight tie or pocket square for a touch of seasonal flair.

If you prefer a more casual wedding look, consider a seersucker suit or a linen-blend blazer with chinos or dress pants.

Don't forget to consider your wedding venue's terrain; if you'll be walking on grass or uneven surfaces, choose shoes with good traction.

Winter Wedding Considerations

Winter weddings call for warmth and sophistication. A classic black or charcoal gray suit in a heavier wool or wool blend fabric is a timeless choice. You can also opt for a velvet blazer or a tuxedo with a sleek overcoat for added warmth and style.

Don't forget to accessorize with a stylish scarf or pocket square to complement your look.

Fabrics and Colors

The fabric and color choices you make can significantly impact the overall look and feel of your wedding attire. Here are some popular options to consider:

Fabrics

- **Wool:** A classic and versatile choice, suitable for both suits and tuxedos
- **Linen:** Lightweight and breathable, perfect for warm-weather weddings
- **Cotton:** Affordable and comfortable, great for casual or rustic weddings
- **Silk:** Luxurious and smooth, often used for tuxedo jackets or dress shirts
- **Velvet:** Rich and elegant, ideal for winter weddings or formal affairs

Colors

- **Black:** A timeless and formal choice for tuxedos or suits
- **Navy blue:** Sophisticated and versatile, a navy suit is a popular option
- **Gray:** Stylish and modern, available in a range of shades from light to charcoal
- **Khaki or tan:** Relaxed and casual, perfect for outdoor or beach weddings
- **Burgundy/plum:** A rich and bold color choice for a touch of drama
- **Light blue:** Fresh and summery, a great option for warm-weather weddings

Suit and Tuxedo Fits

Not all suits and tuxedos are created equal when it comes to achieving that perfect tailored look. Understanding the different fit styles is key to selecting an option that flatters your body type:

- **Classic fit:** The classic fit provides a more generous, relaxed cut through the chest, waist, and legs. It's a safe choice for most body types.

WEDDINGS

- **Modern/slim fit:** Slimmer through the chest, waist, and arms with slightly tapered legs. This streamlined silhouette creates a sharp, contemporary look popular with younger grooms.

- **Super slim/skinny fit:** Ultra-slim and tailored throughout for an exceptionally trim silhouette. This edgy style works best for very slim builds.

- **Athletic fit:** Cut with more room in the shoulders/chest but a trimmer waist and seat for a masculine, confident look on muscular frames.

Getting the Right Fit

While off-the-rack suits can look great, getting professionally measured and fitted by a tailor provides an unbeatable customized look and feel. Even small adjustments like nipping in the waist, hemming sleeves or adjusting the pant length can drastically elevate the fit.

Personalizing Your Look

Even if adhering to tradition is a priority for your wedding day, adding a few personal touches can help you stand out and showcase your unique wedding style. Consider incorporating elements that reflect your personality or the wedding's theme, such as these special touches:

- Patterned socks or fun shoelaces

- Colorful pocket squares or boutonnieres

- Unique cuff links or tie bars

- Custom embroidery or monograms

- Stylish suspenders or braces

Shirt Selection

While the wedding suit or tuxedo jacket gets most of the attention, the shirt you choose is equally important in completing your overall look. The right shirt can elevate your outfit and add a personal touch.

For Formal Weddings

If you're going with black-tie attire, a crisp white shirt is the classic choice. Look for dress shirts made from high-quality cotton or cotton blends with a subtle sheen. French cuffs lend an extra dapper touch.

For Semi-Formal/Casual Weddings

With a wedding suit, you have more flexibility with your shirt's style and color. Light colors like pale blue, pink, or lavender can inject some fashionable flair. Or go for subtle patterns like micro-checks, stripes, or herringbone designs. When it comes to fabrics, opt for high-quality cotton, linens, or cotton-linen blends that breathe well.

Shirt Fit

No matter which style you want to wear, proper fit will be crucial. Your shirt should follow your form without being overly tight or billowing. Leave enough room to move freely, but the fit should be sleek enough to tuck crisply into your pants. Consider having your dress shirt professionally altered for a tailored silhouette.

Finishing Touches

Pay attention to the small details that can make a big impact: cuff links, tie bar, or collar stays. These accessories allow you to further personalize your shirt while keeping your polished look. Having spare shirts on hand is also wise in case of any spills or mishaps on the big day.

Shoes

Your shoes are just as important as the rest of your wedding day outfit. They'll help shape your look and have a big impact on your comfort. Opt for well-crafted, comfortable dress shoes that complement your suit or tuxedo.

Classic options include Oxford or Derby shoes in black or brown leather. For outdoor or rustic weddings, consider a pair of stylish boots or loafers.

Coordinating with Your Groomsmen

Decide on a color scheme and style that complements your own outfit, and provide clear guidelines to your groomsmen on what to wear. You can mix and match suits and tuxedos or have everyone in identical outfits—the choice is yours.

CHAPTER 10

Close Family and Wedding Party

Courtesy of Always Us Photography

DUTY CALLS! HOW TO SHINE WHILE SERVING AS MAID OR MATRON OF HONOR

So, your best friend is getting hitched, and you've scored the top job — you're the maid (or matron) of honor! Congrats! The gig is sure to come with invites to all the pre-wedding parties and, best of all, an up-close-and-personal view of your bestie's big day.

However, with all of these perks comes a certain amount of responsibility that must be taken seriously, from pulling together a bachelorette party to helping the bride organize airport pickups.

For some, this important role can be a little overwhelming and even threaten to ruin the fun of the event. If that's you, take a read through this quick guide to some of the maid/matron of honor's primary responsibilities, tips for tackling them, and the best ways to support your friend while saving your sanity.

What's Expected of You

- **Party planning.** As the bride's No. 1 gal, one of your most important tasks is organizing the bachelorette party. Of course, the bride's wishes should be tops in your decision-making process, but it's also your job to make sure she considers the guests' financial means and availability before settling on the details. Whether the bride opts for an intimate dinner party or an all-out, weekend-long, out-of-town bash, take care that those who are invited will have fun and that the event won't break their budget, or worse, prohibit them from attending.

- **Accompanying the bride during dress shopping.** Every bride-to-be needs opinions when selecting her dream dress, so be sure to save the date for when she heads to the boutique. In addition to giving your honest (but gentle) feedback, have an idea of what type of style she likes so you can help gather some options for her to try on. It may even be fun to arrange for a post-shopping ladies' lunch for your entourage, which will likely include the bride's mother, future mother-in-law, members of the bridal party, and other female relatives.

- **Recording the wedding gifts at the bridal shower.** Even in this day of text messages and emails, most people expect a handwritten thank-you note when they give a wedding gift. To make sure the bride has an accurate accounting of who gifted what, plant yourself beside her during the gift-opening part of the bridal shower, pen and notebook at the ready. After the party, type up the list and email it to her for safekeeping and easy access.

Pro tip: To reach the level of maid/matron of honor extraordinaire, you could keep her company and offer thank-you note writing tips when she's struggling with multiple ways to express her appreciation. Be sure to bring snacks!

- **Rallying the troops.** One of the biggest stressors for brides is ensuring the wedding day goes off without a hitch. As maid/matron of honor, you can help make that happen by serving as the unofficial wedding party wrangler. From making sure bridesmaids show up for gown selection to pushing them to order their dresses on time to scheduling their fittings, taking care of these tasks yourself frees up a lot of brain space for the bride—and buys you her eternal gratitude.

- **Being a go-to contact for wedding inquiries and errands.** There's seemingly no end to wedding to-dos, many of them often falling to the bride. To alleviate some of her stress, offer to be a point of contact for some or all of them, including guests' questions, vendors calling for appointments, or even RSVPs.

Also, make yourself available for errands, perhaps carving out a weekend or two for getting them done. Remember, helping your friend pull her big day together with nary a breakdown is part of the maid/matron of honor's job description, so be flexible and responsive to her needs.

- **Making a wedding toast.** It's reported that public speaking is many people's biggest fear, but with proper preparation, it doesn't have to be. When writing your remarks, include a few personal anecdotes about the bride and groom, a dose of humor—if you feel comfortable with it—and a pinch of sentimentality to pull off a toast that encapsulates how you feel about your dear friend's marriage. Also, keep your audience and the tone of the event in mind. Ultimately, if you keep it light, heartfelt, short, and appropriate, you can't go wrong.

WEDDINGS

Courtesy of Josh & Dana Fernandez Photography

- **On the wedding day, hit the dance floor, and bring the bride with you.** Enough said. You both deserve it!

Quick Tips to Help You Get It Right Without Succumbing to Stress

- **Delegate.** Call on your fellow bridesmaids whenever you can. Divide and conquer!

- **Ask the other bridesmaids to share the expense of the bachelorette party.** As these events become larger and grander, so do expenses increase. Divvy up the cost to lessen the financial strain.

- **Plan a wedding-talk-free dinner or night out with the bride.** A relaxing dinner or casual drink may be just what both of you need to shore up your nerves and rest a bit before diving back into planning.

- **Take a breath and advise the bride to do the same.** Assure your friend her wedding will be perfect and, even if there's a snag here and there, you are there to support her and make it right.

Serving as the maid or matron of honor for one of the most important women in your life is likely a memory you'll treasure forever. Taking care to do the job right while keeping it fun is the name of the game. After all, a happy bride and a memorable wedding day are the best rewards you could ask for.

HOW TO BE AN OUTSTANDING GROOMSMAN

Ohio resident David Ryland made headlines when he participated in the Akron Marathon hours before his wedding. One reason he achieved his goal—and made it to the altar on time—was the fact he had the support of his groomsmen. Since they were runners, too, they completed the marathon with Ryland as a marathon team called "Cold Feet."

When *Runner's World* interviewed Ryland about the experience, he said he was moved by his friends' above-and-beyond show of support.

"The fact that they all made the time to fly to Ohio for a weekend to run and then be with me on my wedding day is something you cannot ask more for in friends and family," he said.

If you've been asked to be a groomsman, it's unlikely that you will have to go to such extreme measures to support the groom. That said, the role does come with some built-in responsibilities. And, if you'd like to be the kind of groomsman who's remembered for his unwavering support (without lacing up your running shoes), there are any number of ways you can help.

What Exactly Do Groomsmen Do?

For most people, the word "groomsman" (or possibly "groomsperson" or "groomswoman") evokes a pretty specific image. These are the people who stand beside the groom during the wedding ceremony. But standing by the groom isn't limited to your physical presence; your job is to "be there," to be a source of help and support before and during the wedding. Here's a closer look at what that entails.

Your most well-known pre-wedding duty will be helping the best man plan and execute the bachelor party. Your involvement will depend on the best man, but you might be helping by contributing (and providing feedback on) ideas, helping with arrangements, sharing costs, and being there to add to the fun.

You will also need to attend the wedding rehearsal and rehearsal dinner—and maybe even make a toast there.

You'll be responsible for getting your outfit for the wedding, too.

During the wedding, in addition to participating in the ceremony, you can expect to pose for wedding pictures and, during the reception, lead people onto the dance floor.

Above all, though, you're one of the people the groom knows he can count on: to listen, to encourage, and to lend an extra hand when necessary.

Making a Real Difference

So how can you move beyond doing the basics? Here are some strategies for being an invaluable source of support and assistance as a groomsman:

- **Wearing it well:** Depending on the groom, you may be provided with details on what the groomsmen should be wearing, or you may be asked to share suggestions on clothing decisions. Beyond that, simply picking up your outfit on time, without being nudged, is a surprisingly easy way to ease the bride's and groom's stress.

- **Embracing behind-the-scenes tasks:** You can be a tremendous help, and stress-reliever, by lending a helping hand. This could involve giving relatives rides from the airport to their hotels, picking up supplies, running errands for the bride and groom, and carrying in/packing up supplies on the wedding day.

- **Showing empathy for groom stress:** Some grooms find it a little tough to focus on their wedding day. Groomsmen can help by keeping them on schedule, making sure they eat and stay hydrated, and, again, being a friend they can talk with.

- **Being a friendly face:** As a member of the wedding party, you're sharing hosting duties in a way. So greet guests and be available to answer questions.

  Pro tip: Your most common inquiries will be whens ("What time will dinner start?") and wheres ("Can you point me toward the restrooms?") You can help yourself by asking the bride and groom (or their wedding planner) for the day's itinerary and seating plan and by getting a feel for your venue's layout.

WEDDINGS

- **Coaxing people onto the dance floor:** A wedding is, after all, a celebration. As a groomsman, you'll help set the tone by getting people on the dance floor and encouraging them to have fun.

In the end, if you think of yourself as a source of help, friendship, and support, you'll recognize opportunities to be there for the groom. Act on them, and you'll be a highly successful groomsman.

HOW TO RELEASE YOUR MAID OF HONOR FROM WEDDING DUTIES

Weddings represent love, festivities, happiness, and making memories with family and friends.

So it goes without saying that being forced to "fire" an attendant doesn't exactly fit the fantasy, especially if we're talking about your maid of honor.

This was supposed to be your go-to person (aside from your partner) from the time you began making wedding plans through the moment you made your grand exit from your wedding venue.

However, sometimes pulling your maid of honor or bridesmaid from your wedding party lineup is exactly what needs to happen to pull off the wedding of your dreams and to preserve the relationship.

Now, you may be wondering what exactly could prompt such a drastic move. Well, there are a few surefire red flags that signal someone should not hold a place of honor at your wedding:

- She is causing problems between you and your spouse-to-be, other wedding party members, or close family members.

- She is not holding up her end of the responsibilities, such as showing up for dress fittings, attending parties, planning your bridal shower, or pitching in financially when others are.

- She is acting in any way that is detrimental to your wedding planning or well-being rather than being a source of help and support.

- She is being rude to you or dismissing your ideas and opinions.

- She is not responding to your attempts to communicate with her.

- She is making everything about herself.

- You're starting to have concerns that she'll act out at the wedding.

Dos and Don'ts To Consider

Of course, any reason you believe warrants a demotion from maid of honor to wedding guest is your prerogative, but let me give you some dos and don'ts when it comes to breaking the news and handling the aftermath.

- Don't rush the conversation. Take the time to carefully consider your words and approach the discussion with empathy and understanding, recognizing that this may be a difficult moment for both parties involved.

- Do be honest, up-front, and clear about your reasons for making this decision. Most ways you cut it, this won't be an easy conversation, so if at all possible, schedule a face-to-face sit-down with your friend and talk to her about your decision and why you're making it. Give her a chance to explain her side.

- Don't break the news over email or text. Your friend deserves to hear it from you in person.

- Do stand your ground. You may be tempted to back down, especially if your maid of honor becomes emotional. Be kind and respectful but also firm. Remember, you didn't come to this decision lightly.

- Do express gratitude for her past support and friendship. Emphasize the fact that your decision is based on what you believe is best for both of you in the context of the wedding-planning process.

- Do extend an invitation to the wedding and any related events.

- Don't make a scene or guilt-trip her if she decides not to attend.

- Do alert your groom, parents, and other bridesmaids about your decision. Keep private details to a minimum.

- Don't gossip about her after cutting her from the wedding party. This only creates a toxic environment for other bridal party members and may cause problems, especially if she is a friend of one or some of them.

- Do reimburse her for the bridesmaid dress.

- Don't reimburse her for the bachelorette party or other soiree expenses.

- Do ask one of your other bridesmaids to step into the role if you have to replace your maid of honor.

- Don't waffle once your decision is made. Going back on it and reversing course will only cause confusion and stress for those still involved and for you and her as well.

- Don't dwell on the decision indefinitely. Once you've communicated your decision and allowed for discussion, focus on moving forward positively and maintaining the friendship, even if the dynamic has shifted slightly in the context of the wedding preparations.

Keeping Your Friendship Intact

You may be wondering if your relationship can weather such a public storm. The truth is it can, but, as with most sticky situations, it depends on how you handle it. When you sit down to talk to your friend about your decision, taking an honest and forthright approach is best. Don't sugarcoat the situation, but don't be unnecessarily harsh either. Maybe offer your friend an easy way out or allow her to save face by telling others that she had to bow out for her own reasons. If the friendship is important to you, express that clearly and say that just because the maid of honor duties didn't work out doesn't mean it bodes badly for your friendship.

Of course, maybe her behavior in the lead-up to your wedding was a wake-up call for you in terms of your desire to continue the relationship. If that's the case, honesty is, once again, your best weapon. Be direct, forthright, and firm in ending the relationship and wishing her well.

Whatever you decide, make sure the decision lies peacefully on your heart as you walk down that aisle and into the next chapter of your life.

HOW TO ROCK YOUR ROLE AS MOTHER OF THE BRIDE

As the mother of the bride, you have an important part in the planning and execution of your daughter's special day. Naturally, you really want it all to go right. As you embark on this most significant of journeys, it's important to remember that, even though you're not the star of the show, you are certainly playing a crucial supporting role. And that, if we're being honest, makes your task all the trickier.

Weddings, with their endless instances of stress-inducing decisions, are notorious for bringing up anxieties and annoyances between the players. Here is where you can shine. You have an opportunity to smooth out differences and to offer experience-based advice, a calming touch, and even a bit of fun to the planning, making for a seamless wedding-day experience for the bride and groom. Here are a few dos and don'ts to keep in mind:

> *Note:* As the mother of the bride, you may be pitching in with the cost of the wedding or footing the bill completely, and these suggestions are made with your potential financial contributions in mind.

- Do establish open communication with your daughter. Once the engagement is announced, sit down with the soon-to-be newlyweds and talk about how much of a role you'd like to play and what they want/expect from you. Setting clear expectations and boundaries should prevent many conflicts down the road.

- Don't impose your style on the bride. Chances are your daughter has colors, flowers, and dress styles in mind. She may have her heart set on a specific venue or wedding theme. Even if none of her choices suit your taste, as long as they fit into the overall budget, your wishes should not override hers when it comes to how she wants her wedding to look and feel.

- Do offer your opinion if asked. If your daughter asks your opinion on any of her choices, give it freely and truthfully, but let her know you support whatever decision she makes.

WEDDINGS

- Don't let others push your daughter and her groom-to-be into making plans that don't fit their needs, wants, or budget. People have lots of ideas about what makes for the perfect wedding, but unless they're the ones walking down the aisle, providing professional services, or writing the checks, they shouldn't have a deciding vote. Make sure your daughter knows you're there to help her to stick to her guns, and make sure to offer a supporting hand when it comes to asking others to take a step back.

- Do allow for others' opinions to be floated if your daughter is seeking them. Serving as the gatekeeper of would-be advice-givers might be one way to support your daughter, but be flexible. If she's seeking out help, particularly from those in the wedding industry, consider taking a step back and listening to what they have to say. Afterward, you can serve as a sounding board or counselor to steer her decisions in her best interests.

- Don't take over the guest list. Sure, you're eager to invite some of your nearest and dearest to witness the wedding of your child, but any guest decisions must be made in accordance with the betrothed couple's wishes at the forefront. That means close family from both sides and the couple's good friends come first.

- Do consult with your daughter before you purchase your dress. As you hope she'll include you in the fun of choosing her wedding dress, ask for her opinion on what you should wear. Get her views on the fit and style of the dress as well as how it fits in with the vibe she's going for. With so many options to choose from, it's likely you'll land on something you both love, although the final decision is yours.

- But don't aim to overshadow the bride. Although it's hard to upstage a bride in her wedding dress, keep in mind that you are not the star of the show, and what you wear should reflect that. Of course, steer clear of white or ivory and instead choose a color that flatters you and suits the occasion. Think subtle and elegant. You can and should be one of the best dressed there, but avoid an attention-getting gown and let your daughter shine.

WEDDINGS

- Do share family heirlooms. If your daughter is interested in the tradition of having "something old, something new, something borrowed, and something blue" with her on her wedding day, help her find items with special meaning. They might include a pair of gorgeous earrings, the veil you wore on your wedding day, a family love letter, or the recipe for a beloved family dish.

- Do help to smooth ruffled feathers where you can. Unfortunately, hurt feelings and misunderstandings are often par for the course during wedding planning. As the mother of the bride, you have the opportunity to help defuse those situations or even prevent them by setting a supportive example for the bride and groom. If a sticky situation does arise, ask your daughter if you can help by intervening in spots where you can make a difference, rather than leaving all the mitigation to her. Unruly groomsmen and catty bridesmaids will likely take direction from a mother figure, and you'll spare your daughter the headache of dealing with them.

- Don't create issues with the groom's mother. Instead, recruit her as your partner in crime, so to speak. She'll appreciate the thought, and you'll head off any lingering tensions at the pass.

- Do plan your toast in advance. Mothers of the bride don't always make a speech at their daughter's wedding, but it's not unheard of. If you're planning on it, take time to reflect on what you want to express, put it down on paper, and practice it a few times before your wedding-day delivery. Remember to keep the focus on your daughter and her new husband.

- Don't sweat the small stuff. When it comes to throwing a beautiful wedding, there's no shortage of ways it can come together. In that spirit, don't argue with your daughter on small things that you feel are unnecessary or that make you cringe, but that bring an element of uniqueness to the event or simply make her happy. If it's not going to adversely affect the overall look and feel of the wedding, put it out of your mind and don't let it stress you needlessly.

- Do join in on the wedding-day bridal suite fun. After so many months of planning, putting out fires, and lending the all-important supportive and sympathetic shoulder to your daughter, try to relax and enjoy a day of pampering with your best girl and her squad. Slip on your beautiful dress, have some wine (but not too much!), let the bridesmaids include you in fun pics, and enjoy the rest of the day!

Watching your daughter walk down the aisle to begin her married life can be a wonderful moment as a mother. Bonding with her over the wedding planning process can create memories you'll cherish for a lifetime. With that in mind, approach your mother-of-the-bride role with grace, wisdom, patience, and love. Your daughter will thank you for it.

MAKING RING BEARERS AND FLOWER GIRLS SHINE: SWEET WEDDING IDEAS

Your wedding day is not only a celebration of love between you and your partner but also a day to share joy with your family and friends. Two of the more adorable participants in wedding ceremonies are the ring bearer and the flower girl, who add an extra touch of sweetness and charm to the proceedings.

Ring bearers and flower girls symbolize innocence, purity, and the future of the couple's union.

The ring bearer, usually a little boy, traditionally carries the wedding rings on a pillow or cushion. The flower girl's big job is to scatter petals along the aisle as a lead-up to the bride's entrance.

Selecting a Flower Girl or Ring Bearer

Including children in your wedding ceremony is completely optional. Couples who want a flower girl and/or ring bearer in their wedding usually choose children that one or both of them are close with, or the children of a close friend or family member.

Age recommendations for these young members of your wedding party range roughly from 3 to 8. Ideally, they should be old enough to understand and carry out their duties. If you want a particularly young child to participate, younger than 3, you can always recruit a helper to carry them or walk them down the aisle.

WEDDINGS

If you have children in mind, talk with their parents about the possibility of including them in your wedding. Discuss what the children's roles entail, for both them and their parents. The parents, for example, will need to talk with their children about what to expect and buy their children an outfit. Also, the flower girl and ring bearer, in many cases, attend the rehearsal dinner, creating another commitment for their family. Be sure the parents feel that being a flower girl or ring bearer will be a positive experience for their child.

When It's Time To 'Propose'

Inviting a child to be a ring bearer or flower girl can be an exciting moment for both them and the couple. Consider going the extra mile when you propose. It will make the moment even more meaningful to them and show them that they're valued. Here are some creative ideas to make your proposal extra special:

- **Personalized invitation:** Creating printed invitations addressed specifically to the little ones you want in your wedding will move them and give them a special reminder of your proposal. You can design the invitation with their favorite colors, cartoon characters, or themes that reflect their interests. Include a heartfelt message expressing why you would love for them to be part of your wedding day.

- **Treasure hunt:** Organize a treasure hunt leading to a hidden treasure box containing the invitation and a small gift, such as a toy or a treat. Leave clues around the children's home or a favorite location, guiding them on an exciting adventure culminating in the surprise proposal.

- **Personalized keepsake:** Present each child with a personalized keepsake, such as a custom-made puzzle or storybook featuring illustrations of the bridal party. As they piece together the puzzle or flip through the pages of the book, they'll discover your message inviting them to be your ring bearer or flower girl.

- **Video message:** Work with your partner to create a video that explains why you would love for the child to be your ring bearer or flower girl. To make the proposal more meaningful, include personal anecdotes or memories of occasions you've shared with the child. You can deliver the video request in person or send it digitally for a surprise reveal.

- **Special outing:** Plan a fun-filled day with your prospective ring bearer or flower girl, such as a visit to their favorite park, zoo, or ice cream shop. Use this opportunity to casually broach the topic of your wedding and express how much it would mean to have them participate in it. Present them with a small gift or token of appreciation during the outing as a symbol of the proposal.

- **Family gathering:** Incorporate the ring bearer proposal or flower girl proposal into a family event like a birthday party or holiday gathering. Bring everyone together for a special announcement, where you can formally ask the child to be part of your wedding. Celebrate the moment with cake, balloons, or other festive decorations.

- **Enlist their parents' help:** Coordinate with the child's parents or guardians to plan a surprise proposal that really resonates. Maybe your ring bearer proposal can include a message tucked into his favorite storybook. Or your flower girl's proposal can be delivered in a beautiful gift box decorated in her favorite colors.

Getting Them Down the Aisle

It will be important to talk with the flower girl and ring bearer about their parts in the wedding. The more you build up their importance before the big day, the more likely they will be to cooperate when the time comes.

Also, if you and the children's parents give them some chances to practice, they'll be more confident at your ceremony.

Even if all of your preparations go off without a hitch, it's possible that stage fright will strike at the ceremony. Talk with the children's parents about having a treat ready for them at the end of the aisle; it may be just the enticement they need to start walking toward it.

A parent stepping in to accompany them can help, too, but if a child still refuses to begin walking down the aisle, it's better to graciously let them bow out.

WEDDINGS

Special Touches for the Ring Bearer

One decision you'll need to make with the children's parents is whether to keep their involvement in your wedding simple and traditional or to incorporate creative elements into their journey down the aisle.

If you want, instead of having the ring bearer carry rings resting on a traditional pillow, you can have him pull them to the altar in a miniature wagon.

For cuteness overload, you could enlist a beloved pet to accompany the little man down the aisle.

Baby Ring Bearer Ideas

Having a baby as your ring bearer is an incredibly sweet and adorable way to include the youngest member of your family or friend group in your wedding ceremony. Here are some ideas to make your baby ring bearer's role extra special:

- **Wagon ride:** Instead of having the baby walk down the aisle, have them pulled in a decorated wagon, stroller, or other wheeled vehicle. Adorn it with ribbons, flowers, and signs like "Here Comes the Bride/Groom."

- **Family attendant:** Assign a family member or trusted friend to be the baby's personal attendant for the day. This person can calmly guide them down the aisle while you exchange vows.

- **Mini tuxedo:** Outfit your baby ring bearer in an adorable mini tuxedo or an outfit that coordinates with your wedding colors and style. Add a cute newsboy cap or baby's first bow tie for extra charm.

- **Ring bearer pillow alternative:** Instead of a traditional pillow, have the baby present the rings in a special box, basket, or pouch attached to their wagon or stroller. Get creative with the container.

- **Stuffed animal:** Give your baby ring bearer a special stuffed animal "buddy" to hold onto as they make their way down the aisle. It can provide comfort and be a keepsake afterward.

Remember, flexibility is key with babies. Having backup ring bearers ready and focusing on making beautiful memories is most important.

Flower Girl Ideas for Your Wedding

Enhance the flower girl's role by offering her creative alternatives to traditional flower petals. Consider having her scatter confetti, bubbles, or even feathers along the aisle.

For a whimsical touch, adorn her basket with ribbons, flowers, or fairy lights. Encourage her to walk at her own pace, allowing her to savor the spotlight and enjoy her special moment.

Here are more creative ideas to make the flower girl's part of your wedding even more delightful:

- **Fairy wings and wand:** Transform the flower girl into a magical fairy character by outfitting her with delicate wings and a sparkling wand. Encourage her to sprinkle fairy dust (biodegradable glitter or confetti) along the aisle as she walks.

- **Floral crown and basket:** Adorn the flower girl with a beautiful floral crown that matches the bridal bouquet or the wedding theme. Pair it with a charming basket filled with petals, flowers, or herbs like lavender or rosemary.

- **Ribbon wands:** Replace traditional flower petals with ribbon wands for the flower girl to wave gracefully as she walks down the aisle. Choose ribbons in your wedding colors or opt for a mix of pastel hues for a whimsical effect. Guests can wave their own ribbon wands in celebration as the flower girl passes by.

- **Balloon bouquet:** Instead of flowers, have the flower girl carry a bouquet of balloons in assorted colors and shapes adorned with ribbons or streamers.

- **Pomander ball:** Create a pomander ball for the flower girl to carry, featuring a spherical arrangement of flowers, foliage, or fabric blooms. Hang the pomander from a ribbon or decorative handle, so she can carry it with ease as she walks down the aisle.

- **Parasol or umbrella:** Shield the flower girl from the sun or rain with a charming parasol or umbrella embellished with floral motifs or decorative trim. Choose a parasol in a color that complements your wedding palette.

WEDDINGS

Older Flower Girl Ideas

While the role of flower girl traditionally falls to young girls, there's no reason why older flower girls can't add their own unique charm to your wedding ceremony. Here are some delightful ideas to make older flower girls feel special and included in your big day:

- Give older flower girls special responsibilities to make them feel more involved. This could include assisting with wedding planning tasks, helping younger flower girls with their duties, or even giving a reading during the ceremony.

- Allow older flower girls to have a say in their attire, whether it's choosing a dress style that reflects their personality or selecting accessories like jewelry or hairpieces.

- Instead of scattering petals, older flower girls can carry a small bouquet of flowers down the aisle. Work with your florist to create a personalized bouquet that complements the overall floral theme of your wedding.

- If you have multiple flower girls, consider pairing older flower girls with younger ones to provide guidance and support during the ceremony. This can help younger flower girls feel more at ease while giving older ones a sense of responsibility.

More Ideas

- Incorporate the ring bearer and flower girl into your wedding photo shoot, capturing candid moments of their excitement and joy. Have your flower girl pose with the bridal party while the ring bearer poses with the groomsmen.

- Provide age-appropriate entertainment and activities to keep the little ones engaged during downtime at the reception, such as coloring books, puzzles, or a designated play area.

Saying Thank You

Think about getting your flower girl and ring bearer a gift to express your appreciation for them. Select something age-appropriate that matches their personalities and interests.

It also would be nice to write them a special thank-you to tell them how happy you are that they were part of your wedding.

Consider gifts, or at least thank-you notes, for the children's parents, too. Without their help, it wouldn't be possible to have their children in your wedding.

CHAPTER 11

The Ceremony and Special Wedding Moments

Courtesy of CivicPhotos

THINKING OF WRITING YOUR WEDDING VOWS? HERE ARE SOME PROS, CONS, AND TIPS

I have a quick quiz for you. Does the idea of creating personalized wedding vows strike you as:

A) A beautiful way to make your ceremony more meaningful?

B) A form of torture rivaled only by a root canal?

C) Something you'd love to do if you didn't find the idea so daunting?

Or …

D) A lovely idea for other couples?

There is no right answer. Creating your own vows can make the wedding more intimate and memorable, but unless you and your partner love the idea—and feel comfortable reading what you've written in front of family and friends—it may not be an ideal choice.

If you're on the fence about this approach, the pros and cons I've compiled might help you decide. And if you're in love with the idea of writing something special for your ceremony, I have a few tips for you.

Upsides to Personalized Vows

Why have personalized wedding vows been such an enduring trend? For one thing, they allow couples to create a ceremony that's uniquely about them.

Writing your vows lets you decide what you're promising. You're not going with something generic; you're expressing your commitment to each other on your terms. Whether you're promising to travel the world together or to never stop encouraging your partner to follow their dreams, your vows will be poignant to the two of you.

Working on vows also helps you put the stress of wedding planning in perspective and focus on why you want to spend the rest of your lives together. In the midst of interviewing vendors, making deposits, and completing a long list of other to-dos, the time you spend writing about your first date or the moment you knew your partner was the one can be particularly valuable.

Not only can a personalized ceremony be memorable for you, but it also can lead to a magical, emotional experience for the loved ones sharing the moment. Granted, you shouldn't write your vows simply to please your guests. But if you like the idea of a personal approach, it may encourage you to know that you'll be touching your loved ones, too. For those who care about you, it doesn't get much better than hearing your soon-to-be spouse sharing why they want to live out their life with you.

When Personalized Vows Aren't a Good Fit

Creating personalized vows is not the right choice for every couple. If that applies to you, don't give it a second thought. Going with the approach that's right for you is key to planning an unforgettable, meaningful wedding.

One challenge related to vow writing is that it can create tension between the bride and groom. Maybe one of you is significantly more enthusiastic about vow writing than the other. Or perhaps you both agreed to write vows, but your partner is seriously procrastinating. This doesn't mean they don't love you. Some people just don't feel comfortable with writing or with saying something personal in front of an audience. Many doubt their ability to craft something special enough for a wedding. You can offer to write your vows together if you think that would help, but ultimately, I encourage you to let it go if it's driving a wedge between you. You still can have a beautiful wedding and all the good feelings that go with it.

Another reason to let the vow writing go: You could have very different ideas on how to approach it. Maybe one of you wants to weave intimate, deeply felt reflections into your vows, and the other wants to try their hand at stand-up comedy or share a story that they find hilarious—and you find cringeworthy.

Also, depending on your faith, some religious wedding ceremonies don't include vows, or there are specific requirements for what's said. In other cases, the officiant might ask to approve what you've written. That doesn't mean personalized vows are out of the question; you just may have to extend more effort, and possibly be willing to compromise.

Keys to Vow-Writing Success

If you and your partner agree that personalized vows are the best way to go, we have some tips that could help:

- **Talk with your spouse-to-be in advance.** This goes back to the risk of differing ideas on what your vows should be. How

WEDDINGS

does each of you feel about humor? Are there stories that one of you would just as soon keep to yourselves? Address these issues before moving forward.

- **Give yourself time.** No matter how strong your feelings are, expressing them clearly can be a challenge. If you wait until the last minute to write your vows, you're making your task much more stressful and setting yourself up for less-than-ideal results.

- **Go for a walk.** Many writers will tell you that stepping away from the keyboard is one of their most effective cures for writer's block. Let your mind wander a bit. Reminisce about special moments you and your partner have shared. That will help provide a framework for your writing.

- **You don't have to reinvent the wheel.** While writing vows is a powerful way to personalize your wedding, there's nothing wrong with finding examples from books, TV, or movies and making them your own. You might find additional inspiration in old messages, cards, and even gifts that bring back special memories.

In the end, remember that you don't have to be Shakespeare to do this. Your words don't have to be clever, romantic, or deeply insightful. Just speak from the heart. Tell your partner you love them and why. Make promises that are relevant to the two of you, whether you vow to always be there for your partner or pledge to root for their favorite college football team.

Keep it sincere, and you will have created the unforgettable wedding you've been hoping for.

SELECTING A WEDDING OFFICIANT

One of the most important items on your to-do list, when you're planning a wedding, is selecting your officiant: the person who conducts your ceremony.

This is the person who, depending on what you're looking for, can help you prepare to make a lifetime commitment to one another. They can be an invaluable source of guidance and support, and they'll set the tone for the whole point of your wedding: becoming a married couple.

To help you with the selection process, I've put together a list of commonly asked questions about selecting an officiant, along with my answers.

What Is an Officiant?

A wedding officiant, also known as a celebrant, is someone who can legally conduct a marriage ceremony. It can be your pastor, a justice of the peace, or your best friend.

What Are Our Ceremony Options?

From a big-picture perspective, you can look for an officiant who can conduct a religious ceremony, a secular event, or an interfaith wedding.

You also may want to ask yourselves, if you do want a religious ceremony, whether you prefer it to be traditional or if you'd like to make a few adjustments. And some couples might want help creating a wedding they consider spiritual but not religious.

Where Can We Find Officiants?

If you don't have someone specific in mind to conduct your ceremony, try asking married friends and family members if they have recommendations. You also can consult with your venue, your wedding vendors, and your place of worship.

Another option is to use online resources such as the Celebrant Foundation & Institute or The Celebrant Directory.

How Can We Research the Officiants We're Considering?

I encourage you to ask your prospective officiants for references, and, if possible, check online reviews from other couples. The officiant also should provide proof that they meet all local and state requirements for conducting a wedding.

Once you've narrowed down your choices, see if the officiants can provide videos of themselves conducting marriage ceremonies. Do they seem confident? Are you comfortable with their style and their ability as a speaker?

In the end, one of the best ways to make a final choice is to interview your final candidates. That will help you get a feel for each other and make sure you have a good fit for the kind of ceremony you want.

WEDDINGS

Some possible questions to ask:

- Do you have any restrictions we should know about?

- Do you offer/require pre-wedding counseling or classes?

- Can we read your ceremony script? Will you let us make any changes?

- How do you feel about couples writing their own vows?

- Are there any songs or readings you include in your ceremonies?

- How long, on average, are your ceremonies?

- Tell us about one of your favorite ceremonies.

- Tell us about one of your least favorite ceremonies.

How Much Should We Expect To Pay?

In the U.S., the average cost for officiating services is $200-$450. Some officiants don't charge for their services; instead, it's customary to donate to their place of worship. The suggested donation amount typically ranges from $100 to $300.

Keep in mind that you are paying someone not only to help you exchange vows, but also for their preparations. Ideally, they'll get to know you and be able to conduct a ceremony that is meaningful to you and your partner. What's more, they will most likely participate in, and even run, your wedding rehearsal.

You also are paying for your officiant's travel expenses and for them to make sure your marriage license is properly completed, signed, and submitted.

What If We Want a Friend To Conduct the Ceremony?

Increasing numbers of people are asking friends or family members to marry them. Some find the idea of being married by someone close to them comforting; others feel it will make their ceremony more meaningful.

Keep in mind, a friend or family member will add emotional impact to your ceremony—but their lack of officiating experience may be evident, too.

If you want to go this route, I encourage you to go beyond asking if they're willing to conduct your ceremony. Consider asking these questions as well:

- If they anticipate any scheduling conflicts or something that could come up to force them to cancel at the last minute

- If they feel comfortable speaking in front of crowds, including other close friends and family members

- If you can cover their costs to become an officiant

If they don't feel comfortable accepting your invitation, accept their decision gracefully. It's a serious commitment.

If they say yes, and they need to get ordained to conduct wedding ceremonies, there are a number of sites where they can get ordained, including the following:

- American Fellowship Church

- Universal Life Church

- Universal Ministries

When Do We Need To Make a Final Decision?

Try to have your officiant lined up at least seven months before your wedding.

What Can We Do To Ensure a Positive Experience?

Make time for you and your officiant to get to know each other. While the number of conversations you have is not set in stone, it is important to clearly communicate your hopes for the ceremony. And, to help your officiant get to know you, we recommend sharing stories about how you met and fell in love.

Ultimately, you and your partner should both feel comfortable with the person who conducts your ceremony. You want someone focused on creating the experience you want, someone who's in your corner. I hope these answers help you find that person.

WEDDINGS

YOUR GUIDE TO WEDDING PROCESSIONAL AND CEREMONY ORDER

The walk down the aisle is a moment etched in memory forever. It's the culmination of anticipation, excitement, and all the love that led you to this very spot.

But before you steal the show (let's be honest, you will), there's the beautiful choreography of the processional.

Here, we'll explore the meaning behind the order and how you can personalize it to make your big moment even more special. You'll also find information about the overall order of the wedding ceremony itself.

Family Members and Seating

The ceremony often begins with the seating of family members. In a traditional Western wedding, the bride's immediate family members, such as parents and grandparents, are typically seated in the front row on the right side of the aisle. The groom's immediate family sits in the front row on the left side. This arrangement allows the couple's closest loved ones to have a front-row view of the proceedings.

In a traditional Jewish wedding, the seating arrangement differs; the bride's family is seated on the left side, while the groom's family occupies the right. This arrangement is based on the belief that the bride is the most important person at the wedding, and therefore her family is given the place of honor.

It's important to note, however, that seating arrangements can vary widely depending on the couple's preferences and the specific traditions of their culture or faith. Some couples may choose to have a more egalitarian seating arrangement, with family members from both sides seated together, or they may choose to have mixed seating arrangements that reflect the diverse backgrounds and traditions of their families.

The Wedding Processional

Once the guests are seated, the processional begins.

The *processional* refers to the choreographed entry of the wedding party, where each participant walks down the aisle in a specific order.

It usually starts with the groom, who takes his place at the altar or in front of the ceremony space, awaiting the arrival of the bride. The groom may be accompanied by his best man, who will stand by his side.

WEDDINGS

Next are the ring bearer and flower girl. The ring bearer is a child who carries the couple's wedding rings on a small pillow. The ring bearer walks along the aisle to symbolically present the rings to the couple. Following the ring bearer, the flower girl (also a child) gracefully strews flower petals along the aisle, creating a beautiful path for the bride. (Including a ring bearer and flower girl is a lovely tradition, but having children in your wedding is completely optional.)

From there, the bridesmaids and groomsmen, also known as the attendants, walk down the aisle. The number of attendants can vary, but it's generally recommended to have an even number to create a balanced, symmetrical appearance. The bridesmaids and groomsmen may walk individually or in pairs, depending on the couple's preference. The maid of honor typically walks last, just before the bride.

The Jewish Wedding Processional

The Jewish wedding processional order is traditionally a bit different. The groom, accompanied by both his parents, leads the procession, symbolizing the importance of the groom's family and the passing down of tradition from one generation to the next. The groom's parents are often referred to as the "kvatter" and "kvatterin" and are responsible for escorting the groom to the chuppah (the wedding canopy). Next, the bride, escorted by her parents, makes her entrance. The bride's parents traditionally walk her down the aisle and then remain at the chuppah as witnesses to the wedding ceremony. The bridesmaids and groomsmen then follow, walking in pairs. This processional order is symbolic of the support and community that surrounds the couple as they begin their new life together.

More Unique Traditions

Here are a few more examples of cultures with unique and meaningful approaches to the wedding day processional.

Korean Weddings (Pyebaek)

The bride enters with her mother, symbolizing the importance of the maternal bond. After the wedding ceremony, the Pyebaek takes place. This is a formal tea ceremony in which the couple bows to their elders, such as parents and grandparents, as a sign of respect and gratitude. During the Pyebaek, the elders present the couple with gifts, often in

WEDDINGS

the form of money, jewelry, or other valuable items. The Pyebaek is an important part of the Korean wedding tradition and is a way for the couple to show their respect for their elders and seek their blessing as they start their new life together.

Ethiopian Orthodox Weddings

The couple proceeds in together, symbolizing their unity from the start. The wedding ceremony is rich in chanting and hymns, with the couple, priests, and congregation all participating. The ceremony is led by a priest, who guides the couple through the various elements of the service, including prayers, scripture readings, and the exchanging of vows. It is a solemn and joyful occasion, filled with music, dance, and the warm embrace of community. The focus of the Ethiopian Orthodox wedding ceremony is on the couple's commitment to each other, as well as their commitment to building a strong and healthy family based on the teachings of the Ethiopian Orthodox Church.

Vietnamese Weddings (Lễ Cưới)

During a traditional Vietnamese wedding, the groom's procession (known as đại giỗ) will typically carry symbolic gifts, such as fruit, betel leaves, and areca nuts, to the bride's family home. These gifts are presented as a sign of respect and a way of asking for the bride's hand in marriage. After the groom's procession has been received by the bride's family, the couple will often walk down the aisle together, symbolizing their unity and commitment to each other.

The Bride's Entrance

The bride's entrance is often the most anticipated moment of the wedding ceremony.

In a traditional Western wedding, the bride is escorted down the aisle by her father, who "gives her away" to the groom. This symbolic gesture represents the father's blessing and the passing of the bride's care from the family to the groom.

In some cultures, the bride may be escorted by both parents or by other family members, such as a brother or grandparent. The bride's entrance is a powerful moment, as she makes her way toward her partner, signifying the start of their new life together.

The Ceremony

Once the bride has reached the altar, the officiant (who may be a religious leader, a civil celebrant, or a close friend or family member) begins the ceremony. The ceremony typically includes vows, readings, and the exchange of rings, among other elements. The specific order and content of the ceremony can vary greatly depending on the couple's religious or cultural traditions.

The Recessional

After the ceremony is complete and the couple has been pronounced husband and wife, the recessional begins. This is when the newlyweds and their wedding party leave the altar, leading the way for the guests to follow. The order of the recessional is typically the reverse of the processional. The newlyweds lead the way, followed by the best man and maid of honor. Next come the bridesmaids and groomsmen, the flower girl and ring bearer, and, finally, the parents of the bride and groom. The recessional is a joyous moment, as the couple and their loved ones celebrate the beginning of their new life together. It's a time for the couple to bask in the love and support of their community as they embark on their married journey.

Nontraditional Processionals

Now that we've explored traditional approaches to the wedding processional and ceremony order, let's explore some creative ideas for those of you who want to try something different.

Together We Walk

Both partners enter the ceremony together, symbolizing their journey as equals in the relationship.

Grand Entrance with the Squad

The wedding party walks down the aisle together, either as a single group or in pairs (bridesmaids with groomsmen, or all bridesmaids followed by all groomsmen). This creates a more inclusive and celebratory atmosphere.

Family Spotlight

Instead of bridesmaids and groomsmen, couples can choose to include grandparents, siblings, or other important family members in the processional.

The Grandparents' Walk

Grandparents of the couple can walk down the aisle together, followed by the parents and then the couple. This is a sweet way to honor their role in your lives.

The Pet Parade

For animal lovers, including a well-behaved pet (a dog walking down the aisle with a ring tied to its collar, for example) can add a touch of personality.

Tips for a Smooth Processional

Now that you've envisioned your dream processional order, let's ensure it unfolds flawlessly on the big day. Here are some practical tips to keep your ceremony entrance smooth and stress-free:

- Plan the order of your processional in detail and create a timeline to make sure everyone knows when to enter.

- Designate a trusted friend or family member to coordinate the flow of your processional, making sure everyone is lined up and ready to walk on cue.

- If you have a complex processional with multiple groups entering, consider having a quick rehearsal before the ceremony.

Even with the best planning, unexpected things can happen. Take a deep breath, smile, and focus on the joy of the moment.

WEDDING FIRST LOOKS: PROS AND CONS, TIPS, AND MORE

When HuffPost asked 22 grooms what was going through their minds when they saw their spouses-to-be on their wedding day, the answers were surprisingly transparent—and touching.

Several of the couples had participated in a first look: a private, often emotional moment when a bride and groom see each other before the wedding ceremony.

One of the grooms interviewed, Wayne Memmott, told HuffPost that the minutes leading up to his first look with his bride seemed to

Courtesy of Becca Lee Photography

stretch out forever—but their moment together before the ceremony was worth it.

"The door to the courtyard opened, and as soon as I heard her heels on the brick path, I started to tear up," Memmott said. "She tapped me on the shoulder, and I turned, and I burst into tears for what would be one of many times that day. I remember looking at her and realizing that my life was going to be forever better because of her, and our day would be everything we wanted it to be, and it was."

If this kind of moment sounds appealing, I have some considerations and tips that can help you decide if an intimate first look is right for you, and if it is, how to make it unforgettable.

The Growing Popularity of the First Look

First looks can be traced back to celebrity weddings in the 1990s and 2000s when cameras captured emotional moments of couples seeing each other for the first time on their wedding day. However, the trend didn't take off for everyday couples until the late 2000s.

As more couples sought to make their weddings unique and create more private time together on their busy wedding day, first looks began increasing in popularity. As of 2019, about 76% of U.S. couples were having a first look on their wedding day.

While some couples still prefer to save the moment of seeing each other for the altar, many find first looks to be a meaningful way to savor some calm intimacy before the energy and events of the rest of the wedding day sweep them up.

Upsides to a First Look

When it comes to deciding whether a first look is right for you, there is no right or wrong. It's simply a matter of personal preference. Here are some benefits of planning an intimate moment to see one another before your ceremony:

- **It allows you to have a private moment.** This special moment belongs just to the two of you to take each other in, say a few words, and exchange gifts before being surrounded by family and friends the rest of the day.

- **It can help you feel more relaxed for the ceremony.** After letting go of the nervous jitters, you and your future spouse will be able to be more present and enjoy the ceremony more.

- **It facilitates a gap between the ceremony and the reception.** With photos done, you can take a break to attend cocktail hour with your guests while finishing any last reception details.

- **Your first reactions are genuine.** At the altar, the groom's reactions can seem staged or feel awkward as he waits for the bride to get closer. A first look allows photographers to capture authentic emotion.

Potential Downsides To Consider

While a first look offers many perks, there are a few downsides to consider:

- **You lose that aisle moment.** Some couples dream of that first-look moment as the bride comes down the aisle, and they want to experience it simultaneously with guests.

- **It goes against tradition.** While it's less common now, some couples prefer to honor long-standing wedding customs.

- **Overeager guests could sneak a peek.** Be sure to pick a private first-look spot to protect the intimate moment you've been anticipating.

- **You still need some post-ceremony photos.** While you can take the bulk beforehand, you'll still want photos of the wedding party, extended family shots, and possibly more candid photos during cocktail hour.

Tips for a Memorable First Look

If you opt for a first look, follow this advice to make the most of the experience:

- Choose an out-of-the-way location for privacy, like a tucked-away garden corner or inside a limo.

WEDDINGS

- Think about writing letters to read aloud to each other. This adds meaningful words to complement your emotions.

- You also might want to exchange small gifts, whether symbolic like a locket or quirky like his-and-hers socks.

- Ask close friends and family to give you both a few minutes when you are truly alone before they come for group photos.

- Schedule at least 30 minutes for yourselves to relax and soak in the moment.

- Arrange for last-minute makeup touch-ups afterward so you look fresh before guests.

Capturing Your First Look on Camera

Your first-look wedding photos will be some of the most treasured from your special day. Follow this advice to get stunning shots:

- Hire a professional photographer with expertise in capturing emotional moments and who can scout and frame interesting backdrops.

- Make sure the lighting is optimal; avoid harsh midday light or dark shadows.

- Have a variety of shots planned: facing each other, reactions when walking up, holding hands, embracing, foreheads touching.

- Bring meaningful accessories for some shots, like a love letter, gift, or family heirloom.

- Apply makeup that looks great up close, since the camera will capture your joyful tears. Waterproof is a must!

- Do some solo shots of each of you to build up anticipation and capture your expressions before coming together.

- Once you're together, forget the camera and immerse yourself in the moment. Your wedding photographer will fade into the background.

While you'll need to decide what's right for you, first looks offer an excellent opportunity to privately ground yourselves in love and gratitude before the wedding celebrations commence.

When thoughtfully planned, your first look can be a profoundly meaningful moment you'll cherish forever.

THE GRAND EXIT: ENDING YOUR WEDDING IN STYLE

As the final moments of your wedding reception wind down, the excitement starts to build for one last memorable wedding day event — the grand exit.

This departure marks the official conclusion of festivities (unless you're planning a wedding after-party), so couples aim to leave guests with a lasting, positive impression. Consider these tips when orchestrating your own distinctive, showstopping exit.

Defining the Grand Exit

The big moment when the bride and groom depart their wedding goes by several names, including the wedding send-off, the grand exit, the getaway, and the farewell. Whatever you call it, this event transpires after you complete any final reception traditions.

The DJ or band typically announces the couple's impending departure and invites wedding guests to gather. In most modern weddings, attendees form two parallel lines, creating a pathway for the newlyweds to pass through on their way out. Guests will cheer, wave glow sticks, blow bubbles, toss flower petals or confetti, or partake in other activities to celebrate and bid the couple farewell.

The exit may occur from the reception venue, hotel lobby, or another nearby location en route to your post-wedding transportation.

Purpose and Significance

Beyond concluding festivities on a high note, the wedding send-off carries deeper symbolic meaning. Passing through the channel of loved ones ushers you into your next adventure as a wedded couple. The images also make for emotive photographic mementos that capture the outpouring of love and support from your friends and family.

WEDDINGS

Creative Wedding Send-Offs

Here are some wedding send-off ideas to inspire you:

Bubbles

Supply guests with individual bubble bottles or bubble wands. Have everyone blow bubbles enthusiastically during your wedding send-off. This option, by the way, photographs fabulously both day and night. Plus, bubbles symbolize hopes floating into the future.

Flower Petals

Some couples adorn their exit path with flower petals for wedding guests to grab and toss.

Roses provide classic romance, but any petals can work. Consider sustainability by using faux or dried petals. For added symbolism, use flowers from your bouquet or floral arrangements. Let nature's beauty bless and surround your departure.

Ribbons

For a whimsical effect, hand out ribbon wands for people to wave during your send-off. Choose ribbons in your wedding colors. As you pass through sparkling ribbons dancing in the air, you'll be creating a vibe of love and childhood delight.

Beach Ball Exit

Provide your family and friends with a beach ball (or mini beach balls) printed with "Just Married" or the names of the bride and groom and your wedding date. Yes, beach balls are more casual, but they add to the fun of your wedding send-off.

Glow sticks

At your evening reception, give each guest a glow stick, bracelet, or necklace. As you walk through the magical glowing path, have your wedding photographer snap epic long-exposure photos. Glow sticks and similar items double as dance floor accessories earlier in the reception.

Paper Airplanes

Another playful idea is to hand out markers and paper airplane templates, which family and friends customize with sweet notes and then toss as you depart.

Bells

Have family and friends ring handbells as you exit to create a festive, jubilant feel.

Have your photographer capture images of smiling faces and bells mid-shake during your wedding send-off. (Of course, if you hold your wedding at The Bell Tower at 34th you'll also be able to incorporate the ringing of the bells in our tower into your wedding celebration. Bells are a time-honored wedding tradition.)

Thematic Ideas

For maximum impact, match your wedding send-off style to your wedding personality or your wedding theme. Here are some thematic concepts:

- **Romantic:** rose petals, lanterns, sparkling lights, limo exit

- **Whimsical:** bubbles, ribbons, parasols, vintage car

- **Bohemian:** flower crowns, loose flowers, glow sticks

- **Classic elegant:** luxury car, champagne toast, black-tie attire

- **Beachy:** seashell confetti, tropical floral leis, "Just Married" sign on vintage surfboard

- **Winter wonderland:** sleigh ride exit, fur wraps, falling snow machine, lanterns

Etiquette and Logistics

When planning your wedding send-off, keep these pointers on timing, location logistics, and etiquette in mind:

- Announce the exit 10-15 minutes prior so guests can prepare.

- Thank guests and say some of your individual goodbyes before your wedding send-off, if possible.

- Have supplies ready and assign someone you trust to organize guests. Recruit the DJ/band or coordinator to assist.

WEDDINGS

- Choose an exit spot with space for guests to gather safely. Ensure good lighting at night.

- Provide clear instructions on throwing items before your wedding send-off. Have ushers oversee.

- If you're considering glitter, confetti, or loose petals for your send-off, respect your wedding venue policies and cleaning fees.

- Be prepared for an exit in inclement weather. Have umbrellas or an alternative indoor area planned.

Capturing Your Grand Exit

Discuss these camera-ready tips with your photography team to get the wedding photos you want:

- Light the area sufficiently for quality images. Use string lighting if the wedding send-off will be outdoors at night.

- Request wide shots of the entire spectacle along with close-ups of emotional expressions.

- Ask your photographer to capture guests waving, cheering, and engaging actively in your send-off.

- Request shots in black and white or sepia tones for classic dramatic looks.

- Ask your photographer to be creative with angles, including low perspectives, faraway zoomed shots, movement, and panning effects.

Create the Exit You Want

Not every bride and groom will feel comfortable as the center of the spectacle for long periods.

If you'd rather escape sooner than later, keep your wedding exit short and simple. Waving quickly as you dash toward the car still makes an impression.

Or if you'd rather avoid a big public scene altogether, discreetly sneak off early without major farewells. Determine what level of drama and attention suits you best.

CHAPTER 12

Common
Wedding Questions

Courtesy of Oryan Photo and Video

HOW DO I CHANGE MY NAME IN TEXAS?

(Note: While this was written for brides in Texas, where my venue is based, most of the information applies to people who live in other states, too.)

If you're a newly married Texan and have been wondering how to legally change your name after marriage, I have some good news for you: An easy name change after marriage is within your reach.

All you need are some key vital records, completed forms, and legal documents, along with a list of the government entities you'll need to notify.

If you're wondering where to get your name changed, you should know that there is no one-stop shop — or government entity — that will handle your post-wedding name change. You'll need to work with multiple entities individually.

If you don't want to work on this on your own, you can find a name change service with Texas expertise, but that isn't a requirement. The only warning I have for you is that although it's not complicated, changing your name after marriage is not a particularly speedy process.

Below I will explain how to legally change your name, and I'll offer a few tips that can simplify each step. My goal is to save you time and help you make wedding memories with minimal stress and distractions.

Change of Name Due to Marriage: First Things First

Before you can start the process of changing your name, you'll need legal proof of your marital status. You can get that with certified copies of your official marriage certificate from the office of the county clerk that originally issued it. In most cases, you can order copies of your marriage certificate (your marriage record) online. I recommend requesting several copies.

Keep in mind that a photocopy is not the correct marriage certificate to use for this process. You need a certified copy. Be specific when you make your request.

Pro tip: If you're still preparing for your wedding and you intend to change your name, you might be able to order the certified copies of your marriage certificate with your original marriage license to save yourself some time.

WEDDINGS

Know What You Want

Have you decided what kind of name change you'd like? You can either hyphenate your last name with your spouse's name or make a complete switch and take your spouse's last name.

What you won't be able to do is use your marriage certificate to change your first name. The law also doesn't allow for changing your current middle name, creating a double middle name, or making up a new last name.

Court Requirements? Not In Texas

I've seen articles about changing last names in Texas that instruct readers to file a name change petition with their district court clerk. These articles mention court costs or filing fees and the need for a brief court hearing.

You should know that while filing a court petition is necessary for a legal name change in Texas, that requirement does not pertain to those filing for a changed last name after marriage. You will not need a court order.

Instead, you'll be approaching individual government agencies with a name-change request, providing one of your certified marriage certificate copies, and submitting name-change forms.

I recommend starting with the Social Security Administration.

How To Update a Social Security Card After Marriage

Changing your name with the federal government and getting a new Social Security card calls for completing an SS-5 form. If you want, you can start the application process online on the Social Security Administration website before making an appointment to visit your local Social Security office.

Another option is to call 1-800-772-1213 to request a form by mail.

In addition to a certified copy of your marriage certificate and your signed, completed SS-5 form, you'll need to be able to show the following:

- Evidence of your age, which ideally would be your birth certificate. Other options could be a U.S. hospital record of your birth, a religious record established before you were 5 years old, a passport, or a final adoption decree.

- Evidence of your identity, which could be a U.S. state-issued driver's license or identification card or your U.S. passport.

- Evidence of U.S. citizenship, which could include your U.S. birth certificate or passport, a Consular Report of Birth, a Certificate of Citizenship, or a Certificate of Naturalization.

The Social Security Administration requires original documents or certified copies in all cases, so while you can submit your application by mail, remember that you'll need to include your supporting documents as well. If you go that route, Social Security will return your documents with your new card.

If you'd like to submit your application and documents in person, you can find your nearby office on the Social Security Administration's website. You can expect a processing time of three to four weeks.

A Texas Driver's License Name Change

Once your new Social Security card arrives, your next step will be to complete the Texas Department of Public Safety's (DPS) Form DL-14A, which you can find online, to change your name on your Texas driver's license or ID.

If you supply the information for questions 1 and 2 on the form, you also can start the process of updating your voter registration.

In addition to your signed, completed Form DL-14A, you will need a certified copy of your marriage certificate, your new Social Security card, your passport (in your previous or married name), and your current driver's license or state ID, for a name change on a driver's license in Texas.

If you don't have a passport, the DPS accepts other documents, including a U.S. birth certificate. You can find the complete list of accepted documents on the DPS website.

You'll also need two documents that show you're a Texas resident. They can include your current driver's license or ID if it has your current address. Additional options are a utility bill, a pay stub, a bank or credit card statement, or a postmarked bill.

Take all of your documents to your local DPS office. You can avoid long lines by scheduling an appointment on the DPS Texas Scheduler site.

The DPS does charge a fee for updating your license or identification. Processing takes two to three weeks.

The DMV and an After-Marriage Name Change

After receiving a new driver's license reflecting your married name, your next step is to update your car registration and title.

Here's how to work with the Texas Department of Motor Vehicles (DMV) on a name change after marriage:

- Gather necessary documents. You will need to bring your current car registration, new driver's license, a certified copy of your marriage certificate, and a completed title and registration application. The title application must be completed in your new married name.

- Visit your local TxDMV office to process the car title and registration name change in person. Locate your closest office by searching online or calling.

- Pay applicable title and registration fees. There is a small title fee to reissue the car title in your new name. You'll pay standard registration renewal fees if you're also renewing the registration.

- The DMV will issue new car title and registration documents in your updated married name. Make sure all information is correct before leaving the office.

- Contact your auto insurance provider with your new name and updated vehicle docs to reflect the changes on your policy.

Passport

If you have a passport, I suggest getting a new passport as soon as possible so it's available when you need it. To do that, use the DS-82 Form, available for download online.

Mail your completed, signed form to the U.S. Department of State. Once they receive it, standard processing time ranges from eight to 12 weeks; expedited processing is five to seven weeks.

If you're enrolled in the U.S. Global Entry program, which provides expedited clearance for preapproved, low-risk travelers upon their arrival in the United States, you'll also need to visit a Global Entry enrollment center to update your information.

Your Health Insurance Card

After changing your name legally in Texas, one of the many items you'll need to update is your health insurance information.

The first step is to get in touch with the customer service team for your insurer. Let them know that you've recently changed your legal name due to marriage and need your name updated in their system and on your insurance card.

You'll need to provide legal name change documentation. Your insurer will likely require a certified copy of your marriage certificate.

Your insurer might have specific forms or applications for processing a name change on an account. Be prepared to fill these out with your new legal name.

Once you submit your name change request and documentation, ask your provider how long it will take to receive an updated insurance card and when the name change will take effect in their system. There is often some processing time.

Once you receive your new card, contact your doctors, dentists, specialists, and other health care providers to update your insurance information in their files. Provide them with the updated card.

If you have a spouse or dependents also covered under your policy, make sure to request enough new insurance cards so each covered member has an updated card.

Updating Your Name on Employment Authorization

If you have legally changed your name in Texas due to marriage, and you have employment authorization documentation, you'll need to update that as well.

The validity period, expiration date, and requirements to renew the card vary based on your immigration status.

Reach out to the U.S. Citizenship and Immigration Services (USCIS) office that issued your employment authorization document to inquire about requirements.

Next, submit your application and documentation. You'll likely need to file Form I-765 with USCIS to request a corrected employment authorization document reflecting your new name. Include supporting documents like your marriage certificate.

Allow processing time. It may take two or three months for the updated card to arrive. Continue working legally with your current card in the interim.

Once your new employment authorization arrives, make sure your name is correct. Contact USCIS immediately if any changes are still needed.

Let your employer know about your name change and updated work authorization document. Provide them with a copy for their records.

Taking these steps ensures you remain legally authorized to work under your new name. Reach out to USCIS or an immigration attorney if you have any questions about the process.

Banks, Credit Cards, and More

After you have your updated Social Security card, along with your driver's license and/or passport, you'll be able to change your name on your bank accounts, credit cards, and other forms of identification.

Banks and credit card issuers may have varying procedures for updating your name. Check their websites or contact their customer service departments to understand their specific requirements and processes.

While changing your name, take the opportunity to review and update other account information as necessary, like your mailing address or contact information.

After requesting a name change, watch for correspondence from your bank or credit card issuer confirming the update. Review any documents or statements carefully to ensure that your new name is reflected accurately.

Along the same lines, monitor your bank and credit card accounts regularly to make sure all transactions and account activity are accurate. Notify your financial institutions immediately if you notice any discrepancies or unauthorized activity.

Name Change FAQs

Here are answers to some frequently asked questions:

Do I need to hire a lawyer to change my name?

In most cases, you do not need legal representation to change your last name after marriage. As long as you have the required documents, like a certified marriage certificate, you can navigate the name-change process on your own by working directly with each government agency and account you need to update.

How should I list my name when I apply for something before the change is complete?

When filling out applications during the transition period, list your previous or maiden name as your current last name. You can note your new name with "as married" in parentheses or in the "Other Names Used" section. This ensures that records accurately reflect your legal name at that time. Once the name change process is fully complete, you should list your new name as your legal name on all applications and accounts.

Is there a time limit to change my name after marriage?

There is no time limit for changing your name after marriage in most locations. However, it's recommended that you begin the process soon after your wedding to minimize complications of having documents and accounts in your maiden name. Many people start the process one to two months after marriage.

Will my signature need to change?

Most likely, yes. Once your legal name has changed, you'll sign documents like checks and contracts with your new full name. While your signature itself doesn't need to drastically change, signing with your new last name solidifies your name change.

SHOULD WE GET A PRENUPTIAL AGREEMENT?

It's not at all unusual to feel uncomfortable with the idea of a prenuptial agreement. I've heard people say they don't like the idea of thinking about divorce before they even get married. And that's understandable.

But avoiding a potentially uncomfortable topic is not necessarily a good idea, either. It could be worth the effort to decide as a couple whether a prenuptial agreement—also known as a prenup or a premarital agreement—is right for you.

You should also know that more and more couples are seeing value in setting up some kind of premarital agreement. A 2022 survey on prenups by market research firm Harris Poll found that out of 1,000 people, 15% of married or engaged respondents had signed a prenuptial agreement, a considerable increase from 3% in 2010.

What's more, setting up a prenup does not increase a marriage's likelihood of ending in divorce.

While I can't provide a comprehensive guide on prenups, I have some basic information for you to review, in case you've been considering this option. I encourage you to learn as much as you can so you and your partner can make an informed decision, one that will give you peace of mind on your wedding day and beyond.

What Is a Prenuptial Agreement?

A prenuptial agreement is a legally binding contract, signed by both parties prior to marriage, that determines what happens in case of a future divorce.

Specifically, a prenup outlines how assets and debts will be divided if the marriage ends. Beyond that, they can also address various other matters, such as spousal support, property rights, and estate planning considerations.

While some may view prenuptial agreements as anticipating the end of a marriage, they can actually strengthen communication and foster transparency between partners, laying a foundation for a strong and secure relationship.

The Benefits of a Prenup

There are good reasons why a couple may want a prenuptial agreement.

For one thing, it protects assets you owned before the marriage. Without one, state laws apply.

What's more, establishing a prenup requires open talks about finances, debt obligations, spending habits, and other personal finance topics that couples sometimes are reluctant to discuss. Getting it all out in the open prevents surprises down the road.

A prenup promotes planning for inheritances and family businesses as well. If one partner expects to receive a large inheritance or already owns part of a family business, premarital agreements can ensure that those assets stay with the intended recipient.

The Downsides of a Prenup

However, there are some disadvantages to consider as well before saying "I do" to a prenup.

They include up-front cost. Having an attorney draft a solid prenup costs $2,000+ in legal fees.

They also can seem unromantic. Some partners feel prenups undermine trust and commitment. It's always a good idea to approach conversations about prenups sensitively to avoid hurt feelings.

Another consideration: The terms could change. Much can happen during a marriage, so if you create a prenuptial agreement, it will be important to revisit it occasionally to amend terms as needed.

What Couples Can and Cannot Include in a Texas Prenup

When developing a prenup in Texas, you and your future spouse have broad flexibility in coming up with mutually agreeable contract terms about how to divide your property if you later divorce.

However, there are a few limitations imposed by Texas law on prenup content. They include:

- How to split marital property and debts
- Plans for spousal support if you divorce
- What happens to benefits and rights from wills, trusts, retirement accounts, annuities, and similar accounts and documents
- How to handle the commingling of community property with separate property
- How future earnings will be classified

While Texas generally gives wide latitude on prenup terms, there are certain stipulations Texas law does not permit in domestic contracts like prenups. They include:

- Anything promoting divorce
- Limiting child support payment amounts
- Blocking child custody/visitation rights
- Forcing one spouse onto government assistance
- Requiring illegal or morally objectionable acts

Any provisions found by a judge to encourage divorce or keep a dependent spouse impoverished risks nullifying sections or the entire prenup. This is why enlisting an experienced attorney is crucial for crafting an enforceable agreement. They keep you safely within allowable boundaries under Texas statutes.

Broaching the Topic

Because prenuptial agreements do require what may be an awkward financial conversation, here are some tips for making it easier:

- Bring up this subject early to avoid surprises.

- Frame talks positively — explain why you want the protection.

- Be honest about all assets, debts, and property ownership details.

- Listen to any concerns your future spouse expresses.

Get an Attorney's Help

While online templates make setting up prenups seem like a quick and easy way to save money, having an experienced family law attorney customize your prenuptial agreement is highly advisable. Judges scrutinize DIY prenups more closely for enforcement issues than they do those created by legal professionals.

An attorney can handle all the required formalities and legal language intricacies involved with prenups to ensure that yours stands against legal challenges if necessary down the road. They can also advise you on what can and cannot be included based on Texas statutes.

Fostering Peace of Mind

While it's certainly not essential, more and more couples see the wisdom in outlining financial ground rules for marriage ahead of time through prenups.

For those bringing significant personal assets into a marriage or looking to safeguard future inheritances, prenups can provide invaluable peace of mind.

WHAT IF SOMEONE OBJECTS?

Have you ever imagined yourself in the following scenario? Your wedding officiant says, "If anyone objects to this union, speak now or forever hold your peace," and someone actually speaks up. Awkward!

WEDDINGS

While it's rare for someone to say "I object" at a wedding, it does happen occasionally. Here's what you need to know about wedding objections and how to handle one with grace in the unlikely event it happens on your wedding day.

What Is a Wedding Objection?

Wedding objections refer to when someone speaks up to oppose the marriage during the traditional "speak now or forever hold your peace" portion of the wedding ceremony. Typically, the officiant will ask if anyone has a reason why the couple should not be legally wed. An objection occurs when someone speaks up after this question is asked.

Why Would Someone Object?

There are a few reasons why someone might speak up during a wedding ceremony:

- They have a legal reason: They believe one or both people are already married to someone else. This could happen if someone had a previous marriage that they never legally dissolved.

- They know of a serious reason the couple should not marry, such as the relationship being unethical or illegal in some way.

- They consider it a last-ditch effort to have a relationship with you. Maybe they harbor unrequited romantic feelings or jealousy and are acting on emotion rather than logic.

- They are intoxicated and causing a scene.

- They're doing it as a prank or dare (not recommended!).

Do You Have To Include the Objection Question?

These days, the "If anyone objects" sentence is often omitted from wedding ceremonies. But you might find it's part of your ceremony script if you're holding a religious ceremony as a member of an Anglican or Episcopal church. The statement comes from the Book of Common Prayer's marriage liturgy section.

If your denomination requires the "if anyone objects" statement and you're concerned about the possibility of someone answering, consider having a private legal marriage ahead of time, then excluding this portion of the script from your symbolic ceremony.

Of course, it's still possible (however unlikely) that someone will speak up without waiting for the officiant's cue.

Preventive Measures

If you're worried someone may object during your wedding day, here are some measures you can take to help avoid it:

- Don't invite anyone you think would intentionally ruin your day. Only share wedding details with trusted friends and family.

- Give potentially challenging guests a role in the wedding so they feel included and are less likely to object.

- If you think someone close to you harbors unresolved feelings, speak to them honestly ahead of time. They may need closure.

- Remind your wedding officiant that they can ignore frivolous interruptions and continue with the ceremony.

- Line up security to politely escort out any drunken or disorderly guests before the objection point.

What Happens If Someone Objects?

So, can you still go forward with your wedding vows if anyone objects? Most likely. Generally, a wedding objection cannot legally halt the ceremony.

Your officiant can ignore it and continue with the wedding if they wish. That said, a legitimate legal objection, such as proof that one partner is already married, may result in the wedding officiant pausing the ceremony to address it. But a casual objection without legal merit cannot stop the proceedings.

How Should You Respond?

Stay calm. Take a deep breath and try not to react in the moment. Look to your officiant to handle the situation and do not engage directly with the objecting party. The officiant may intervene and remove the person if necessary.

If the officiant pauses the ceremony, respectfully comply, but ask to reconvene privately after investigating the objection.

Above all, do not let an objection ruin your special day. Stay beside your partner and focus on your love and commitment. An objection says more about the person objecting than about you.

Overcoming the Awkwardness

If someone causes an awkward scene with an objection at your wedding, try to defuse tension with humor and grace. Laughter and lightness can help smooth over discomfort. Possible responses could include the following:

- "Duly noted. Now let's get to the good part!"

- "We appreciate your concern, but this train has already left the station!"

- "If you have any additional relationship advice, you can write us after the honeymoon."

- "Thank you, next!" (A nod to Ariana Grande's hit breakup song.)

- "Bless your heart, but we've got this covered." (This response is perfect for a Texas wedding, but say it with a smile to take the edge off.)

- "We'll be sure to keep that in mind at our 10-year vow renewal!"

- "We know you mean well, but today is about love, not objections."

The key is keeping it lighthearted rather than mean-spirited. A bit of humor can help diffuse the awkward tension and get things upbeat again.

If an objection occurs, I also encourage you to look to your wedding party, family, and community for reassurance and support. Focus on those there to celebrate your love, not the one person trying to undermine it.

CORPORATE AND NONPROFIT EVENTS

CHAPTER 13

Event Planning
Considerations

NEED THE PERFECT VENUE FOR YOUR CHARITY EVENT? HERE'S WHAT TO LOOK FOR

When planning a charity event, your goal is to do what it takes to raise as much money as possible for your cause. This means one thing: Your guests—also known as the ones who will be opening their wallets—are king! With that in mind, booking the right venue to wine, dine, and entertain your donors is tops on your priority list.

Below is a list of considerations—in no particular order—to keep in mind when deciding where to stage your fundraising event.

1. **Cost.** Everyone knows you can't raise money without spending money, but that doesn't mean you should throw thriftiness to the wind and book the most expensive place in town. Shop around for places that fit your budget. You can even ask your top contenders if they're willing to give you a break on some of the costs in light of the fact that you're hosting a fundraiser for a good cause.

2. **What's included and what isn't?** Think through your entire event and inventory everything you need to make it happen, then create a checklist and take note of what is and isn't included in the cost of the venue. Ask lots of questions. Do they offer on-site catering? Can you bring in extra tables and/or equipment? Do they provide podiums or projectors? Do any of these extras cost more money? Is there an event coordinator to work with?

3. **Menu options.** People have to eat, and it's your job to make sure they have plenty of tasty bites to choose from. Scan the menu to make sure your venue offers a range of meats and vegetarian/vegan dishes and a good sampling of sides. Now's also the time to decide if and how you're going to serve cocktails and/or before-dinner hors d'oeuvres.

4. **Easy access to parking.** Make sure your guests can park easily and that they know how to navigate the parking situation once they get to your venue. Be sure to let folks know if they'll be expected to pay (although this isn't ideal, and you should try to work a deal with your venue to avoid it if possible). If nearby parking just isn't possible, arrange a bus service from a nearby meeting spot or organize ride-sharing options.

5. **Proper audio/visual capabilities.** Most charity events feature guest speakers, a presentation, and some sort of auction. For these activities to go off seamlessly, you'll need the proper equipment, particularly a good PA system, microphones, a projection screen, and maybe more. Just be sure you know what you need and that your venue can support it, and do a dry run with the equipment before your event. Don't forget to ask about lighting and sound capabilities, as well.

6. **Reliable Wi-Fi.** Nowadays this is a must. People have to be able to quickly access the internet, whether it's to check in with their babysitter or to participate in an online auction.

7. **Size, look, and comfort of the space.** Never underestimate the importance of aesthetics when you want to wow people and inspire big donations. That means you need a space that fits the mood and vibe of your event and/or organization, and one that fits your guests comfortably but isn't too big, so as to make the turnout look meager, or too small, cramming the space.

   Pro tip: Check out the facility's bathrooms. There should be enough stalls so that your guests don't have to wait in line. And—this goes without saying—they should be clean and well-stocked. There's nothing worse at a fancy event than inadequate or (shiver!) gross bathrooms.

8. **Location.** Where do the majority of your guests hail from? Are you interested in throwing your bash in a particular part of town? Do you want a space that is centrally located, with easy access for the greatest number of attendees? These are all questions you need to ask yourself when narrowing down a location.

9. **Staff.** A great party deserves a great staff making it all come together and ensuring guests are kept happy and well-fed. When scoping locations, ask your venue about how well the staff works together and how many experienced servers they have.

Though not exhaustive, this list is a good place to start when planning an amazing charity event venue, but you should never be shy about asking questions and getting the answers you need to throw a mem-

CORPORATE AND NONPROFIT EVENTS

orable event that inspires guests, creates a positive impression of your charity, and, of course, inspires people to support your organization.

9 TIPS FOR CORPORATE EVENT PLANNING

Organizing a corporate event, from a party to a seminar, can be intimidating. But putting together a successful event that guests will remember is doable, even if this is new territory for you.

Detailed planning and organization will be important, along with consideration for your attendees and their needs. Although this isn't a comprehensive guide, I have some suggestions that can help you plan successfully.

Here are your nine tips for planning a corporate event.

1. **Be clear about your event's primary purpose.** Is it team building? Launching a new product or service? Helping employees feel appreciated? You'll need solid objectives before you can start figuring out how to make them happen.

   When you clearly identify your goals, you'll be better able to manage your resources, stay on task, make decisions that support your primary purpose, guide your team, and measure your effectiveness.

2. **Develop a comprehensive plan.** Once you have a big-picture view of your event's purpose, develop your strategy for achieving it, whether that's creating a fun, unforgettable party that your colleagues will never forget or finding a motivational speaker that will truly energize the company.

   Then map out your tasks — the building blocks of your event — from finding the perfect venue to ordering supplies.

   Plan elements might include the following:

   - A planning timeline

   - A budget

   - Specific tasks, who will be responsible for completing them, and deadlines for each

Corporate And Nonprofit Events

- Internal communications or marketing to get the word out about the upcoming event

- A chain of command for decision-making

- Venue research

- Your guest list

- An itinerary for the event

- Food and drink details

- Audio/visual needs

- Tech requirements

- Transportation/parking

- Entertainment, if applicable

- Logistics for setting up and tearing down

3. **Start your preparations early and allow for interruptions and delays.** Life happens, especially when you're on a deadline. Giving yourself as much time as possible to pull your event together will help minimize your stress and increase the likelihood of success.

4. **Select product and service providers carefully.** Make sure they have experience with corporate events and have positive references.

5. **Remember to have a contingency plan in place.** Your Plan B may save the day if something goes wrong, whether it's a miscommunication with your caterer that results in no lunch deliveries or a sound system that refuses to cooperate.

6. **Consider a rehearsal.** Couples hold wedding rehearsals; why shouldn't you? If your event has elements that need to come together without a hitch, possibly an award presentation or a snappy audiovisual display, having a run-through will give everyone more confidence and help you catch potential problems before the real event.

7. **Depending on what you're planning, a theme can be an effective way to add a sense of energy and excitement to your event.** Aim for something fun and look for creative ways to work it into the day, from food and drink offerings to signage. Humorous touches will help, as long as they're not off-color and are appropriate for the type of event planned. (Humor is perfect for team building but may not land well at a shareholders' meeting.) A word of warning: If you don't have the time and resources to develop and execute a theme effectively, skip it. That's better than a last-minute or cheesy theme, which will work against the positive energy you're trying to create.

8. **Don't lose sight of your attendees' needs.** Whether you're working on a party or a product launch, the goal should be to keep participants comfortable and engaged. Employees are much more likely to retain the information presented during a day of interactive, hands-on activities at a workshop, for example, than they would be after hours of PowerPoint presentations. Also, give attendees plenty of breaks and consider the temperature of your setting.

9. **Don't underestimate the importance of good food; it will shape participants' overall perception of your event and add to the fun.** Consider healthy options that will keep people energized, or offer decadent comfort food and dessert stations (or both).

As you make menu choices, it helps to consider what will be taking place. Will attendees be hearing complex data that will require sharp focus? Consider proteins like lean meat, poultry, fish, and vegan options. Will the day be a bit of a marathon? Offer foods that will boost attendees' energy, like nuts, complex carbohydrates (whole-grain breads and pastas, brown rice), and vegetables.

HOW TO CREATE AN EVENT COMMUNICATIONS PLAN

In a 2015 LinkedIn article, public relations pro Erika Turan transparently wrote about several special event planning fails she has experienced and what they taught her.

One of her examples involved planning a public event for a hospital service. Everything seemed to be coming together beautifully until the coordinator Turan was working with provided an incorrect number for call-in registrations. No one caught the mistake until the phone number was printed on event invitations and would-be attendees started using it. A wrong number is one thing, but it turned out that this particular number happened to belong to an adult entertainment hotline.

Just reading about this gives me sympathy stress for everyone involved.

Turan said that incident forever cemented in her mind the importance of having someone—ideally someone unrelated to the project—double-check numbers, emails, and website addresses before mailing or publishing them.

I agree and applaud Turan for sharing her experience so others can learn from it.

I would add that mishaps like that are just the kind of thing event communication plans can help prevent. Planning your communication with the people involved in delivering an event, and those who will be attending it, is a great strategy for keeping everyone on the same page and identifying potential miscommunications before they happen.

Event Communication Plans 101

Event communication plans are similar to event plans but with a focus on disseminating information. They can focus on marketing and PR: your "what, when, where, and how" for getting your event messaging out. But they also can include strategies for communicating with event planning team members, clients, service providers, speakers, and performers.

Whatever way you approach it, an event communication plan is meant to be a tool that helps you do your job more effectively.

Start with the Who

I suggest beginning your plan by asking yourself who you'll need to communicate with before, during, and after your event and creating a list.

Then focus on each person, organization, or business you've listed, and identify your communication goals for them. Do you want to make sure the band you've hired is aware of the event venue's policies for bringing in equipment? Will you need to keep your client up to date on your planning progress and be accessible for their questions?

CORPORATE AND NONPROFIT EVENTS

Do you need to develop and implement a social media campaign to attract attendees? Do you want to make sure team members' tasks haven't fallen through the cracks?

Once you know what you want to achieve communications-wise, you can start developing a budget, timeline, and strategies for carrying out your objectives.

More Details to Gather and Share

In addition to the examples above, you might need to make plans to communicate the following:

- **Location details:** Address, parking information, entrances, transportation options, area construction or road closures, and toll roads.

- **Communication channels:** Phone numbers, emails, websites, messaging apps, meeting apps, social media, and event apps.

- **What-ifs:** Your contingencies for severe weather, cancellations, and emergencies; plans for communicating changes in plans; and team member assignments.

- **Event details:** The people getting the word out about your event will need speaker and entertainer names, bios, images, and videos (if possible). They'll need to know about vendors, exhibits, demonstrations, scheduled activities, and other relevant elements.

- **Food and drink details:** If attendees are spending a significant amount of time at your event, they'll want to know what kind of food and beverages will be available. They'll also appreciate options to request alternatives if they have allergies or dietary restrictions.

- **Dress:** If you want team members, entertainers, or anyone else involved to dress a certain way at the event, be sure to provide clear information well in advance.

Drawing Attendees

Naturally, communicating with the people you hope to attract to your event is a major goal. Depending on the size of the event and your budget, your event communication planning might incorporate your approach to invitations, an event website or landing page, advertising, publicity, social media, and e-blasts.

Your plan should take a detailed look at every tool you'll be using to bring people to your event. If you'll be distributing invitations, for example, you'll need to establish a time frame for sending them (ideally, two months in advance). You'll need to decide who will be responsible for invitation wording (along with proofreading and double-checking details), appearance, approval, distribution, confirmations, and reminders.

If you plan to have an online event registration site, you'll need to follow a similar process: establishing a time frame and delegating team members to handle content writing and editing, design, site approval, site publishing, registration monitoring, and the handling of questions or tech glitches.

Every strategy you use to draw people to your event, from introducing a unique hashtag to pitching articles to the media, will require detailed planning, delegation, a timeline, and a means of ensuring open, back-and-forth communication to make sure the plan is moving forward and everyone is on the same page.

And as Turan would tell you, keeping communication flowing and making sure everyone is on the same page are well worth the time and effort.

A COMPREHENSIVE GUIDE TO TEAM-BUILDING EVENTS

With AI, online meetings, and remote work arrangements becoming the norm in today's business world, fostering trust and camaraderie among team members is becoming increasingly important—and challenging.

Corporate team-building events have emerged as a powerful tool to strengthen the bonds within a team. These events are designed to enhance collaboration, communication, and trust among team members.

The Benefits of Trust-Building Events

One of the primary pluses of these events is that they create opportunities for team members to get to know each other better. This, in turn, promotes a sense of camaraderie and belonging within the team.

Here are a few additional benefits of events designed to foster team building.

- **Improved communication:** Effective communication is at the core of any successful team. Trust-building events with team-building activities encourage open dialogue, making it easier for team members to share ideas and work together more effectively.

- **Increased productivity:** Team members that trust each other are more likely to work cohesively and efficiently. This can lead to higher productivity and better results.

- **Conflict resolution:** Trust-building events often include activities that require problem-solving and conflict resolution. These skills can be applied in the workplace to resolve conflicts more efficiently.

- **Employee satisfaction:** Team members who feel a sense of trust and belonging are typically happier and more satisfied in their roles, which can lead to better retention rates.

The Four Cs of Team Building

If you decide to arrange a team-building event, you should know about the "four Cs" that underlie effective team building: communication, collaboration, creativity, and camaraderie.

- **Communication:** As I mentioned, effective communication is the cornerstone of any successful team. Encourage open dialogue, active listening, and constructive feedback during your event. Games and team-building activities that require clear communication will help participants understand the importance of sharing information, ideas, and goals.

- **Collaboration:** Teamwork and collaboration go hand in hand when it comes to solving problems and achieving common goals. Team-building activities that require participants to work together and harness their individual strengths promote a sense of unity and collective accomplishment. Emphasize the idea that every team member plays a unique role that contributes to the overall success of the team.

- **Creativity:** Creativity is often the key to innovative problem-solving. Encourage your team to think outside the box and approach challenges with fresh perspectives. Team-building activities like collaborative art projects and cardboard boat building can tap into the creative potential of your team members. And that contributes to a culture of innovation and resourcefulness.

- **Camaraderie:** A strong sense of camaraderie creates a positive work environment where team members trust and support one another. Foster a spirit of friendship and unity during your event. Social activities, shared meals, and fun team-building exercises will help.

Best Practices

Planning with the four Cs in mind is helpful, but as you plan, you should also ask yourself if there are any specific objectives you want to achieve. Maybe you want to build bonds after a return-to-the-office (RTO) mandate or build leadership skills among young professionals. Plan activities with your goals in mind.

Here are some more planning tips.

- **Budget wisely:** Set a budget and stick to it. This will help you make informed decisions on your venue, activities, vendors, food, and other event details.

- **Choose the right venue:** Selecting the right event venue, by the way, will be one of your most important decisions. Make sure it offers the necessary space, facilities, technical capabilities, and ambiance to create an environment conducive to trust-building activities.

- **Consider your team's preferences:** Not everyone enjoys the same types of team-building activities. You'll be more effective if your programming caters to different personalities and generations. For example, the introverts on your team might prefer quiet, reflective activities like a book club discussion or mindfulness sessions. Millennials and Gen Z team members might enjoy interactive and tech-based activities like virtual escape rooms or collaborative online games more than Generation X and baby boomers would.

- **Think about engaging a professional facilitator:** In some cases, it may be worthwhile to hire a professional facilitator to guide the team through programming and team-building exercises. A professional can provide valuable insights and the necessary expertise to create a successful event.

- **Make assignments:** Delegate tasks to responsible team members and provide a clear timeline for completion.

- **Develop an agenda:** Create a well-structured agenda with a balance of team-building activities, discussions, and downtime. This will help the event flow smoothly and keep participants engaged.

- **Keep safety first:** Keeping team members and participants safe during activities is a must. Pay attention to any physical and emotional boundaries, and be ready to adapt activities if necessary.

Team-Building Activity Ideas

Now that we've explored the importance of trust-building events and the best practices for planning them, let's dive into the heart of these gatherings: the activities that will bring your team members closer together.

Team-building activities will be the building blocks of your event. They challenge individuals, promote teamwork, and create lasting memories. Below, you'll find some of the best team-building activities I've observed at my venue.

- **Trust falls:** This is a classic team-building activity in which team members take turns falling backward, relying on their colleagues to catch them. This promotes trust and teamwork.

- **Escape room challenges:** An escape room experience is great for problem-solving and teamwork. Teams work together to solve puzzles and "escape" from an area within a set time limit.

- **Outdoor adventure activities:** Fun activities like ropes courses, zip-lining, and hiking encourage teamwork and camaraderie while taking advantage of the outdoors.

- **Collaborative art projects:** Get creative with group art projects that require participants to work together to create a masterpiece.

- **Team-building workshops:** These workshops can cover topics like effective communication, conflict resolution, and leadership skills.

- **Cooking classes:** Another effective team-building exercise is to cook or bake something together. A cooking class can foster collaboration, sharpen communication skills, spark creative thinking, and instill a sense of accomplishment among team members.

- **Scavenger hunt:** A scavenger hunt is a fantastic team-building activity that encourages problem-solving, communication, and collaboration. During the scavenger hunt, teams decipher clues and find hidden items or complete challenges. This friendly competition promotes trust as each team member relies on the others' abilities and support to succeed.

- **Board games:** Playing board games, or even holding a board game tournament, is a fun team-building strategy. Board games offer a relaxed yet effective way to build trust. Games like Monopoly and The Game of Life require negotiation, teamwork, and decision-making, fostering strong interpersonal bonds. They encourage healthy competition while also enhancing problem-solving skills and strategic thinking.

- **Two truths and a lie:** In this team-building activity, team members take turns sharing two true statements and one false statement about themselves. The group then has to guess which statement is the lie. This game promotes active listening, communication, and understanding within the team.

- **Cardboard boat building:** Challenge teams to design and build a boat using only cardboard and tape. Afterward, test the boats' seaworthiness in a fun and engaging water-based competition. This activity promotes creativity, problem-solving, and teamwork.

- **Trivia:** Organize a trivia competition based on your company's history, industry knowledge, or pop culture. Teams work together to answer questions, fostering a competitive but still collaborative spirit.

CORPORATE AND NONPROFIT EVENTS

- **Egg drop challenge:** Teams are tasked with creating a protective contraption to keep an egg from breaking when it's dropped from a height. This challenge encourages creativity, problem-solving, and innovation while reinforcing teamwork and trust.

Team-Building Theme Ideas

Another dimension to consider as you plan your event is the possibility of establishing a theme. A well-chosen theme can set the tone, ignite enthusiasm, and add an extra layer of fun and meaning to your event. Here are some possibilities to consider:

- **Around the World:** Each team represents a different country and takes on challenges that reflect that culture.

- **Movie Mania:** Base your event around popular movies, with activities and decorations inspired by famous films.

- **Survivor Challenge:** Mimic the popular reality TV show by creating a series of physical and mental challenges for team members to overcome.

- **Carnival Extravaganza:** Transport your team members to a carnival with games, popcorn, and cotton candy.

- **Garden Retreat:** Host your event in a beautiful garden setting, fostering a sense of tranquility and relaxation.

- **Sports Spectacular:** Incorporate sports-themed team-building activities to promote cooperation and friendly competition.

More Planning Considerations

Here are a few more strategies for creating an effective, memorable event and, ultimately, achieving your team-building objectives.

- **Communication:** Keep the lines of communication open throughout your planning process. Regularly update participants and provide any necessary information.

- **Accommodations:** If your event involves travel, provide comfortable, convenient accommodations for participants.

- **Feedback and reflection:** After your event, gather feedback from the participants to understand what worked well and what could be improved. Keep this information in mind when you plan your next corporate event.

Corporate team-building events are much more than a fun day away from the office. They're a strategic investment in your company's success.

CORPORATE PARTY THEMES FOR A MEMORABLE EVENT

Boosting employee morale, impressing clients, and generating buzz around your brand—these are just a few of the potential benefits of a well-themed corporate event. But how do you go beyond a simple color scheme or generic concept to create something truly unique and memorable? I have some suggestions.

Take It Outside.

A game of cornhole, lawn Jenga, or a giant version of Connect Four, anyone?

Simple fare like burgers, hot dogs, and brats make menu planning easy, but don't forget to include something vegetarians will savor, too, possibly potato salad (admit it: almost everyone likes that), a Caprese pasta salad, or a grilled veggie sandwich. Vegans and gluten-free guests alike might enjoy lettuce wraps stuffed with a savory blend of tofu, mushrooms, onions, and water chestnuts.

Want to take the outdoor theme to the next level? How about a country fair theme with traditional midway games like pick a duck or a water coin drop?

Or if you really want to go big, consider a corporate camping trip, even one that's not a sleepover. Although it couldn't really be defined as roughing it, one company recently treated their employees to a mock camp-out at a resort. The event featured custom-constructed A-frame tents, a s'mores bar, and a campfire.

Go Behind the Screens.

Binge-watching is a popular guilty pleasure. One way to connect with guests is to hold an event that salutes programs and films that people are talking about.

Let the setting and plot be your guide. For a *Stranger Things* party, decorate with string lights and alphabet wall displays, and serve Eggo waffles. Feeling more upbeat and adventurous, like in *The Mandalorian*? Incorporate Star Wars-themed decorations and perhaps a Baby Yoda photo booth.

A trivia tournament or a *Jeopardy!* or *College Bowl*-style competition is a sure way to test your guests' TV and movie knowledge. Not only can contests like those improve engagement, interpersonal skills, and team dynamics, but some people believe they can actually make you smarter!

Travel the Globe.

Take your guests on a global adventure without ever leaving the venue. Set up stations representing various countries, complete with traditional foods, drinks, and décor. For example, you could have a Parisian café with croissants and café au lait, a sushi bar for Japan, and a taco stand for Mexico.

Enhance the experience with cultural performances, music, and interactive activities like a passport-stamping game in which guests collect stamps from each "country" they visit.

Or Try Time Travel.

Transport your guests to different eras with a time travel-themed event. Create zones that reflect various decades or historical periods, such as the Roaring '20s, the Fabulous '50s, or the Groovy '70s. Decorate each zone with period-appropriate décor and offer themed food and drink options. Encourage guests to dress up in costumes from their favorite era, and provide fun activities like a '50s dance-off or a '70s disco contest.

A LOOK AT EVENT PROFESSIONALS AND WHAT THEY DO

Do you know the difference between event planners and event producers? How about event coordinators—do you know what they do?

If you're a little fuzzy on what these roles involve, don't feel bad; you're in good company. Many, even those in our field, get a bit confused about who does what in the events industry. But there are important distinctions that you should know about.

This section can serve as your guide. Once you have a solid understanding of what distinguishes event producers, planners, and coordinators from one another, you'll be better able to make educated decisions about seeking their services. And you'll be able to fully realize the benefits of their knowledge and skills.

Planners and Producers: There Is a Difference

While most people have at least heard of event planners, few outside of the event industry are familiar with event producers. That's ironic, because planners actually are a subset of producers.

"The event planner is responsible for designing a strategy and taking care of the small details, while the event producer is responsible for using their production expertise to deliver a good experience for both the attendees and the client," event solution provider Vario wrote in a blog.

As RGI Events puts it, "Event production goes above and beyond traditional event planning by combining event management with creative and technical production, focusing on the overall event experience. All producers are planners, but not all planners have the technical skills and knowledge of a producer."

Producers often map out and manage the technical aspects of an event, from directing production staff to making sure audiovisual equipment is set up properly.

But the differences between planners and producers don't stop there.

Planners help clients identify a purpose, vision, and budget for their events and determine what steps will be necessary to realize the client's goals, from selecting the event location to lining up speakers.

A producer then figures out the best approach to executing those steps and does what it takes to ensure their success.

Event producer Stephanie Jayko, founder of Knock Out Productions, contrasted the roles of event producers and planners during an interview with Event Planning Blueprint.

"On the event-planning side ... they're putting together what the client wants and needs and all the little pieces into a spreadsheet, whether it's in their mind or a real one. They're building the road map that becomes the event.

"As a producer, we come in and work on the road map that has already been laid out for us," Jayko continued. "We look at all of that and determine what is needed to accomplish those different things, how to build the world within each stop on that road map. We're a little more on the technical side and a little bit more on the creative side."

Where Producers Shine

Wondering what that looks like?

Depending on the event, a producer's responsibilities could include developing strategies for executing clients' visions, reviewing and editing event proposals from other team members, implementing the vision of the event by hiring appropriate vendors, and managing event logistics, among other tasks.

A Closer Look at Event Planners

While event planners often are members of the teams that organize large events like those described above, they also can help with personal events, from anniversary parties to weddings.

Examples of tasks that event planners handle include meeting with clients to discuss their event's purpose; working with clients to establish an event's time, location, program, and cost; helping clients develop event themes; researching lodging, transportation, and services surrounding the event; and coordinating with venue staff members.

And, if you enlist a planner for your wedding, they can help with such tasks as serving as your overall wedding advisor, helping you select a wedding venue, guiding you through contracts with vendors (photographers, entertainment, flowers, etc.), scheduling and attending vendor meetings, coordinating hotel rooms and transportation for your guests, providing input on wedding design and fashion, building your wedding website, mailing invitations, and tracking reservations, among other things.

What About Event Coordinators?

Basically, event coordinators do the legwork required to implement what's been planned. They often assist event planners.

"Generally speaking, the planner makes critical decisions regarding what, when, who, and how," Geoff Beers wrote for The Balance Small

Business. "An event coordinator, on the other hand, is responsible for making sure all of the details are executed, and that each vendor shows up on time and performs appropriately."

According to Beers, large organizations may have two coordinators for every planner, and smaller operations may have one coordinator on call for all the event decision-makers.

"Either way, there is typically a direct line of supervision over the coordinator position," he wrote.

On the day of events, coordinators generally are at the venue, working as a go-between for the client, vendors, and the venue staff.

So now you know who you can turn to for help with planning your wedding or event.

The important thing to remember is that whatever you have in mind—whether it's a party, corporate gathering, charity gala, or your wedding—you can find event professionals with skills and expertise that match your needs.

CREATING YOUR EVENT TIMELINE

If you're a big believer in spontaneity—or you're struggling to stay on top of your planning—you may find yourself questioning the value of creating a detailed event timeline.

I can tell you from experience that in most cases, a good timeline is a sanity saver, for you and everyone who will play a part in your event.

Think of all the businesses that will have a role in your event, from caterers and entertainers to your venue and photographer. And what about your event team and volunteers? Unless you provide them with guidance, you have a recipe for confusion, frustration, and awkward moments.

A timeline helps everyone know what to expect, and what's expected of them.

And even though a timeline is an investment in, well, time, it returns the hours you put into it with interest. Not only does it bring order to a potentially hectic and chaotic period, but it also can remind you of details you hadn't thought of and spark creative ideas.

So go ahead and start your timeline. You can use the tips and suggestions I'm sharing here to get started.

Break Down Your Event

Start by listing the key activities and moments that will take place during your event, from the welcoming of attendees to the closing entertainment—everything that will take place. These items will be the building blocks of your timeline.

After You Identify Your 'What,' Consider Your 'Who'

Identify everyone who will have a role in your event and what they'll be doing, so you can add them to your timeline. Specify the times and locations each person will need. In the case of your vendors, for example, specify arrival times and windows of time they'll have to complete specific tasks.

Seek Input

By now, you may be thinking, I have no idea when my videographer should arrive or how long the band will need to set up. You don't have to figure all of this out on your own. You can seek advice from your venue, which probably has seen an event or two in its time. Vendors and service providers can help, too, by giving you a feel for what they do on the day of the event and, roughly, how long they expect it to take to bring in equipment, complete flower arrangements, or do their sound check.

A Timeline Is More Than a Schedule

The more detail you can build into your timeline, the better.

If you've hired a DJ, for example, not only will they need to know when to bring their equipment to your venue, they'll also need to know where they should set up and who they'll need to coordinate with when they get there. Later, because they might be your emcee, too, they'll need to know when people will eat and the timing for the other key moments of the day.

As you block off times for people and businesses, be specific. An example might be, *4 p.m.: The videographer arrives, loads their equipment through the side entrance, and checks in with the venue manager.*

Include names, if you have them, and people's contact information.

Don't Expect Everything To Run on Schedule

Your planning will help keep your day on track—up to a point. Life happens. People run late. Technology fails to cooperate, and activities can stop aligning with the time frame you had in mind. So, to prevent stress and a chain reaction of delayed events, build buffers of five or 10 minutes into your timeline. And try to keep your sense of humor.

Plan with Photography in Mind

As you create your event's itinerary, note the moments and activities you'd like your photographer (and possibly your videographer) to capture.

You'll be able to use that information to make a shot list, complete with the people you want included. Working from your timeline will save you time and simplify your planning.

A GUIDE TO CHOOSING THE SHAPE OF YOUR EVENT'S MEAL TABLES

If you're planning a corporate celebration, deciding on the shape of the tables may sound like an insignificant detail, but this design element is more important to your event than you might think. Table shape impacts how a room will look and flow, how much space attendees will have to mill about, and the overall vibe of your celebration.

Here you'll find a summary of your options and their pros and cons.

CORPORATE AND NONPROFIT EVENTS

Courtesy of Pam Ashley Photography

Round tables

Pros: This classic choice is often the most cost-effective route, for several reasons. First, many venues already stock round tables, which eliminates the need for rentals. Second, standard sizes, including 36-, 48-, 60-, and 72-inch options, seat anywhere from four to 12 people comfortably, more than other shapes. Third, the more folks you can fit at the table, the fewer tables you'll have to decorate, saving you money on centerpieces. Finally, there is no limit to how many linen options you'll find.

Cons: Really, there are few cons to round tables unless you simply don't like the look of them. Round tables tend to have a traditional vibe. If you'd prefer a different feel to your celebration, you have plenty of other options.

Rectangular tables

Pros: Also called banquet tables, rectangular tables can create a beautiful, streamlined symmetry in your seating design. What's more, they can fit from four to 10 people, depending on how long they are. A fun way to work with this style is to link several together to create a dramatic, long setting. This allows for ease of conversation, but make sure you don't overdo it on the centerpieces and block people's line of sight between one another. This style is also ideal for outdoor events where you may have more space to spread out.

Cons: Going with rectangular tables will likely cost you more, as they don't fit as many folks as other styles and take up more floor space to seat the same number of guests as round tables. They don't typically work for events with a large guest list; they're more suited to intimate gatherings.

Square tables

Pros: Like round tables, squares can handle large centerpieces while keeping the setting intimate for attendees. Plus, they tend to work in most event venue spaces, so they can be a good, modern alternative to rounds, depending on how many people will be attending and how much space you have to work with.

CORPORATE AND NONPROFIT EVENTS

Cons: Square tables tend to take up a decent amount of floor space, so if your venue is on the smaller side you may want to consider round tables. Also, renting square-shaped linens isn't always easy, as vendors largely carry round and rectangular-shaped selections.

Serpentine tables

Pros: Pushing several curved tables together to create a winding seating arrangement can add a fun and interesting visual element to your celebration. As long as you can fit all the attendees in your curvy, creative space, this option will be an attention-grabber and conversation starter.

Cons: A serpentine setup calls for a decent amount of space and likely won't be achieved indoors.

WHAT YOU SHOULD KNOW ABOUT LINENS

Ever wondered why place settings look more elegant on a certain linen? Or why some tablecloths cost a small fortune? The world of event linens can be more involved than you might think.

With that in mind, I've pulled together a guide for you that includes materials and uses along with tips, trends, and some creative ideas to help you make informed choices during your event planning.

Materials

Let's start by looking at the tremendous variety of materials available to you.

- **Cotton:** Lightweight, breathable, and affordable, cotton linens are a classic choice for events of all kinds. They come in a variety of colors and patterns, which makes them versatile and easy to coordinate with your event theme (if you have one).

- **Damask:** Damask linens are known for their intricate, woven patterns and luxurious feel. They add an elegant touch to tables.

- **Embellished:** If you'd like to infuse your event with a touch of glamour, embellished linens adorned with beads, sequins,

CORPORATE AND NONPROFIT EVENTS

or embroidery can add a hint of sparkle and sophistication to your tables.

- **Linen (the fabric):** Linens made of linen fabric have a rustic charm and a slightly textured feel. They're perfect for creating a relaxed but elegant vibe.

- **Organza:** This sheer, lightweight material can be used for overlays or runners. If you'd like to add a touch of whimsy to your tables, organza is a perfect choice.

- **Polyester:** Yes, polyester is a more affordable choice, but using this material doesn't mean you can't create beautiful event tables. Polyester linens are available in a large range of colors and work well with most event formats and themes.

- **Raw silk:** With its natural luster and subtle texture, raw silk linens exude a sense of luxury and sophistication. It's a beautiful option for formal events and celebrations.

- **Satin:** Smooth and glossy, satin linens have a rich, elegant feel. They can be used for tablecloths, napkins, or opulent chair covers.

- **Taffeta:** This fabric is known for its crisp, slightly rough texture and sheen. Consider taffeta if you'd like to add a touch of drama and visual interest to your tables.

- **Velvet:** Plush, luxurious velvet is ideal for creating a cozy, intimate atmosphere. It works especially well for winter or evening events and adds an element of warmth to décor.

Uses: More Than Just Tablecloths

While tablecloths might be the most obvious linen choice, a whole world of other options exists to elevate your event décor. Each type of linen serves a unique purpose:

- **Liners:** Often the unsung heroes of table settings, liners are placed beneath tablecloths to provide an extra layer of protection against spills and stains. They also help to smooth out any imperfections in the table surface and create a more polished look.

- **Overlays:** Want to add a touch of drama or a burst of color? Overlays are your answer. These decorative cloths are placed on top of tablecloths, offering an opportunity to introduce texture, patterns, or a contrasting hue. Popular choices include sequined overlays for a glamorous feel or lace overlays for an elegant, vintage touch.

- **Runners:** Long, narrow runners are typically positioned along the center of tables. They can be used to create a visual focal point, drawing the eye down the length of the table. Runners are also an excellent way to incorporate a bold pattern or color without overwhelming the entire table setting.

Linens for Chairs
Chair covers, sashes, and bands can transform ordinary chairs into elegant statements. They can be used to coordinate with your table linens or to add a contrasting accent. Using chair linens is a fantastic opportunity to tie your entire décor scheme together and create a cohesive look.

Sizes for Rental
When renting linens, it's important to know the standard sizes to ensure a proper fit.

Tablecloths typically come in sizes such as 90x90 inches for a 60-inch round table, 108x108 inches for a 72-inch round table, and 120x120 inches for an 84-inch round table. For rectangular tables, common sizes include 90x156 inches for a 6-foot table and 90x180 inches for an 8-foot table.

Tips for Selecting Linens
The right linens can elevate your event décor from ordinary to extraordinary. To make sure your choices harmonize with your overall vision, consider these factors:

- **Theme and color palette:** Select linens that complement your event's theme and color scheme. For a rustic or bohemian event, natural fabrics like linen or cotton would be fitting, while a glamorous affair might call for luxurious satin or velvet.

- **Venue style:** Consider your event venue's ambiance when choosing linens. A formal ballroom might demand elegant, floor-length tablecloths, while a relaxed outdoor celebration could be enhanced with breezy, lightweight linens in pastel hues.

- **Mix and match:** Try experimenting with textures, patterns, and colors. Layering different linens can create depth and a more personalized look. For instance, pair a textured linen tablecloth with a smooth satin runner for a sophisticated touch. Just take care to maintain a cohesive look.

Fabric Care

Before committing to a particular fabric, check the care instructions. Some linens require special handling or professional cleaning, which might not be practical for your budget or timeline. Opt for durable, easy-care fabrics if you prefer a hassle-free approach.

10 CHAIR OPTIONS FOR YOUR CELEBRATION

When planning an unforgettable celebration, the right dining chairs can make all the difference. They're not just a place for your guests to sit—they're a key element in setting the tone and enhancing the overall vibe of your event. As you research venues and chair rentals, it will help to have a feel for some of the more popular chair options available, from sleek and modern to plush and opulent.

Here's a guide to dining chairs to get you started.

1. **Bentwood chairs:** Available in multiple colors, Bentwood chairs feature a rounded wooden back. These chairs are simple, attractive, and comfortable.

2. **Chameleon chairs:** Also known as "fanfare chairs," these metallic chairs usually have cushions or fabric covers that tend to blend in with event décor. These chairs are attractive and comfortable.

3. **Cross-back chairs:** Also known as "vineyard chairs," they are a popular choice for rustic and garden events. As their name says, the backs of these dark wooden chairs have crosspieces forming an X.

4. **Chiavari chairs:** The backs of these chairs feature vertical and horizontal bars. Chiavari chairs are usually made of wood or resin and are an elegant, comfortable, and popular choice for formal affairs.

5. **Folding chairs:** These are one of your more affordable options, and these days they're available in a range of materials, from metal to wood, along with stylish designs. Folding chairs are a great choice for outdoor events.

6. **Ghost chairs:** These clear acrylic chairs add a modern note to your event. Because they're transparent, they give your space a more open feel. On the other hand, ghost chairs are not necessarily the most comfortable option you can offer attendees.

7. **King Louis XVI chairs:** These classic chairs feature an upholstered oval back. They're a popular choice for formal events, and one of your more expensive options.

8. **Marais chairs:** These chairs, inspired by French neoclassical furniture designs, are often made of carved, gilded wood with upholstered seats. Their curved, cabriole legs give a graceful silhouette. These chairs are perfect for bringing a touch of formality or old-world glamour to an event. They work well with chic and vintage themes.

9. **Slotted chairs:** These chairs evoke the feel of a sidewalk café. Slotted chairs are available in wood and plastic and work well with simple, casual events and more formal affairs. They're also a great option for creating rustic or industrial vibes.

10. **Versailles chairs:** Also known as "Napoleon chairs," Versailles chairs have a scalloped back with vertical spindles, along with a cushioned seat. They typically feature intricate carvings and gold leaf/gold paint accents. Their timeless baroque style communicates grandeur and luxury. Versailles chairs are a great rental option for formal events. They make a wonderful backdrop for photos, too.

CORPORATE AND NONPROFIT EVENTS

18 FAVOR IDEAS FOR YOUR NEXT CORPORATE PARTY

Favors—gifts for party guests—may have evolved over the years, but the practice of giving them is alive and well. They're a way of expressing appreciation and gratitude.

The goal is to select items people will actually want to keep — or enjoy in the moment.

If you're leaning toward offering favors at a corporate party you're planning, you may be wondering how much to budget for them. Generally, about $5 to $20 per person is a good rule of thumb.

Now all you have to do is select your favors. Here are some ideas:

- Packets of seeds (herbs or flowers) in customized packaging

- Packages of coffee, whole or ground beans

- Test tubes filled with cocoa mix, with customized tags attached (or the same approach with tea leaves)

- It's hard to disappoint with chocolate favors: engraved bars, packets with a variety of treats, or s'mores kits

- Customized notebooks or journals

- Portable phone chargers

- Packets of seasoning blends, meat rubs, or spices

- Frosted sugar cookies

- Butterfly garden kits

- Luggage tags

- Reusable stainless-steel straws

- Jars of honey, jam, or maple syrup

- Go Texas: Lone Star magnets, barbecue sauce, hot sauce, pecans, Texas wildflower seeds, or mini bottles of tequila

- Eco-friendly tote bags

- Small bottles of olive oil

- Unique bottle openers

- Tiny succulents

- Favors that tie in with your party's theme. Are you planning a movie-themed celebration? Give guests gourmet popcorn kernels. Will your party have a disco vibe? Give disco ball keychains. Will your event take place in the summer? Give travel-size sunscreen, sunglasses, and flip-flops in a cute beach bag. Another summer option would be s'mores kits.

10 TIPS FOR AN AMAZING OUTDOOR EVENT

While the allure of an outdoor event is undeniable, their logistics can be a bit more complex than those of their indoor counterparts. Weather, permits, and unexpected obstacles are just a few of the factors to consider. That said, if you invest some time in careful planning and preparations, there's no reason why your outdoor event can't be a smashing success.

Before we get into my tips, let's take a closer look at outdoor events. They're not always a good fit. Here are a few of their pluses and downsides.

Outdoor Event Pros

- Attendees can enjoy the sights and sounds of natural surroundings and scenery, not to mention the feel of an open-air environment.

- You'll have the freedom to be creative with your décor, lighting, and layout.

- You'll have more accommodation options for larger events.

Outdoor Event Cons

- Weather is an uncontrollable factor (rain, wind, heat).

- You'll need backup indoor options.

- Outdoor events require careful coordination of rentals like tents, floors, and lighting.

- You could encounter issues with bugs, sun exposure, or noise.

If you decide to move forward with an outdoor event, these tips can bolster your planning:

CORPORATE AND NONPROFIT EVENTS

1. **Have a rain plan.** One of the biggest concerns with outdoor weddings is rain. Have a backup plan like rental tents or an indoor venue option, or just embrace "rain plan" decorations, such as clear umbrellas.

2. **Prepare for other weather issues.** Things like wind, humidity, heat, and bugs can disrupt an outdoor event. Have cooling stations, bug spray, and accessories like parasols or fans. Time key activities to correspond with mild temperatures.

3. **Rent the right lighting.** As the sun goes down, proper lighting is key. String lights, lanterns, and candles create an inviting glow. Bring in professional lighting to make sure no areas are too dark.

4. **Keep attendees comfortable.** Shaded spaces can contribute greatly to your attendees' comfort. Rent umbrellas or have a tent where people can escape the sun. I also recommend blankets for colder evenings and possibly a station with bug spray and sunscreen.

5. **Focus on ventilation.** Even a light breeze can disrupt an outdoor event or dinner. Use structure tenting to block wind and enhance airflow in key areas.

6. **Create ambiance with décor.** Enhance the natural landscape with décor tailored to your event venue. Try wooden pieces, floral installations, hanging greenery, and similar elements.

7. **Make parking convenient.** Have parking attendants and golf carts to help everyone get around.

8. **Incorporate locally sourced elements.** Use in-season florals and food from local sources. It's eco-friendly and allows you to highlight your locale.

9. **Embrace nature in photos.** An outdoor setting offers endless amazing photography opportunities with natural backdrops, unique perspectives, and gorgeous golden-hour lighting.

10. **Plan for audio.** Make sure you have the right audio equipment and setup to accommodate speeches, music, and other audio needs. Use wind guards on microphones and sound systems to ensure clarity.

CHAPTER 14

Preventing and Dealing with Event Challenges

Courtesy of Pam Ashley Photography

SELF-CARE DURING EVENT PLANNING

Event planning is a whirlwind of creativity, logistics, and high-stakes problem-solving. While the results can be incredibly rewarding, the journey itself can take a toll on even the most seasoned professionals.

With that in mind, I've put together some thoughts on the importance of self-care for event planners along with practical strategies for maintaining your well-being throughout your planning process.

Yes, self-care should be a priority.

When you're trying to select the ideal event venue, line up entertainment, and finalize countless other details, the stress can add up. It could impact your health and diminish your effectiveness as a planner. Keeping yourself well in the lead-up to your event—and, of course, during the event itself—is part and parcel of creating a memorable experience.

Taking time for yourself doesn't have to be very involved or even expensive. The primary idea is to take steps that leave you feeling refreshed and minimize your stress. Here's what they could look like:

Physical activities help.

Consider scheduling weekly or monthly massages in the lead-up to your event. Even one massage could work wonders! If exercise is your happy place, you could try a yoga class or any other workout session. Or keep it simple and commit to regular walks after dinner or on a weekend morning.

Make wise food choices.

Putting thought into what you eat can be considered self-care, too. To be clear, I'm not recommending dieting. Instead, think about foods that will improve your energy, overall health, and well-being.

High on the list of stress-busting foods is celery. The phthalide it contains can help reduce stress hormones and lower blood pressure. Foods high in omega-3s, like avocados, salmon, and trout, are great stressbusters too, and foods with magnesium, including nuts and seeds, help reduce anxiety.

Lean on your support network.

Don't feel bad about turning to people in your life for support. They can also offer a great escape and be an element of self-care. You could schedule a lunch date with a friend or family member with the agreement that event planning will not be a topic of discussion.

Try mindfulness and relaxation techniques.

Incorporating mindfulness and relaxation techniques into your daily routine can be a game-changer for managing stress. Practices like deep breathing exercises, progressive muscle relaxation, and guided imagery can help you stay calm and focused. Apps like Headspace and Calm offer guided meditations that are easy to fit into your busy schedule. Even taking just a few minutes to practice mindfulness each day can make a significant difference in your overall well-being.

Use time management tools.

Effective time management is another valuable aspect of self-care for event planners. Harness tools like planners, to-do lists, and scheduling apps to keep track of your tasks and deadlines. Break your tasks into smaller, manageable chunks and prioritize them. This will help prevent you from feeling overwhelmed and keep you on top of your responsibilities. And, of course, it's perfectly OK to delegate tasks to team members or hire extra help when needed.

Don't sacrifice sleep.

Quality sleep is often one of the first things to be sacrificed during the hectic planning process. But maintaining good sleep hygiene provides a powerful boost to your mental and physical health. Create a bedtime routine that promotes relaxation. Try reading a book, taking a warm bath, or listening to soothing music. Make your bedroom a sleep-friendly environment by keeping it cool, dark, and quiet. Aim for seven to nine hours of sleep a night, and odds are good that you'll wake up refreshed and ready to tackle your day.

There is no doubt that pulling together all the elements of a successful event can throw even the best of us into a full-blown breakdown if we're not careful. Investing in self-care is not indulgent; it's a strategy that will help you be more effective as a planner.

CORPORATE AND NONPROFIT EVENTS

MINIMIZING NO-SHOWS AT YOUR FREE EVENT

Hosting free events can be a great way to attract attendees and promote your business.

However, one extremely common problem with these events is the risk of no-shows—people who RSVP but don't attend. If you're an event organizer, you're acutely aware that no-shows can be frustrating and costly.

Root Causes

A free event intrinsically attracts more no-shows than paid events do. When there is no financial commitment or penalty for not showing up, attendees feel less obligated to honor their reservation. Here are some common reasons for this pattern:

- **Double-booking:** Attendees RSVP for multiple events on the same day and choose one later.

- **Schedule changes:** Other obligations like work or family come up between the time someone registered and the event day.

- **Low investment:** As I mentioned, with no money paid, attendees feel less committed.

While no-shows can be understandable, particularly in the context of free events where attendees may not feel as invested, they still pose significant challenges for you as an event planner. Not only do no-shows disrupt event logistics and planning efforts, but they can also result in wasted resources like unused seating, catering, and promotional materials.

Additionally, no-shows can hurt the overall attendee experience, leading to diminished engagement, decreased networking opportunities, and potentially lower satisfaction levels. From a financial perspective, no-shows can represent lost revenue opportunities, as sponsors and vendors may base their support on expected attendance numbers.

And consistently high rates of no-shows can damage the reputation of both the event and the organizing entity, potentially deterring future attendance and sponsorships.

So if you're an event planner, what can you do to minimize no-shows at your next event?

Use RSVP Limits

Implementing RSVP limits can be a strategic approach to mitigate the risk of no-shows at your free-to-attend events. By setting a maximum number of RSVPs and adhering to it diligently, you not only ensure that your guests don't exceed your event venue's capacity, but you also enhance the perceived value of your event and urgency among attendees.

Here are some tips for effectively using RSVP limits to discourage no-shows.

- **Understand your venue capacity.** Before setting RSVP limits, assess the capacity of your event venue. Consider factors like seating arrangements, standing room, and safety regulations so you don't inadvertently overbook, which could lead to overcrowding and potential dissatisfaction among the attendees.

- **Establish a realistic limit.** In addition to considering your venue, you can base your RSVP limit on such factors as your event type and expected attendance. It also helps to consider past event turnouts and any promotional efforts that could impact attendance.

- **Communicate clearly.** Announce your RSVP limit on your event invitations, website listings, and social media promotions. It also helps to provide a compelling reason for attendees to RSVP early. Emphasize limited spots or any special perks reserved for early registrants. I also would clearly state that once your RSVP limit is reached, no further registrations will be accepted.

- **Monitor RSVPs closely.** Regularly monitor RSVPs as your event date approaches. Keep track of the number of confirmed attendees and be prepared to close RSVPs promptly once the limit is reached. Use event management tools or dedicated RSVP platforms to manage this process and track RSVPs accurately.

- **Implement waiting lists.** In case RSVPs fill up quickly, be ready to implement a waiting list system to capture additional interest. Notify people on the waiting list promptly if spots become available due to cancellations, and allow them to confirm their attendance within a specified time frame.

- **Ask for confirmations.** Encourage the people who RSVP to reconfirm their attendance closer to your event date. Send out timely reminders by email or text. Along with your reminder, share important event details and reiterate the importance of honoring their RSVP commitment.

Try a Refundable Deposit

You can also reduce no-show rates by implementing a refundable deposit system. You collect a nominal fee when people register, typically ranging from $5 to $10, with the promise of a refund after their arrival at the event. This approach helps mitigate the risk of no-shows and fosters a sense of accountability among attendees.

Here are some points to consider when implementing a refundable deposit system.

- **Establish clear terms.** Outline the terms of the refundable deposit system in your event communication and registration process. Explain that the deposit will be refunded upon attendance at the event, and provide details on how attendees can claim their refund.

- **Highlight the benefit.** Emphasize the benefits of the refundable deposit to prospective attendees. Explain that it helps ensure accurate attendance projections and enhances the overall experience for everyone involved. Frame it as a way for attendees to demonstrate their commitment and contribute to the success of the event.

- **Keep the deposit amount reasonable.** Set the deposit amount at a level that's affordable and reasonable for attendees. A small $5-$10 fee should be enough to encourage commitment without creating a financial barrier to participation.

- **Automate your refund process.** Use event management tools or registration platforms that support automated refund processing. That will simplify the refund process for you, your team, and the attendees.

- **Monitor deposit refunds.** Even with the help of technology, I recommend keeping track of deposit refunds and making sure they're processed promptly. Regularly reconcile attendance records with deposit payments to identify any discrepancies or issues that may arise. Promptly address refund requests or inquiries from attendees to maintain transparency and trust.

Partner with Influencers

Collaborating with influencers can be a powerful way to promote your events and attract a larger audience. Here's how to effectively partner with influencers to increase RSVPs.

- **Identify relevant influencers.** Research and identify influencers in your event presenter's niche who have a strong following and engagement with your target audience. Look for influencers whose values align with the presenting organization's brand.

- **Build relationships.** Reach out to influencers and build genuine relationships with them before pitching an event collaboration. Engage with their content, leave thoughtful comments, and share their social media posts to show your support and appreciation. Building rapport with influencers makes them more likely to consider partnering with you and promoting your event to their followers.

- **Craft compelling offers.** Develop attractive offers and incentives for influencers to promote your event. This could include free tickets, exclusive access, behind-the-scenes experiences, or affiliate commissions for ticket sales generated through their referral links. Tailor your offers to each influencer's interests, audience, and promotional preferences to maximize their impact.

- **Provide valuable content.** Equip influencers with valuable content and resources to help them promote your event effectively. This could include high-quality images, videos, event details, key selling points, and promotional materials that they can share with their followers. Make it as easy as possible for influencers to create engaging and persuasive content that drives RSVPs to your event.

- **Express gratitude.** Show appreciation to influencers for their support and promotion of your event. Thank them publicly on social media, share their content with your audience, and consider offering them additional perks or incentives for their efforts. Building positive relationships with influencers can lead to long-term partnerships and ongoing promotion of your events.

While some no-shows may be inevitable when there's no charge for your event, utilizing creative strategies like communication, small refundable deposits, RSVP limits, and partnering with influencers can help significantly reduce your no-show rate. With better attendance, you can improve the attendee experience and get a solid return on investment for event expenditures.

WHEN SOMETHING GOES WRONG

In event planning, it's practically a given that something will go wrong sooner or later. It might be a minor hiccup like on-site registration that drags out longer than expected, vegan attendees who don't like their menu choices, or a full-scale disaster like a missing keynote speaker. Problems come with the territory in this field.

Yes, you can minimize the risk of problems with strategic planning, but some things will be outside of your control.

When things do go wrong, your response will shape your client's perception of you and your services. A prompt, honest, and professional reaction will earn respect much more than placing blame or panicking.

I've put together a few guidelines and suggestions that will help you respond effectively to unwanted situations at your events.

A Few General Rules

- **Don't panic.** If your client, or their guests, see you lose your cool, the magnitude of the problem will seem much, much bigger. Besides, worry and panic are contagious—try not to spread them.

- **Be accountable.** When something goes wrong, be it a missing delivery or a climate-control malfunction, don't make excuses. Instead, work on resolving the situation. Communicate clearly with your client and be honest if the problem can't be fixed.

- **Consider resources that can help.** In a recent blog post, Reinventing Events recommends evaluating your resources when things go wrong. "If the badge vendor didn't send enough badges, is there a FedEx Print Center you can call to see if they can do a quick print? If a sudden storm is knocking down your outdoor signage, is there a volunteer who can help you pick them up?"

- **Make sure your team is prepared, too.** Make time to train your staff on how to respond when something goes wrong. Not only should they be focused on remaining professional and taking good care of event attendees, but they also should know what steps they should take. Maybe you want them to contact a specific manager to ask for instructions. Or maybe you'll want certain staff members to step in to help resolve a problem, possibly by fixing malfunctioning equipment or bringing in backup supplies.

Be Your Own Best Friend

One of the best things you can do for yourself, and your clients, is to have just-in-case plans, processes, and tools in place. Each event should have a custom contingency plan, which should be completed in the earliest stages of your planning. You can't prepare for everything, but start your plan by asking yourself what the most likely, or most devastating, scenarios would be.

One example could be the possibility of a no-show (or extremely late) guest speaker. Your contingency plan should include professional speakers who can fill in on short notice. Your plan should also have information about the event attendees: In an article for Associations North, business speaker Thom Singer suggests pulling together an expert panel of four or six subject matter experts or admired people attending your event. He also encourages planners to find the best emcee they can to moderate.

"Have the moderator interview all the panelists about their best ideas in regard to an important industry topic, then allow the audience to participate in Q&A with these masters of knowledge," Singer writes. "With four or six on the panel no one individual needs to carry the whole presentation."

Another logical topic to address in your plan is the possibility of severe weather or a natural disaster. Be prepared to move to another location, reschedule, or—if possible—shift to a virtual event. Speak to your venue in advance about severe weather policies. Have contact information on hand for area airports, public safety officials—even hospitals. (Along with your plan, consider getting event postponement and cancellation insurance.)

As you develop responses to potential problems, think about who will be responsible for which measure. Will you call the caterer when they misunderstand your order, or do you want another team member to take charge? Who will call the valet service if you need a larger parking team? Who will handle your internet connectivity issues? After selecting the best team members for each responsibility, make sure they understand exactly what you want them to do. Provide detailed written procedures for them, and talk it over to make sure there are no misunderstandings.

I also recommend creating an emergency kit. It's not unusual for brides to pack items that will help save the day when (not if) minor mishaps like a stained dress or broken heel occur on their wedding day. You should do the same with your event in mind. Events company East of Ellie wrote in a blog post that they always bring a bag of random supplies to live events.

"A laptop, printer, and laminator on-site for any last-minute jobs is a must. We also have Post-it notes, Sharpies, pens, rubber bands, binder clips, a hot glue gun, paper, and anything else that can fit for event day."

Along the same lines, insist that the vendors you work with, from the venue to the entertainers, take the same approach. They should have backup equipment and supplies in place and ready to go if they're needed.

One more thought: Try to remember that event mishaps aren't failures on your part. The best you can do is prepare for as many possibilities as possible—and be calm and professional about situations you couldn't control or anticipate.

PLANNING A CORPORATE GATHERING? HERE ARE 8 MISTAKES TO AVOID

When putting together a company gathering, be it a holiday party, product launch, or special event to mark a major success or honor a valued employee, the details can make or break your affair. After all, bringing together co-workers who may or may not socialize outside of work can be tricky, so it's important to make the right decisions at every step of the planning process.

Read on for a list of potential planning pitfalls and how to avoid them.

1. **Not Researching Your Event Date**
   Sometimes you have no choice about your event date. It may tie in with an anniversary, for example, or be the only day a speaker is available. But, whenever possible, I suggest taking measures to prevent a scheduling conflict with other events in your community or area of interest. You don't want to lose potential attendees. Check event calendars and industry news updates to see if something else is planned on the date(s) you're considering. I also suggest avoiding major holidays and holiday weekends when people may have personal obligations.

2. **Not Properly Vetting the Venue**
   Where you host your event should be one of your top priorities. Make sure the venue you're considering—its catering services, size, look, cost, and list of amenities—fits your needs and the purpose of your party. You'll also want to be sure you have the details in writing and have carefully discussed and considered what the venue has to offer before you book.

   Pro tips: Look for a staging area if you're hiring a band. Try to avoid places with stairs if you have an older workforce. Also, make sure the restroom facilities are top-notch.

3. **Not Delegating Responsibilities**
   Event planning, particularly for a corporate function, should be a team effort. If you're the ringleader, be sure to assign specific tasks to each of your helpers and give them a deadline to get it done. Be available to help and offer alternatives if their plans fall through, and don't neglect your own to-do list. Better yet, if your company has the budget, hire a corporate event planner and work closely with them.

CORPORATE AND NONPROFIT EVENTS

4. **Not Having Enough Food**

It should go without saying that no one should go hungry at your event. Can you say morale buster? Get an accurate head count and then prepare a little bit extra. When choosing your caterer, look for a company that's experienced in your type of event and can accommodate a number of different tastes. Be sure to survey the attendees beforehand about any special dietary needs and see if the menu includes at least a few vegan options as well as dairy- and gluten-free dishes.

Pro tip: If possible, offer to provide advertising for your caterer or promote them on social media in exchange for a discount.

5. **Not Limiting the Free Drink Service**

Of course, a cocktail hour can be part of the fun of an event, but getting drunk in front of your boss and co-workers is poor form. You can help your attendees avoid that scenario by limiting drinks. Tickets for one to three spirits on the house is a nice touch, and drunkenness is discouraged when people have to pony up for additional drinks.

6. **Not Having a Set Agenda**

I'm sure you want your employees to enjoy your special event, but if the time is too loosely structured you may not achieve what you set out to do. Have a time frame for different elements of the event and stick to it. To keep things moving, designate someone who will announce what's happening and direct employees' attention to the order of events.

7. **Not Planning Entertainment or Background Music**

Though this might not apply to every corporate event, it will for many—particularly holiday parties, honoree events, company milestone celebrations, or any occasion where you aim to keep things light and social. Whether you go with a live band or a sophisticated string quartet, the music should reflect the spirit of your event. Ask around about talented local ensembles and artists, and discuss your musical expectations beforehand.

CORPORATE AND NONPROFIT EVENTS

8. Not Having a Backup Plan

Inebriated attendee? Better have transportation options like Uber or Lyft on speed dial. Your guest speaker canceled at the last minute? Have an activity in your back pocket that your guests can enjoy instead. You get the idea. Though you certainly can't plan for everything that could possibly go wrong, being prepared to deal with common issues will keep you ahead of the game and your event going strong.

A LOOK AT EVENT POSTPONEMENT AND CANCELLATION INSURANCE

No matter how thoroughly you've mapped out your upcoming event, it's impossible to prepare for everything.

Sometimes life steps in and unravels what you've been working toward.

Since my venue opened for business, we have been encouraging clients to purchase event postponement and cancellation insurance, which covers customers if an emergency interferes with their big day. This is not the same as vendor liability insurance, which protects you if a vendor is responsible for an injury or property damage during your event.

Here's a closer look at event postponement and cancellation insurance and how it works.

The Basics

With event postponement and cancellation insurance, you pay a one-time fee to cover an event if an unexpected circumstance, like hazardous weather or a serious injury, impedes your ability to move forward with your plans.

Depending on the policy you choose, it will reimburse you for nonrefundable payments you've made to book an event venue and vendors (food, entertainment, etc.).

EventInsuranceQuote.com puts it this way: "Event Cancellation Insurance provides coverage for the loss of revenue derived from OR expenses committed to an event due to a cancellation, abandonment, interruption, curtailment, postponement, or relocation caused by covered perils as defined in the policy as covered perils."

Notice the "as defined in the policy" phrase. If you do invest in postponement and cancellation insurance, be sure to take the time to research multiple providers and plans. Find out exactly what the policies you're considering will cover. Are there any exceptions you should be aware of?

Money and Other Considerations

How much can you expect to pay for event cancellation and postponement insurance? The cost of your policy will vary by provider and the level of coverage you want. From what I've seen, buying policies in the $400 range meets most clients' needs.

Here are a few more things to keep in mind as you research your options:

- **Purchasing windows:** Some insurers won't sell policies more than two years in advance or later than 16 days before a special event.

- **Changes of heart:** In the case of weddings, policies rarely cover brides or grooms backing out of a wedding, though there are exceptions.

- **Budgeting:** Many insurers require payment in full up front; they will not accept installments.

Do I Really Need Event Cancellation Insurance?

You may be wondering if cancellation insurance is worth the money, especially with all of the other event expenses you're facing. But the idea behind getting cancellation and postponement insurance is to protect the money you (or your client) will be investing.

From my perspective, while event cancellations and postponements don't occur frequently, they do happen. That's why we recommend it to every client, and prospective client, we speak with.

Coverage Options

Being forced to postpone or cancel an event is one of several situations you can cover with insurance. Here are a few other possibilities to ask your prospective insurer about:

- A major vendor, such as the florist, doesn't deliver agreed-upon services.

- Special attire or jewelry is lost or damaged.

- Gifts are lost, stolen, or destroyed.

- Event photographs are destroyed.

- In the case of a wedding, an immediate family member, event participant, or your officiant cannot attend because of a military deployment.

While shopping and purchasing event cancellation insurance involve some extra time and expense, the coverage you purchase can protect you from significant loss and stress in the long run. And having coverage in place frees you to focus on planning and enjoying your event.

TIME MANAGEMENT TIPS FOR CORPORATE EVENT PLANNING

Missed deadlines, forgotten details, and last-minute scrambling—these are the nightmares that can haunt you when you're planning a corporate event. But it doesn't have to be this way. With the right techniques and tools, you can transform chaos into calm and increase the likelihood that your event will run smoothly from start to finish.

Plan Your Planning

Even if you're not a to-do list kind of person, a checklist can truly be your friend when you're planning an event. Create a list with major tasks (like hiring a photographer) and related subtasks (like researching photographers online and checking references). Give yourself a deadline for each major task.

Next, map out times to achieve the goals you've just set for yourself, along with your other responsibilities.

Don't forget to give yourself some extra time, or buffers, to make up for unexpected events that don't care about your carefully scheduled week, from a client meeting that runs long to car issues that demand immediate attention.

Another point to keep in mind: Finding large blocks of time for selecting the right venue or designing the centerpieces you want to make

might not be realistic. Instead, schedule smaller chunks of time, maybe 15 or 30 minutes, and continue working toward your goal gradually.

As far as prioritizing goes, try to get the toughest, most complicated tasks done sooner rather than later. What those things are will depend a little on you and your personality. Some people dread creating a budget, while others worry about décor details. Getting the most challenging tasks done early will reduce the temptation to procrastinate and will smooth the remainder of your planning.

Organization Can Be a Stressbuster

You may be a Type A person who believes everything has its place ("Doesn't everyone color code?") or a bit more relaxed ("The piles on my desk are the perfect filing system.")

It's not realistic, or desirable, to change who you are in order to plan your event. But even if you fall into the more relaxed category, I encourage you to embrace a few basic organizational principles for now. It will save you time and stress in the long run.

For one thing, try keeping all of your event information in one or two designated places. You might have a binder for printed materials and documents and a folder on your laptop or an app for storing digital information.

If someone is helping with your efforts, possibly a professional planner, you can set up a Dropbox or Google Drive folder for sharing checklists, contracts, and other documents.

And while we're talking about help from others, designating tasks is an excellent organizational strategy and a sanity saver. Giving small projects, such as stuffing invitation envelopes, to trustworthy team members will free you up to accomplish your own to-dos.

Another organizational strategy: Give yourself as much time as possible. Granted, life happens, and sometimes you just don't get the amount of time you'd like to plan your event. But as much as possible, start tasks early.

A few more tips:

- Capitalize on your vendors' and venue's expertise. Instead of spending hours looking for good videographers, for example, ask the photographer you've lined up for recommendations. Your venue likely will be able to recommend businesses — and provide additional event-planning tips and resources, too.

- Use your lunch hour. This can be an ideal time to conduct online research, call vendors, or work on your event timeline.

- Harness technology. You may want to enlist the help of an app for event-planning. Apps are available to help you create to-do lists and check items off, keep up with deadlines, and stay on top of payments and deposits.

WHY WE INSIST ON INSURED WEDDING AND EVENT VENDORS

When you're planning an event, the benefits of hiring insured vendors are fairly straightforward. If something goes wrong at your event, and a vendor is responsible for someone or something being harmed, that vendor's liability insurance covers the cost of the damage. Their insurance ensures that neither they nor you, their client, are left holding the bag financially.

Having that protection is extremely important and a big reason why The Bell Tower on 34th requires clients to hire insured event vendors. But it isn't the only reason.

CORPORATE AND NONPROFIT EVENTS

We see our requirement as a way to protect our ability to consistently achieve The Bell Tower on 34th's key objective: delivering excellent events that no one will ever forget.

Sure Signs of Professionals

Basically, there are part-timers and hobbyists in our industry, and there are full-time pros. Given our choice, we'll work with the pros every time. That's true for planners and for all event professionals, from caterers and florists to photographers and entertainers. All of them.

One way to identify professionals is that they almost certainly carry liability insurance, along with errors and omissions coverage. The latter is a specialized form of liability insurance that protects businesses and professionals if they're sued for inadequate work or negligence.

We know that if you're making your living providing a product or service, there's a good chance that you are a responsible business owner. And responsible owners know they aren't going to be making a living very long if they don't continuously take care of their business. That includes having the proper insurance.

All event service and product providers, from planners to caterers to bakers, should have both liability and errors and omissions insurance. It's a sign that they know what they're doing and they're serious about their craft.

Those who understand that — the vendors who invest in the insurance they need — are the professionals The Bell Tower on 34th wants to partner with to deliver excellent events.

Professionals want to — and know how to — ensure success for their clients. Look at professional event DJs, for example. Yes, they know their music and have the right equipment, but they also know how to work seamlessly with the other vendors at the event. They treat guests with courtesy. They know when to eat, that they shouldn't drink on the job, and how to help keep the event itinerary moving forward. A customer just isn't going to get that with an old college roommate.

We prefer to limit our interactions with vendors willing to work at events without liability insurance. Doing so suggests that the vendor isn't concerned about sustaining a full-time future in the event industry. They're certainly not concerned with protecting their clients.

If they don't have insurance, they probably are not an event industry pro.

We'll Take the Heat

Our insurance requirement for vendors provides a secondary benefit to our clients. It helps them avoid uncomfortable conversations with family members, friends, and acquaintances who volunteer to help with their event.

The client can throw us under the bus, so to speak, and say, "I appreciate your offer, but my venue insists that I hire vendors who can provide a certificate of liability insurance. It's even in our contract." And they'll be telling the truth.

To be fair, some clients don't want that out; they'd prefer to accept their friend's or relative's offer to take a vendor's role at their event. While that's not advisable, we usually will make an exception to our insurance requirement if the client feels strongly about it. But we also make it clear that by going that route, they accept 100% of the financial responsibility for their uninsured vendor(s).

Using insured vendors is always the best choice, the one we try to steer our clients toward. It protects them from liability, and because it results in professional vendors working with us on events, it helps protect our ability to deliver excellence.

CORPORATE AND NONPROFIT EVENTS

CHAPTER 15

Food, Drinks, and Attendee Comfort

SERVING FUN, FANCY, AND DELICIOUS MOCKTAILS AT YOUR EVENT

To some, a party, wedding, or corporate event without a spirit to sip as they make their rounds simply isn't appealing; many folks equate the free flow of adult beverages with fun and letting loose.

But this definitely isn't the case for everyone. In fact, there are a number of reasons some guests will pass on alcohol, including religion, health issues, personal convictions, or aversion to the taste. These guests deserve tasty, interesting drink options too, and, as the event organizer, it's up to you to deliver.

To that end, let's talk about creative ways not only to serve non-alcoholic drinks but to present them, as well.

- **Have a conversation with your venue.** To get started on planning a full bar experience that serves up trendy specialty drinks with or without the alcohol, make sure to discuss your plans with your venue. Their bar staff may have experience mixing up unique and yummy concoctions, and they might even boast a signature mocktail or two. You also should ask if your venue is open to taking recipe suggestions from you in case you have some ideas in mind. If they are, you can ask friends and colleagues for recommendations.

- **Do better than straight soda.** Yes, soda (or soda pop, or pop, depending on your region) is standard, go-to nonalcoholic fare and the first drink of choice for a dry bar, but for some, it's boring. How about a soda station, where your guests can create custom refreshments with a selection of ingredients? You could stock the station with syrups laced with fruit flavors or options like mint, berries, ginger, honey, rosemary, crushed flowers, and other fun and surprising choices to spice up their soda. Also, mixing limes and lemons with Sprite or a similar beverage makes for a tasty limeade.

- **Try some refreshing water ideas.** If you're looking to offer fun, light water options, there are many ways to go about it. Lemonade is always a good idea, but you can also provide water infused with lime, cucumber, or strawberries. Not only do these drinks mix well with dinner, but they make a great accompaniment to midday lunch events or brunches.

- **Go crazy for kombucha.** You may have heard of kombucha, a fermented and sweetened black or green tea, but did you know it mixes well with cherries, rosemary, lavender, or berries to make a great alcohol-free beverage? Put it on the drink menu at your next event and delight your attendees.

- **Serve alcohol-free cider.** For teetotalers, cider is a suitable substitute for champagne for making toasts, so why not jazz it up with fruit juices for a flavor kick. Try blackberry, cranberry, or grape juice mixers.

- **Present a pressed-juice station.** Liven up your juice staples of apple, white grape, and orange with pomegranate juice for an outside-of-the-box option.

- **Offer herb-infused options.** Mix lavender lemonade with honey, or shake up a ginger-apple mocktail using ginger, lemon slices, ginger beer, and apple juice. Mint, basil, and rosemary can be combined with soda, too. How about a mint julep made from ginger ale, lemon juice, and mint? You have so many choices!

- **Choose the fancy glasses.** This is a big one! One of the joys of having a nice drink is partaking from a beautiful glass, like an elegant tumbler or a champagne flute. Don't leave your sober guests out when it's time to toast or have a drink in hand—make sure their glass, like everyone's, matches the tone of the event.

- **Have all drinks made at the same bar.** This keeps your guests mingling while ensuring that those passing on the alcohol don't stand out.

As you can see, there are plenty of ways to liven up a dry bar and make sure all your guests have fun, interesting, and tasty drinks throughout your party.

A final tip: I suggest offering at least three nonalcoholic options at your event. With the many ideas included here, that shouldn't be a tough task.

CORPORATE AND NONPROFIT EVENTS

CORPORATE CATERING TRENDS

While the pandemic is now behind us, its impact on corporate events lingers on. Companies, and event planners working on their behalf, are continuing to work to make guests feel safe and welcome—and to accommodate the public's growing interest in staying healthy.

If you will be attending or planning a corporate event soon, here are some of the catering trends you can anticipate.

Serving and Sizes

When it comes to food, caterers are responding to increased requests for individually sized portions. What does this look like? It can range from miniature food items (sliders and desserts in shot glasses) to individual cheese and charcuterie boards.

That's not to say customers are turning their backs on buffets and food stations.

"I believe that the buffet will continue to exist, and it's going to evolve in the way that it's serviced," internationally recognized event producer Lenny Talarico told video teleconferencing software provider RingCentral Events (formerly Hopin).

Buffets and food stations are accommodating corporate customers by organizing serving tables to minimize crowding and long lines, individually wrapping snacks and desserts, and offering pre-plated entrées upon request.

Healthier Choices

Customers, now eager to go a step beyond healthy foods, have been requesting immunity-boosting selections for their corporate events. These requests include probiotic foods that support good bacteria in the gut and bolster the immune system. Examples of probiotics include Greek yogurt, which caterers can offer in parfaits, dips, and dressings; artichoke, perfect for meat and vegetable dishes, even bruschetta; and cabbage, which can be part of salads and vegetable dishes.

I'm also seeing interest in *pre*biotics, foods that set the stage for a beneficial probiotic environment by feeding the friendly bacteria in our gut. Many prebiotics are good fits for catered dishes, either on their own or as ingredients, including asparagus, blueberries, cranberries, cashews, edamame, garlic, onions, leeks, bananas, oats, and apples.

The following are also high in demand for their immunity-boosting qualities:

- Dishes made with açaí berries, which are considered a superfood for their immunity-boosting properties (and other benefits). At corporate events, caterers are serving açaí bowls, açaí smoothies, even açaí ice cream.

- Citrus fruits, which are loaded with immunity-boosting vitamin C. Think fresh fruit juices, fruit and green-leaf salads with citrus, and elegant vegetable dishes complemented with citrus. Other ingredients high in vitamin C include red bell peppers (think salads, chili, and hash browns); and spinach (perfect for salads, spinach quesadillas, and Chicken Roulade Florentine).

- Garlic, which contains allicin and is known for strengthening the immune system. Caterers are adding roasted garlic to salads, vegetable dishes, and meat entrées.

- Elderberry, which is loaded with antioxidants and vitamins that help boost immunity. Caterers are delivering it in smoothies and elderberry-infused water.

Flexitarian and Vegetarian

While offering plant-based options is hardly a new catering trend, it's going strong. This includes an interest in "flexitarian" diets, which include vegan (no animal products) choices, along with meats and other animal products in moderation. To keep flexitarians happy, caterers are offering high-quality meats, so flexitarians feel their splurge is truly worth it, and creating delicious, outside-of-the-box plant-based selections.

"The rise in demand (for planted-based food) is most noticeable on the corporate level," Fia Pagnello, founder and CEO of Kiss the Cook Catering, told CFE (Catering, Foodservice & Events) magazine. "Offices are increasingly focused on sustainability, and this is now starting to impact their purchasing when it comes to food."

Caterers also are offering plant-based versions of nonvegetarian menu items such as lasagna, and their vegan and vegetarian selections include international cuisine and dishes made from fresh, locally sourced ingredients.

CORPORATE AND NONPROFIT EVENTS

Mushrooms: The New Kale

Mushrooms are huge in corporate catering these days, possibly because of their taste, versatility, and nutritional value.

Most of the mushrooms being incorporated into caterers' menus are white button mushrooms. Other popular choices are flavorful cremini mushrooms (young Portobello mushrooms), which make an excellent meat substitute, and shiitake mushrooms, known for their light, woodsy flavor.

For a catering menu, think vegetable skewers with mushrooms, sautéed mushrooms with fresh herbs, wild mushroom soup, mushroom quesadillas, filet mignon with mushroom sauce, braised lamb shank with mushrooms … and a multitude of other options.

More Creativity on the Horizon

It has been encouraging to see companies return to live events, and their ability to make that transition, at least in part, is due to accommodating and innovative catering services. I'm confident that the catering industry will continue to evolve to satisfy corporate clients and the people who attend their events.

MINDFULNESS AND WELLNESS: GROWING TRENDS IN EVENT PLANNING

The next time you attend a seminar or corporate gathering, don't be surprised if you notice an area set aside for yoga, a massage station, or a meditation workshop on the itinerary.

Incorporating mindfulness and wellness into events has become a major trend in the last couple of years. It has been influenced to some degree by the COVID-19 pandemic and heightened awareness about staying healthy, along with increasing interest in self-care and maintaining a reasonable work-life balance.

So how are event planners accommodating the world's growing appetite for events that support attendees' overall well-being? Their solutions run the gamut from scheduling more breaks to offering healthy food options.

Right Here, Right Now

Mindfulness is a commonly used word these days, but what exactly does it mean? According to mindful.org, a website devoted to this topic, it refers to being fully in the moment. It's the opposite of being on autopilot. Mindfulness is connected to wellness, the site explains, because it helps us keep our thoughts from going into dark places.

"We so often veer from the matter at hand," mindful.org says. "Our mind takes flight, we lose touch with our body, and pretty soon we're engrossed in obsessive thoughts about something that just happened or fretting about the future. And that makes us anxious."

If you're an event planner, promoting mindfulness makes sense on a practical level, too. You want attendees to fully take in what they're hearing and seeing, to be active participants, and to notice all of the details and special touches you've woven into the day.

One of the simplest ways to promote mindfulness at an event is simply to give attendees some space. Planners are doing that by working breaks into the schedule—giving attendees time for themselves so they can reflect, take care of a task that's weighing on their minds, or grab a quick nap.

But providing time is only part of the equation. Planners also are taking steps to ensure attendees have access to a comfortable environment that promotes rest and reflection. Prevue Meetings & Incentives recently wrote about the "re-charging stations" they work into events. Not only can attendees recharge their phones, but they also can restore their minds and bodies in these areas. Other planners are creating "unplugged" or "screen-free" zones where people can get a break from distractions and the sense of being constantly on call.

Increasing numbers of planners are arranging yoga or meditation workshops for their events as well.

Healthy Options

And the wellness-related activities aren't stopping there. Events have been including kickboxing and spinning courses, boot camps, and even 5K runs.

The key to successful fitness activities is to offer choices. While some attendees embrace demanding physical challenges, others may prefer stretches or group walks. An added benefit of many of these activities is that they get people outside. And that, in turn, can help boost attendees' moods.

Chair massages are popular options at events as well and can be good for the body and the mind. Not only do they help ease stress and anxiety, but they can support good circulation and strengthen the immune system.

Now that we've returned to in-person events, it will be up to planners to find even more creative ways to deliver experiences, information, and special memories—and to do it in a way that's good for the people who attend.

CREATING AN UNFORGETTABLE COCKTAIL HOUR

Offering a cocktail hour can add a real sense of sparkle and excitement to an event.

The idea is to give attendees a chance to relax, and possibly to network, while enjoying some light snacks (usually via passed hors d'oeuvres or food stations) and drinks.

If you decide a cocktail hour and reception to follow is right for your event, these dos and don'ts can help.

Do Consider Bringing Your Cocktail Hour Outside.

Most people love being outdoors. So why not capitalize on that, give your guests some fresh air, and hold an outdoor cocktail hour?

To keep your guests comfortable during your cocktail hour, you want an outdoor space that's light and comfortable, ideally with no cramped spaces. Patios, rooftops, poolside locations, and balconies are ideal settings.

Granted, if you're planning a summer event, an outdoor cocktail hour can be trickier. But if you love the idea, you can always hold your cocktail hour after dusk when temperatures are falling.

If It's Hot, Do Offer Drinks That Will Help People Keep Cool.

From frozen drinks to spiked iced tea or lemonade, the right drinks will help attendees stay comfortable. You also can consider boozy ice pops, a take on the popsicle. Aim for a summer weather signature drink as well.

But If You Go With an Outdoor Cocktail Hour, Do Plan for Rain.

You can prepare for rainy weather by having a supply of umbrellas and towels available and setting up a tent. It also would be considerate to have travel-size bottles of sunscreen on hand, along with insect repellent and fans.

Don't Underestimate the Importance of Comfortable Seating.

Although you aren't necessarily required to provide a seating arrangement for your cocktail hour space, I do recommend making sure your attendees have plenty of comfy places where they can sit, nibble on finger food, and enjoy their drinks.

There also should be plenty of room for people to move around and chat.

Do Pass Drinks as Soon as Guests Arrive.

Your serving team should be ready to offer guests cocktails, beer, and wine from the moment your cocktail hour begins. This makes guests feel welcome and helps reduce the wait time at the bars.

Do Try Innovative Drink Presentations.

Creative drink presentations at your cocktail hour can enhance your guests' enjoyment and complement the vibe you're hoping to create.

Do you want a cocktail hour with a bit of a Texas or country atmosphere? Arrange bottles of cold beer in a wheelbarrow or a galvanized metal tub. Are you going for a creative look? Add some shelves to the rungs of a ladder and load them up with cocktails. Or create an elegant drink station with luxurious linens and lush floral arrangements.

Do Set Up Creative Food Stations.

Food stations are extremely popular at events, but there's no reason why you can't have them at your cocktail hour, too. Aim for presentations that tie in with your overall atmosphere or theme. Some of the trends I'm seeing in cocktail hour appetizers include charcuterie boards and themed stations with tacos, pasta, and pizza.

Do Offer Signature Cocktails.

Your list of cocktail hour ideas wouldn't be complete without signature drinks. This is a highly effective way to customize your celebration.

If you're wondering how many signature drinks to have at your event, one or two options would be ideal. I wouldn't recommend creating more than three; you want your signature cocktail(s) to be memorable and unique to your event.

CORPORATE AND NONPROFIT EVENTS

And if you're wondering about the best signature drinks to include, look to your theme for inspiration. Here are some go-to cocktail recommendations:

- **Classic drinks with a twist:** Customize classics like an old-fashioned, Moscow mule, or gin and tonic by using unique liquors or garnishes.

- **Seasonal sips:** Incorporate fresh seasonal ingredients into drinks, such as mint and fruit in summer or spiced cider and wine in winter. This complements the time of year.

- **Local finds:** Regional wine, beer, or liquor that represents the community where your company or organization is based can make good event drinks.

- **Colorful concoctions:** Vibrant drinks in shades like pink, blue, or purple make a visually striking statement.

- **Passed drinks:** Consider passed champagne, mini margaritas, or shot pairings as a unique way to serve drinks.

Do Take a Creative Approach to Your Signature Cocktail Signage.

You'll want to have cocktail hour signs that inform attendees about your event's signature cocktails and their contents. But think about going beyond the basics and incorporating some artistry or fun into your signs. You can add photos, too.

Do Take a Strategic Approach to Live Music.

If you're interested in entertainment, live music is an excellent way to enhance the mood of your cocktail hour and set a friendly, celebratory tone. Or you can work with your venue to create and play a cocktail party playlist.

Don't Let the Music Take Center Stage.

Cocktail hour is a time for chatting and networking, and you don't want bands or DJs making conversation challenging. Choose something subtle like a string quartet, a jazz ensemble, a strolling violinist, or an acoustic act.

Do Think About Offering a Photo Booth.

A photo booth is a fun way to memorialize the event and capture moments that a professional photographer might miss. Your guests will appreciate the chance to keep printouts of the cocktail hour photos.

And offering the photo booth will add to the fun and encourage guests who don't know each other to mingle and start chatting.

Do Keep Cocktail Hour Etiquette in Mind.

To keep people happy and comfortable, keep the "hour" part of cocktail hour in mind and make a point of moving on to other event activities on time.

Also, keep in mind that you may have some guests who cannot—or prefer not to—drink. Be considerate and offer a variety of nonalcoholic drinks as well, maybe even a signature mocktail. For a summer event, especially if the cocktail hour is outdoors, offer a water station.

Don't Limit Your Planning to These Cocktail Hour Ideas.

You don't have to stop with these ideas and suggestions. I hope this section serves as a springboard for your own creative cocktail hour touches.

YOUR GUIDE TO VEGAN AND VEGETARIAN FOOD FOR EVENTS

In a 2019 article for the magazine *Bon Appétit*, writer and vegetarian Sarah Jampel lamented the lack of entrée variety she was encountering at weddings.

The most common vegan wedding meal option, she wrote, was a pile of roasted vegetables she called a "veggie stack." She even served it on her own wedding day, because it was the only vegetarian choice she and her family could agree upon.

It's not that veggie stacks aren't tasty, Jampel explained, but after eating them at multiple events, she found herself longing for something different—and a bit more filling.

If you've been hoping to offer satisfying vegetarian or vegan options at your event, whether it's a party, wedding, or corporate gathering, don't worry. Jampel went on to say that accomplishing this is indeed possible. It just takes some research and strategic planning.

I agree: Offering crowd-pleasing plant-based food at an event is very doable. And I have a collection of vegan and vegetarian menu items that will help you pull it off.

Vegan Versus Vegetarian: Understanding the Difference

You might be considering plant-based menu options because of the likelihood that some of your event attendees would prefer them. That's a logical conclusion. There are approximately 375 million vegetarians around the world and about 1.5 million vegans.

To accommodate attendees, you'll need to know what they mean if they inform you that they're vegan or vegetarian.

Vegetarians do not eat meat, fish, shellfish, or poultry. And while it's easy to see how that means you'll need an alternative to pork chops or a filet mignon for some guests, you'll also have to be on the lookout for "hidden" forbidden ingredients.

For vegetarian event catering, that means no French onion soup, which is made with beef broth.

No fish-sauce-laden pad thai.

Even Caesar dressing has anchovies in it, putting it on the no-go list.

Vegans go a step further: They avoid animal products altogether. That means they don't eat dairy (no milk, butter, or cheese), honey, or eggs.

Consult the Experts

We suggest talking with your venue or caterer about the plant-based dishes they offer and if they can work with you to create a wide variety of options for your attendees. Ask what gets rave reviews.

As you review their menus, look for ingredients that could make a dish off-limits for a vegan guest. A side dish topped with cream sauce or mozzarella cheese, for example, might be a great choice for a vegetarian, but the dairy content would not work for people who avoid all animal products.

Once you have options in mind, schedule a tasting to make sure the dishes you're considering are what you have in mind.

Appetizer Ideas

At first glance, it may look like the only safe plant-based appetizers you'll be able to offer are trays loaded with fruit or fresh vegetables. And while those options will be appreciated, you don't have to stop there.

Vegetarian foods that work well for hors d'oeuvres include spring rolls (ask about ingredients); spinach mushroom quesadillas; skewers of basil, fresh mozzarella, and cherry tomatoes; mini quiches; and mini pizzas.

For vegans, consider offering vegetables that have been prepared in a creative way. For example, you can offer vegetable tava featuring seasoned, marinated grilled vegetables served on a steel tava (pan), stews with vegetables and legumes in a vegetable broth, whole-roasted cauliflower with Middle Eastern spices, hummus with olive oil and pita bread, or mushrooms stuffed with pesto, mixed vegetables, and, possibly, tofu.

Satisfying Soups

Hot soups are tremendously satisfying and ideal for fall and winter events.

Serve vegetarians tomato soup with grilled cheese for the ultimate comfort food. Vegans can enjoy butternut squash soup (again, ask about ingredients) with hot bread.

Planning a summer event? Offer gazpacho in shot glasses or chilled avocado soup. You can serve these cold soups in carved ice bowls to give your attendees an even more refreshing experience.

Additional options that work for vegans and vegetarians include bean, wild mushroom, or curry lentil soups. As always, you'll need to talk about ingredients to the team preparing your food.

Salads That Go a Step Above

People who avoid meat and animal products eat their fair share of salads. That's not to say you shouldn't offer salads at your event, but attendees might appreciate it if you take your salad game up a few notches. Incorporate ingredients that will add flavors, colors, and textures.

People who avoid meat might enjoy an apple and walnut salad with green apples, arugula, goat cheese, cucumber, and asparagus served with smoked tomato walnut dressing.

For vegans, offer a mix of broccoli crowns, red onions, cranberries, and almonds tossed with olive oil, Dijon mustard, maple syrup, minced garlic clove, and smoked paprika.

Yummy Sides

Looking for creative sides to include in your vegetarian menu? For a delightful array of vegetarian sides, consider adding vibrant options like roasted vegetable medleys drizzled with balsamic glaze, quinoa salad with fresh herbs and lemon vinaigrette, or mushrooms stuffed with savory herb-infused breadcrumbs and vegan cheese. These dishes offer a burst of flavor and color to complement your main course.

For those seeking vegan alternatives, tantalize taste buds with savory options such as creamy coconut milk mashed potatoes, grilled vegetable skewers marinated in a zesty citrus dressing, or a refreshing kale and avocado salad tossed with tangy tahini dressing.

Vegetarian Entrées

One of the main goals when you are planning a vegetarian menu (or a vegan one) is to offer satisfying entrée options.

For those avoiding meats, consider eggplant parmesan with marinara sauce and mozzarella cheese, Asian vegetables stir-fried with tofu, or marinated grilled vegetables and mushrooms topped with mozzarella and marinara sauce.

Or you can offer comfort foods like pizza, tacos, and macaroni and cheese.

Another crowd-pleasing option would be to offer decadent breakfast dishes like pancakes, crepes, or waffles.

Vegan Entrée Possibilities

Again, even if you're offering roasted vegetables at your event, you can add creative touches to make them more appealing. One example is roasted vegetables with rice pilaf topped with Thai coconut curry.

The most satisfying dishes will contain protein. You can achieve this by offering beans, chickpeas, or peas with grains like rice or quinoa.

Additional options include mushroom lasagna with tofu instead of cheese, and dumplings made with sweet potato and vegetables with a savory nut gravy.

Try Indian Entrées

Indian menus offer a wealth of delectable vegetarian meals. For example, paneer (Indian cheese) with bell peppers in a creamy tomato sauce would be satisfying and a chance for your vegetarian attendees to get a break from the routine.

You can find choices for vegans, too. Offer mushroom Manchurian—mushrooms tossed with onion, bell pepper, and garlic—or tala dal/dal makhana, black lentils or yellow split peas slow-cooked in aromatic herbs and spices.

CHAPTER 16

Event Tech, Trends, and Social Media

TECHNOLOGICAL TOOLS THAT CAN ENHANCE YOUR EVENT PLANNING

There's no question that event planning can be quite a juggling act, from the immense list of to-dos you take care of to the challenges of consistently creating memorable, successful events.

It only makes sense to use the many event management tools available today to free up some of your time, simplify your tasks, and, in many cases, up your game as a planner.

Here's a look at some of the technological solutions at your disposal and the benefits they offer.

Event Planning Software

This can be a generic, catch-all phrase for any software you use to support your event planning efforts. It can include software for developing an event timeline; determining staffing needs; and managing budgeting, invoices, and expenditures.

Benefits:

- Makes you more efficient, saving you money and freeing up time to focus on big-picture goals

- Helps you prevent tasks from slipping through the cracks

- Facilitates collaboration and task delegation

- Improves your ability to communicate with team members, attendees, vendors, and the event host (if it's not you)

- Allows you to analyze what you've done and improve your performance

- Helps you develop and strengthen relationships with event attendees

- Allows you to monitor progress and team members' efforts

Event Management Apps

In addition to software designed specifically for event planning, there are also many helpful mobile apps that can assist with organizing and running events smoothly.

Benefits:

- Provide mobile accessibility for managing events and tasks on the go

- Help coordinate communication and collaboration among event staff and vendors

- Allow event planners to handle last-minute changes or issues in real time during the event

- Offer features like interactive floor plans, guest list management, vendor contacts, invoicing, expense tracking, and more

- Help streamline event-day activities like registration, attendee check-in, surveys, ride-shares, and sharing of photos/updates

- Provide guides, checklists, or timelines for key event-planning milestones

- Can automatically sync data with existing event software and platforms (many apps, not all)

- Enable gathering of instant feedback and reviews from attendees via the app

- Allow easy distribution of schedules, maps, speaker info, and other event details to attendees

Having mobile event management apps can provide you with greater flexibility and accessibility to coordinate successful events from anywhere. The right apps help you stay organized, collaborative, and informed throughout the entire event planning and execution process.

CORPORATE AND NONPROFIT EVENTS

Registration Software

Event registration software allows attendees to sign up for conferences, parties, workshops, and other events online. These systems accept attendees' names, contact information, and payment. Some offer special features, including professional name badge designs, logistics management, and the ability to create an event app.

Benefits:

- It saves you and your attendees time. Instead of waiting in line to register in person, attendees complete the process online.

- If you need to add or update event information, you can easily share it with everyone who has registered, which reduces the chances of mishaps and miscommunication.

- Depending on the software you use, you can strengthen the hosting organization's brand by adding its logo and selecting the color theme.

- Your attendees benefit by having an easy way to send questions to the event's designated contacts.

- You can request notifications about questions and respond promptly, which will enhance attendees' experience and perception of the event host.

- In many cases, the software provides logistics data that you and your team will need to requisition supplies, make seating arrangements, enhance safety, and comply with local codes and regulations.

- The software can help you gather information from attendees, including menu preferences and accessibility requests. And over time, it can help you get a feel for event-planning approaches that worked best, from event days and times to promotions and discount codes.

Event Floor Plan Software

This technology allows you to work either collaboratively or individually to map out your physical event space, including seating, food stations, vendor areas, and more.

Benefits:

- Using this technology is more time-effective than attempting to draw event diagrams on paper.

- In most cases, the software features drag-and-drop capabilities so users can "move" furniture, audiovisual equipment, displays, and other elements.

- Some solutions can integrate with other tools, including event registration software, making it easier to assign guests to tables and seats.

CORPORATE AND NONPROFIT EVENTS

Event Marketing Software

This technology helps you promote a brand, drive awareness and interest in your event, and boost messaging. It can be used to design event and product webpages, create and share social media posts, design and distribute invitation emails, and more.

Benefits:

- Helps you keep your messaging consistent

- Can help you identify target audiences

- Can provide analytics so you can refine your efforts—or change your approach when necessary

- Can often be integrated with other tools, including budgeting and event management software, to increase your efficiency

AN EVENT WEBSITE IS A GREAT TOOL FOR YOUR GUESTS. BE SURE YOURS IS UP TO SNUFF

It should come as no surprise that creating an event website or landing page is an important part of your event planning and that your site will serve as a valuable tool to communicate with attendees. However, when it comes to including all the needed elements, you may be unsure of how to effectively arrange it all.

A good way to approach the task is to keep your attendees' event-related needs at the forefront of your mind. After all, they will use the site to access the details they'll want, including the itinerary, local attractions, and lodging, to name a few, so you want to take care not to forget any critical elements.

To make it as simple as possible, I've compiled a list of dos and don'ts for creating your event website.

- Don't clutter your site or the home page with too many details. Keep your website clean, informative, and to the point.

- Do make sure the most important details for your event, such as the day, time, location, registration information, and parking information, are easily accessible, either on the home page or via clearly marked instructions on how to find them. It might even be a nice idea to include a digital map of your event venue where people can spot it quickly.

- Do include a detailed itinerary of the event. This helps guests know what to expect and plan their day(s) accordingly.

- Do provide contact information. Make it easy for attendees to reach out with any questions or concerns. Include email addresses, phone numbers, and a contact form.

- Do suggest hotels where your guests might stay, and include the phone number, address, and website of these establishments. You might also make it easier on your out-of-town guests by conducting research beforehand on pricing and local sites close to different hotels. Details on nearby airports, routes into town, and car rental agencies are a nice touch as well, with links to all.

- Do recommend some local attractions and fun activities for your attendees, particularly those who aren't familiar with the area where your event is set and especially for those who are staying in town for a few days.

- Do include information about how and when people have to RSVP.

- Do offer an FAQ section. Address common questions about the event, such as dress code, accessibility, and any special instructions.

- Do integrate social media. Encourage guests to share their experiences, and use a specific hashtag to create a sense of community before, during, and after the event.

- Do make use of your site to post event photos. Attendees would love to see them, and sharing photos on the site gives them a fun way to remember the event.

Building a website for your event can be a fun task, but remember, the goal is to create an online resource that keeps your attendees abreast of what's going on and gives them the information they need to make the most of attending. Keep your site simple, welcoming, and loaded with the ins and outs of your event.

HIGH-TECH OPTIONS FOR SHOWSTOPPING EVENTS

If you'd like to make a modern splash that your attendees will remember long after your event wraps up, consider bringing some 21st-century tech into the mix. Here are some ideas to get you going:

Drone Drama

Many event videographers now use drones for a variety of shots, but the increasing sophistication and affordability of drones open additional possibilities, especially if you're using an outdoor venue.

Imagine a drone that automatically follows a keynote speaker or lead entertainer wherever they go, providing a unique overhead view. Such technology was only fantasy a decade ago. Today it's available off the shelf and is surprisingly easy to use.

Photo Booth With a Twist

Photo booths have surged in popularity over the past decade, providing a fun and easy way for guests to memorialize the event. Now you can take that up a notch with high-tech booths that take a series of photos and automatically assemble them into a GIF, apply Instagram filters, add special effects, create holograms, and more. Then the booth can automatically share the results on social media, complete with a hashtag you choose.

Quality Selfies Galore

Encourage and enable your attendees to take high-quality selfies by providing selfie sticks they can use to memorialize as they mingle. Attach instruction cards encouraging the use of hashtags so you can go online later and find the shots with a click.

Charging Stations

To ensure no one runs out of power and loses the ability to participate in the electronic extravaganza, provide charging stations to keep the action going.

Be sure to offer plenty of chargers and cables to cover all possible connection types, including Apple Lightning, micro-USB, and USB-C.

3D-Printed Favors

If you can dream it up, a designer can create it. They can 3D-print custom objects for you to give to attendees—or simply to use as unique decorations around the venue. The possibilities are endless, and the proliferation of skilled hobbyists in the 3D printing field means this may be far more affordable than you would think.

Cameras, Cameras, Everywhere

Small, battery-powered video cameras are now plentiful, and you can use a host of them to add unique views of the action. While GoPro is the dominant brand in these devices, there are a huge variety of generic versions available at a fraction of the price that still create great video.

Stash them all around the venue, from food stations to the dance floor to anywhere else that will provide a wealth of candidly captured memories.

If you don't want to deal with the logistics yourself, ask your videographer to handle it for you and edit the results.

Stream It Live

Accommodate those who can't attend your event in person by setting up cameras and live-streaming the entire day. Many venues have video gear in place and can help you facilitate the streaming.

Just Like Being There

If you want to get futuristic, there are now services that will cover and stream your event directly to virtual reality headsets for the ultimate immersive experience. This is likely to be a pricey option, but it's the next best thing to being there.

LED Clothing

It may be kitschy and campy, but if you want to add some wow factor to your event — or to a key activity — provide a variety of lighted clothing for attendees to don, then turn out the lights and hit the dance floor. There's a huge selection of such merchandise out there, from lighted suspenders to bow ties to shirts to caps, laden with glow and twinkle.

As technology continues to advance, more and more ways to enhance the event experience will come alive, but for now, the above choices should help you create a truly unforgettable event.

UNVEILING THE PERFECT EVENT HASHTAG

Event hashtags are all the rage these days. They're showing up on invitations, being printed on napkins and koozies, and, of course, appearing on social media posts.

A customized hashtag for your event is a fantastic way to build awareness of a brand and event. But coming up with a unique, catchy event hashtag takes some thought and creativity.

This section has some tips to help, along with samples for inspiration.

What's Driving the Hashtag Trend?

Hashtags have become a ubiquitous part of corporate and nonprofit events, and for good reason. They help you and your event attendees do the following:

- **Find and share photos:** Attendees can easily use your hashtag when posting photos on social media, allowing you to find and see all event photos in one place. This is especially useful for capturing key moments like networking sessions, panel discussions, and award presentations.

- **Share live updates:** Attendees can post real-time snippets of such activities as keynote speeches, breakout sessions, and live demonstrations. This helps keep the online audience engaged and informed about what's happening throughout the event.

- **Share the experience:** By following the hashtag, remote participants can stay updated and feel a part of the event experience, whether it's a conference, charity gala, or industry expo.

- **Reinforce special memories:** Hashtags become a digital archive of your event that attendees can look back on for years. This is particularly valuable for annual events, where you can showcase their history and evolution over time.

- **Increase engagement:** A well-promoted hashtag encourages attendees to interact with each other and with the event's content. This can lead to greater networking opportunities and a more vibrant event community.

- **Boost event visibility:** When attendees use your event hashtag, their posts can reach a broader audience beyond just those who are present. This can increase the event's visibility and attract more attention to your organization or cause.

How Do You Make a Catchy Hashtag?

With so many events taking place, it can be tricky to think of funny, unique, or quirky hashtags that no one else has used. Keep in mind that the funniest hashtags are easily understood by everyone who sees them. Here are some ideas for you to consider:

- **Keep it short and sweet.** Long hashtags can be difficult to read and remember. Aim for brevity while still conveying your event's theme or purpose.

  Examples: #techsummit2024, #healthexponyc, #greengala

- **Make it memorable.** Having a catchy and memorable hashtag helps attendees remember it and encourages them to use it in their posts.

  Examples: #innovate2024, #impactawards, #leadwithlove

- **Include the event name or acronym.** Incorporating your event name or its acronym makes the hashtag relevant and instantly recognizable.

  Examples: #xyzconf2024, #abcforum, #defcharityrun

- **Add the year or location.** Including the year or location helps differentiate your event from others and adds a sense of timeliness.

  Examples: #techtalksf, #nonprofitnyc2024

- **Play with words.** Use puns, rhymes, or alliteration to make your hashtag stand out and be more engaging.

  Examples: #missionpossible, #innovateinitiative, #futurefocusfest

- **Highlight the purpose or theme.** Incorporate your event's theme, purpose, or focus to give context to the hashtag.

  Examples: #cleanenergyexpo, #techforgood, #artsadvocate

- **Test for uniqueness.** Before finalizing, search your potential hashtag on social media so you can be sure it's not already in use and that it aligns with your event's image.

- **Encourage engagement.** Create a hashtag that encourages attendees to share their experiences and engage with the event online.

  Examples: #shareyourstoryxyz, #techtalkinspire, #volunteervoices

Hashtag Mistakes To Avoid

In your quest for the perfect event hashtag, steer clear of these common pitfalls:

- **Hard to spell:** Stay away from odd capitalization or spellings.

- **Offensive:** Even unintentional double meanings can come across wrong. Google any risky hashtags.

- **References a trend:** Your event should stand the test of time. Avoid dated trends.

- **Bad grammar or typos:** Proofread! You want it to be correct.

- **Hard to pronounce:** If people don't know how to say it, they probably won't use it.

Where Should You Display Your Event Hashtag?

Once you've created a hashtag you love, spread the word by displaying it prominently in these spots:

- **Event website and registration page:** Include the hashtag prominently on your event's website and registration page so attendees get familiar with it early on.

- **Social media profiles and posts:** Feature the hashtag in your social media bios, and use it consistently in all related posts. Encourage your followers to use it when sharing content about the event.

- **Event marketing materials:** Incorporate the hashtag into all your event's promotional materials, including flyers, posters, emails, and newsletters. Make sure it's visible and easy to read.

- **Event app or platform:** If you have an event app or platform, the hashtag should be prominently featured.

- **Event tickets and badges:** Print the hashtag on event tickets, badges, and lanyards. This serves as a constant reminder for attendees to use it during the event.

- **Welcome and information desks:** Display the hashtag on signage at welcome and information desks. Staff can also remind attendees to use it when sharing their event experiences.

- **Event programs and schedules:** Include the hashtag in the event program, schedule, and any printed materials handed out to attendees.

- **Presentation slides and stage backdrops:** Add the hashtag to the bottom of presentation slides and stage backdrops.

- **Social media walls:** Set up a social media wall at your event venue that displays posts featuring the event hashtag. This not only promotes the hashtag but also encourages attendees to join the conversation.

- **Email signatures:** Include the hashtag in the email signatures of your event team. This subtly promotes the hashtag in all correspondence related to the event.

- **On-site signage and banners:** Use banners, posters, and digital displays around the event venue to showcase the hashtag. Make it easy for attendees to spot and remember.

CHAPTER 17

Music and Entertainment for Your Event

Courtesy of Blanca Duran Photography

ENTERTAINMENT GEARED FOR CORPORATE EVENTS

Corporate event attendees these days have more expectations than ever, from food and activities that promote wellness to an overall sense of freshness and creativity. Guests want to feel that you value them and their time.

One way you can inject energy and memorable moments into your event is through the entertainment you offer. If you go the extra mile and line up something special, something that would be meaningful to your particular audience, your attendees are much more likely to remember the event in a positive light. That, in turn, will improve your chances of making a positive and long-lasting impression.

Looking for entertainment ideas for your corporate event? Here are some possibilities.

Create an Interactive Experience

Guests spend plenty of time listening to others at corporate events. Why not give them a chance to be part of what's happening? Your options include technological solutions like virtual reality games or augmented reality experiences, digital recording booths, escape rooms, or the fun of hamming it up in a photo booth.

Set Up an Arcade

Giant human claw machines are a big trend at parties and corporate events. These devices lift guests in the air and place them in a collection of cool prizes so they can try to grab one and take it with them as they're removed. The machines and the prizes can be customized to reflect company branding and your event theme.

You also have the option of renting retro arcade games, Skee-Ball stations, virtual motion simulators, air hockey, and more.

Line Up a Corporate Comedian

Unlike traditional stand-up comedians, corporate comedians keep their humor 100% clean and appropriate for professional events. These entertainers work with you to develop a custom act based on your organization and goals. Many also serve as motivational speakers and leave audiences feeling energized and uplifted.

CORPORATE AND NONPROFIT EVENTS

Have a Video Station
Guests can make a custom video in a branded booth complete with music and stylized lighting.

Bring in a Typewriter for Hire
Yes, a typewriter. This is another entertainment trend, according to Partyslate.com. Guests have 15 minutes to write a poem, a message, a joke—whatever they want.

Or... Bring in a Typewriter Poet
You actually can hire people to type out a personalized poem for each guest on a vintage typewriter. Talk about creating a unique experience.

Host a Band
This isn't exactly new, but that doesn't mean your guests won't love it. Aim for performers who will resonate with your audience.

Hire Celebrity Impersonators
Give your guests an opportunity to mingle with Marilyn Monroe, Elton John, or Tom Cruise.

Offer Fun Classes
You can bring in people to teach cooking classes, the art of mixing drinks, dancing, or crafts.

Organize Lip-Sync Battles
This is another big trend at corporate events. Guests take the stage and perform (sort of) their favorite song with everything they've got. You can award prizes for the best dance moves, the most passionate performance, the best humorous touches, whatever you can think of.

Take a Classic Approach
Depending on the vibe you want for your event, classical music could be a perfect addition. You can line up a string quartet, a harpist, or even professional opera singers.

Channel Your Inner Child

Maybe you'd like your attendees to experience the sense of wonder that circus acts can create. There are agencies that specialize in this type of entertainment and can connect you with professional jugglers, acrobats, belly dancers, trapeze artists—even sword swallowers.

Circus performers do add a certain wow factor to events, and if you arrange for strolling entertainers, they'll encourage mingling among your guests.

Make Some Magic

Of course, one surefire way to make your event magical is to feature a professional magician.

As Close-Up Chris, a close-up magician from the United Kingdom, explained in a blog post, a good magic show can help make an event unforgettable.

"People remember how they felt at an event," he wrote. "It's why you want to be focused on evoking emotions that feel good. Guess what … magic is an easy way to create the vibe you want. For starters, magic involves the audience—so there's no yawning from the sidelines. And because magic evokes a response in people, the collective enjoyment creates an upbeat buzz that will infuse through your event to get everyone smiling."

SHOULD YOU HAVE A BAND OR A DJ AT YOUR EVENT?

You've decided to include dancing at your event, but you're not sure whether you should hire a live band or a DJ. That's understandable. Both options have their pros and cons, and it ultimately comes down to the type of atmosphere you want to create. In this section, I've outlined some considerations that can help you weigh the "band versus DJ" decision and make the best choice for your event.

Your Planning Process

Before we dive into the merits of a live band versus a DJ, it's important to note that booking professional entertainers should be done well in advance. The earlier you book, the more likely you are to secure your preferred choice.

It's also important to consider your entertainment budget and potential costs. The typical event DJ cost averages around $300 to $800 nationally for general events, including corporate gatherings and private parties. The average band, on the other hand, averages about $1,200 to $3,000 for events throughout the U.S. These costs can vary based on such factors such as the event's location, its duration, and the experience level of the performers. I would discuss all your requirements with your DJ or band, so they don't surprise you with unexpected charges.

Musical Styles

The type of music you want to play at your event is key in deciding between a band with live music and DJ services. Professional bands can create a unique and energetic atmosphere, and they also bring a certain energy and emotion to their performance that can't be replicated by a DJ. However, if you have a specific song that you want to be played by the original artist, a DJ might be the better option. In most cases, they can access any song in their library and play it in its original form.

Additional Considerations

- **Event size and venue:** Larger venues may benefit from a band's ability to fill the space with live music, while smaller venues might be better suited to a DJ setup that requires less space and can control volume levels more easily.

- **Event theme and atmosphere:** Consider the vibe you want to create. A band might be perfect for a high-energy, festive atmosphere, but a DJ can offer a wider variety of music genres and styles.

- **Flexibility and requests:** DJs often have more flexibility when it comes to taking requests, and they can switch genres easily to match the crowd's mood. Bands tend to have a set playlist and might not be able to accommodate as many requests on the spot.

Questions To Ask

Once you decide whether you want a band or a DJ, you'll need to research potential candidates. Here are some suggested questions to ask.

Prospective Bands

- How would you describe your musical style and song repertoire? Is it possible to hear samples?

- Do you learn new music for events? Can I provide a must-play song list?

- How many musicians are part of your band? What instruments are included?

- Do you have backup equipment in case of technical issues?

- What's your backup plan if band members can't perform due to illness or other issues?

- Do you have liability insurance?

- How much space do you require for setup?

- Can you provide lighting or other visual elements during performances?

- Can you provide references from other events you've performed at?

Potential DJs

- What music genres do you specialize in? Can I see your music library?

- Do you take song requests from event attendees?

- What sound equipment do you use? Do you have backups?

- How do you keep the dance floor filled and energy up?

- Can you make announcements?

- Do you have liability insurance?

- How do you take breaks? Do you have an assistant DJ?

- Can you provide lighting, a photo booth, or other extras?

- Can I share a do-not-play song list?

- What's your backup plan if you can't make it at the last minute?

LIVE MUSIC OPTIONS FOR YOUR EVENT: GOING BEYOND TRADITIONAL BANDS

We've seen our share of live bands at our venue, but we've also seen string quartets and jazz trios, mariachi bands, and classically trained soloists. And time after time, these unique performers absolutely captivated their audiences.

Of course, traditional bands can be highly impactful, too. My point is, if you want to create an event that lingers in guests' memories long after people leave, creative approaches to live music can be a highly effective way to do that.

There are several reasons why you might want to consider alternatives to bands for your event music—or think about hiring creative entertainment in addition to a great band. For one, you may find that alternative music options can better match the theme or mood of your event. Or you might feel that a traditional band wouldn't fit the style or the overall aesthetic you want. If you plan to have a vintage-themed charity fundraiser, for example, you might want to choose live music that complements that style, such as a bluegrass band or a group that plays period-specific music.

Or maybe you want to create a more intimate atmosphere. A traditional band tends to foster a loud, energetic atmosphere, which is great, but that may not be quite what you want for a smaller, more low-key event. In this case, you might opt for a solo musician or a smaller ensemble that can provide a more subtle and relaxed ambiance.

Beyond that, some people choose an alternative to a traditional band for their event because they want to surprise guests with something unique and memorable. With so many events featuring similar songs and dance routines, you might want to stand out by choosing a band or performer that's unexpected and exciting.

Ideas and Trends

So what are some creative live music options for events? Here are a few ideas and trends that I've been seeing.

- **Mariachi band:** These bands are a fun and festive way to keep your event on a high note. Mariachi bands feature professional musicians playing trumpets, violins, and guitars. They can present a mix of traditional Mexican songs and contemporary hits.

- **Marching band:** Make a grand entrance or exit with a high-energy marching band leading the way. Their lively rhythms and showmanship will create a memorable spectacle for the attendees.

- **Jazz trio or quartet:** Evoke the sophistication and romance of the golden era with a jazz band performing classic standards or modern interpretations.

- **Pianist or harpist:** For an elegant and intimate atmosphere, a skilled pianist or harpist can create an enchanting ambiance for your event, possibly during a cocktail hour or networking activity. These musicians can play a variety of classical and contemporary songs and create a warm and inviting atmosphere.

- **Themed ensemble:** Depending on your event, a vintage swing band or a folksy bluegrass group could be the perfect element to drive home your theme.

- **Guitarist or acoustic duo:** A talented guitarist or acoustic duo can provide a warm, intimate sound for key activities or networking sessions.

- **Singer-songwriter or folk band:** These groups can provide a more laid-back and acoustic atmosphere and can play a variety of original and cover songs.

More Creative Entertainment Options

In addition to the possibilities listed above, you have many other creative music options to consider for your event. Here are a few more ideas:

- A cappella group
- Steel drum band
- String quartet
- Saxophone quartet
- Klezmer band
- Flamenco dancers

- Samba dancers

- Bollywood dancers

Selection Tips

If the idea of less-than-traditional event music appeals to you, but you're not sure how to make the right choice, I have some tips that can help.

- **Establish your vision.** Before exploring options, clearly define the overall vibe and atmosphere you want to create. If you're planning something formal, for example, a traditional band or jazz trio might be the best fit. If you're having a more casual, laid-back event, a solo guitarist or mariachi band might be a good choice.

- **Consider your venue.** Factoring in the size, location, and acoustics of your venue will help you determine the most suitable live music option—or at least rule out those that won't fit. Focus on performances and groups that are well suited to your event space.

- **Attend live performances.** Whenever possible, attend live performances of the acts you're considering so you can get a firsthand experience of their sound, energy, and stage presence.

- **Discuss logistics.** Make sure the musical acts you're interested in can accommodate your specific needs, including setup requirements, performance duration, and any special requests or considerations.

- **Obtain references and reviews.** As you would with any vendor, gather references and read reviews to be sure you're hiring professional and reliable musical acts.

- **Consider your budget.** While alternative live music options might be more affordable than a traditional band, don't forget to factor in costs like travel expenses, equipment rentals, and any additional fees.

- **Have a backup plan.** No matter how well you plan, there's always a chance that something could go wrong. Make sure you have a backup plan in place, such as a playlist of recorded music, in case of emergency.

CHAPTER 18

Event Décor

Courtesy of Genovese Studios

POINTING YOU IN THE RIGHT DIRECTION: SIGNAGE TIPS AND IDEAS

What's the first thing your attendees notice when they arrive at your event? Chances are, it's the signage. But is it making the right impression? Is it guiding, informing, and exciting them? Let's dive into the world of event signage and explore how to make yours truly unforgettable.

What Is Event Signage?

Event signage refers to the various signs event doers use throughout their venue to direct guests, label areas, share information, set a mood, and enhance décor.

Signs serve practical purposes while also contributing to the overall event décor. They help guests navigate the space (think bathroom signs or workshop signs), find their seats, and understand the event timeline.

Types of Event Signs

Event signage falls into several categories. Here's a look at some of them:

- **Welcome:** Greets attendees at conferences, corporate events, or parties

- **Directional:** Directs attendees to registration desks, breakout sessions, restrooms, and networking areas

- **Seating charts:** Shows seating for dinners, award ceremonies, or speaker sessions

- **Informational:** Lists the event agenda, keynote speakers, session details, and food and beverage options

- **Thematic and branding:** Incorporates company branding, event themes, and social media hashtags to reinforce your event's identity

- **Interactive and activity:** Highlights interactive stations, tech demos, networking activities, and other engaging elements

- **Safety and compliance:** Points out emergency exits, safety protocols, and other compliance-related information

- **Sponsor recognition:** Acknowledges sponsors, partners, or key contributors, often with logos and branding

Creative Sign Ideas

Beyond the essential signs already described, some clever sign applications can make events extra meaningful or fun through personalized messages.

Get creative with signs featuring the following:

- Inspirational quotes, lyrics, or poems

- Stories or milestones of the organization or event

- Interesting or humorous anecdotes related to the event

- Nicknames or fun facts about key speakers or team members

- Caricatures or illustrations depicting notable figures or themes of the event

- The significance of the event's theme or purpose

- Rules or guidelines for event activities or games

- Well-wishes, messages of encouragement, or advice for participants

- Professional photos of the team, event highlights, or key moments leading up to the event

Tips For Displaying Signs

To maximize visual appeal, consider these tips when positioning event signs:

- Hang signs at a consistent height based on attendees' line of sight.

- Incorporate signs on tables among floral centerpieces.

- Angle signs so guests walking toward them can read them clearly.

- Place signs in areas with sufficient lighting.

- Secure signs properly so that whether you're placing them on easels, stands, or hooks, they won't fall.

Material and Design Choices

As you consider sign possibilities, choose materials that will withstand the event environment (e.g., outdoor versus indoor). The signs should be highly readable, so aim for large fonts and high-contrast colors.

And beyond practicality, you want your signs to support your event goals and help support the host's brand. To do that, make sure your signs have a consistent design theme that aligns with your event's branding.

Technology Integration

Technology will help your signs have even greater impact. By using digital screens for some of your signs, you can display dynamic content that can be updated in real time. For information kiosks or wayfinding displays, consider using touch screens.

Personalized Messages

Tailor your signs' messages for different attendee groups (VIPs, speakers, sponsors). I'd also include images of logos, mascots, or event-specific graphics to enhance your signs' visual appeal and reinforce branding.

Accessibility

Don't forget to make sure your signs are accessible to all attendees, including those with disabilities. If your event has an international audience, provide translations.

Set the Stage with Stunning Signs

Through thoughtful communication, useful directions, and purposeful designs, signs enhance events on all levels. Determine which signs best suit your event's size, theme, and layout, then craft eye-catching pieces to wow your attendees.

RUSTIC EVENT DÉCOR

Rustic charm isn't just for weddings anymore. I'm seeing this design aesthetic at corporate retreats and retirement parties, charity galas and holiday events. And in each case, this approach infuses warmth, character, and a touch of nature's magic.

If you'd like to incorporate rustic design into your next event, these tips can help.

Natural Touches
One effective approach to rustic décor is to create event backdrops inspired by natural surroundings.

Complement backdrops throughout your event space with greenery, wildflowers, and organic textures. Elements like macramé, leafy garlands, and overflowing flower arrangements help create a welcoming atmosphere as well. And outdoor events can easily incorporate native grasses, branches, stone, and wood textures.

Rustic Color Palettes
Earthy neutrals like beige, brown, and sage green are staples for rustic events. You can make them more impactful with vibrant accent colors, including deep reds, coral, plum, and metallics like rose gold and copper.

Al Fresco Dining Stations
Rustic events are all about a relaxed, informal vibe. Instead of formal plated dinners, set up bountiful buffets and food stations. Grazing tables, BBQs, family-style platters ... all these options provide variety (always appreciated at special events) and encourage mingling.

Rustic Tablescapes
Depending on the formality of your event, you can bring the rustic vibe you're creating right to attendees' tables. Have them adorned with natural elements like wood slices, burlap runners, and wildflowers in mason jars. Mismatched china and vintage silverware add to the charm.

Bonus Tip: Don't forget the little details: Chalkboard signs, wooden crates, and vintage props can all enhance the rustic ambiance of your event.

MAKING YOUR EVENT SHINE: LIGHTING TIPS

Lighting, harnessed strategically, can set the perfect ambiance for your event. Lights are an impressively effective way to make your space feel warm and welcoming, vibrant and festive, or elegant and refined.

In this section, you'll find tips for using lighting to set the mood for your event, along with a look at some of the creative options available. Here are some general tips to get you started:

- **Consider your event venue.** Your venue can greatly impact your lighting choices. Factor in the size and shape of the space, as well as any architectural features that you want to highlight or conceal, as you make your plans.

- **Test it out.** Before your event day, test out your lighting setup to make sure it's working properly and creating the desired effect.

- **Consider LED lights.** LED lights are energy-efficient and long-lasting, and they produce minimal heat. They are also very versatile and can be used to create a variety of looks and effects.

Illuminating Ideas

If it's appropriate for your event, don't shy away from bold lighting choices. Uplighting, patterns, and fun lighting accents can make a celebration feel magical and wow attendees.

During your event planning, consider lighting details like these:

- Bright white or colored uplighting along the walls

- Patterned lighting projected on walls, ceilings, or floors

- A custom monogram or logo pattern on the dance floor

- Stylish chandeliers or suspended lighting over tables

- Accent lighting on display areas

- Custom neon signs with your event name, logo, hashtag, or a cheeky saying (This makes for great photo ops and an eye-catching lighting accent.)

- Suspended unique fixtures like lanterns, globes, or custom pieces at different levels

- Illuminated furniture pieces, like benches or ottomans, for cool lighting accents that also serve a purpose

- Shadow projections on walls or other surfaces that incorporate patterned lights, custom cutouts, or greenery

Outdoor Radiance

While your outdoor event already boasts a stunning natural backdrop, the magic truly begins once the sun sets with the right lighting. Here are some enchanting outdoor lighting options:

- **Strings of bulb lights or lanterns overhead** create a warm, inviting atmosphere with twinkling lights that mimic the stars.

- **Uplighting to highlight trees, sculptures, or a similar focal point** will add dramatic flair by accentuating key elements of your venue.

- **Dance floor lighting or patterns** infuse energy and excitement into the dance area.

- **Drape delicate fairy lights** above seating areas or pathways for a magical, ethereal effect.

- **Incorporate glow-in-the-dark elements** or LED markers along walkways to enhance safety and add a playful touch.

- **Try projection mapping:** Use projectors to cast vibrant patterns or themed visuals onto walls, tents, or natural surfaces to make your event more memorable to guests.

- **Another great option is themed lantern displays.** Choose lanterns that fit your event's theme—whether rustic, modern, or exotic—to enhance the overall vibe.

My Commitment to
Event Industry Success

Planning and executing events can be intense. Any bride who's planned her wedding can tell you that. So can parents who've organized their teen's blowout graduation bash or a manager tasked with putting together the company's annual awards night.

When it comes to events, the stakes are high. There are no do-overs. I don't say this to stress anyone out—or to suggest that an imperfect event is a failure. (A wise planner aims for excellence, not perfection.) What I mean is that when we're responsible for an event, especially one we're personally invested in, its success feels personal.

As someone who produces events and watches thousands unfold at my venue, I'm committed to helping event doers achieve the success they're striving for. I believe that when event planners have the knowledge and insight to make weddings, meetings, celebrations, and other important gatherings truly memorable, they elevate the entire event industry.

This commitment drives the tips I share on my venue's website and the creation of this book. And I'm not stopping there.

As I mentioned at the start of this book, I've had the privilege of working with many people who plan events. Some of them are highly skilled. But I've yet to meet anyone who approaches events quite the way I do. This isn't boasting; it's just that events occupy a significant portion of my thoughts and my life. Over time, I've developed a philosophy around event execution, a detailed framework for delivering excellence, time and time again. And soon, I'll be sharing it.

My goal is simple: to empower event doers to create epic events that will be remembered forever.

Stay tuned.

Wedding and Events Glossary

A la carte: An option to choose individual items or services rather than a complete package, often allowing for customized event planning.

Accessibility: The design and implementation of events and spaces to allow all individuals, regardless of disabilities, to fully participate and engage.

After-party (or wedding after-party): A casual gathering that takes place after the wedding reception to continue the celebration.

Amenities: Additional services or items provided by a venue, such as Wi-Fi, parking, or complimentary beverages, that enhance guest comfort.

Backdrop: A decorative background used in various areas of the event, such as behind the head table or ceremony space, to enhance the visual theme.

Banquet event order (BEO): A detailed document provided by the venue outlining the logistics, timing, and menu for an event. This document serves as the event's execution guide.

Bartender fee: An additional fee charged to cover the cost of a bartender, especially if bar service is not included in the venue package.

Black tie: A formal dress code, typically for evening events, where men wear tuxedos and women wear elegant gowns or cocktail dresses.

Boho: Short for "bohemian," a free-spirited, eclectic style often featuring natural elements, earthy colors, and vintage-inspired décor, popular for weddings and events with a relaxed, artistic vibe.

Breakdown: The process of dismantling and clearing event setups, such as decorations, equipment, and furniture, after the event ends.

Bridal portraits: A photo session focused on the bride, typically done in her wedding dress.

Brunch event: A social gathering or celebration typically held in the late morning or early afternoon, combining elements of breakfast and lunch. Brunch events offer a more casual atmosphere compared to formal evening affairs, allowing for flexibility in attire, décor, and menu options.

Buffet: A meal service style where food is displayed on a table, allowing guests to serve themselves from a variety of dishes.

Cancellation and postponement insurance: A type of insurance policy that provides financial protection to event organizers if an event is canceled, postponed, or abandoned due to unforeseen circumstances.

Carving station: A food station where a chef or attendant slices meats like roast beef or turkey to order for guests.

Cash bar: A bar setup where guests pay for their own drinks rather than the host covering the cost, commonly used as a budget-friendly option.

Centerpiece: One or more decorative objects placed in the middle of a table at a wedding or event to enhance the décor and set the mood.

Ceremony: The part of a wedding when the couple exchanges vows and is legally married, typically involving a processional, readings, vows, and a recessional.

Champagne toast: A celebratory moment, usually after speeches or the first dance, where guests raise glasses of champagne to honor the couple or occasion.

Charger plate: A large, decorative base plate used under dinner plates for presentation purposes during formal events.

Chuppah: A traditional canopy under which a Jewish wedding ceremony takes place, symbolizing the couple's future home.

Cocktail hour: A time for guests to mingle while enjoying cocktails and finger foods. During weddings, cocktail hour takes place after the ceremony and before the reception.

Color palette: A selection of colors chosen to create a cohesive look and feel for an event's décor, attire, and floral arrangements.

Contingency plan: A backup plan to address potential issues, such as weather disruptions or vendor cancellations, so the event can continue smoothly.

Corkage fee: A charge applied by venues for opening and serving alcohol that was not purchased through their establishment, commonly applied per bottle.

Day-of coordinator: A professional who manages the details of an event on the day it takes place.

Destination wedding: A wedding held in a location where neither the couple nor most of the guests live, often in a picturesque or vacation-like setting.

Details meeting: A meeting between the event planner and client (or vendors) to finalize specifics, timelines, and logistics for the event.

DIY (Do-It-Yourself): Refers to elements of the wedding or event created by the couple or organizers rather than by hired professionals.

Drink ticket: A voucher provided to guests to redeem for a free drink, often used to control bar costs by limiting the number of drinks per guest.

Emcee/MC: The Master of Ceremonies, responsible for guiding the event flow, making announcements, and keeping guests engaged.

Escort card: A card used at events to direct guests to their assigned tables. Unlike place cards that specify individual seats, escort cards only indicate the table number. They are typically displayed near the entrance of the event area, allowing guests to locate their table upon arrival.

Event communication plan: A strategic document outlining how information is disseminated before, during, and after an event. It encompasses communication with various stakeholders including event staff, vendors, attendees, and the media. The plan aims to ensure clear and consistent messaging, minimize miscommunication, and promote event awareness and engagement.

Event doer: A person who plans and executes an event. Examples include a bride or mother of the bride planning a wedding, an employee organizing their company's annual celebration, or an adult working on their parents' 60th anniversary party.

Event planner: A professional who oversees all aspects of event planning, from concept to execution.

Event producer: A professional responsible for overseeing and executing the overall production of an event.

Event timeline: A detailed chronological schedule outlining all the activities and milestones of an event from setup to teardown. It specifies timings for vendor arrivals, key program elements, breaks, and transitions with the goal of fostering smooth event flow and coordination among all parties involved.

FAB: Acronym for "food and beverages."

Family-style: A service style where large platters of food are placed on each table, allowing guests to serve themselves and share dishes.

Favor: A small gift given to guests as a token of appreciation for attending the wedding or event.

First dance: A couple's inaugural dance as newlyweds, traditionally held at the beginning of the wedding reception.

First look: A private moment for the bride and groom to see each other before the wedding ceremony. The first look can be captured by photographers for candid, emotional photos.

Flip: The quick setup change at a venue, typically between the ceremony and reception, where staff change décor, layout, or seating arrangements.

Floor plan: A layout map showing the arrangement of tables, seating, and other key areas within an event space.

Food station: A setup where guests can serve themselves from a selection of food options, often organized by type or theme, such as a salad or dessert station.

Force Majeure clause: A contract provision that frees parties from liability due to extraordinary events like natural disasters, that would make performance of the contract impossible.

Golden hour: The period shortly after sunrise or before sunset, known for its warm, soft lighting, ideal for photography.

Grand entrance: The couple's formal introduction at the reception, often marked by music, applause, or a choreographed entry.

Grand exit: The couple's dramatic departure from the reception, often involving guests sending them off with sparklers, confetti, or other festive elements to bring the celebration to a close.

Guest book: A book with blank pages where guests can sign their names and write messages for a wedding couple or guests of honor.

Guest count: The total number of attendees expected at an event, used to determine seating arrangements, catering quantities, and budget requirements.

Head table: A special table reserved for the wedding couple and their immediate family or wedding party.

House brand versus premium brand: Refers to the quality and cost of alcohol served. House brands are typically standard options, while premium brands are higher-end selections, often with an additional charge.

Indemnity clause: A provision in a contract where one party agrees to protect the other from any losses, damages, or legal liabilities that may arise from the contract, often covering costs associated with claims or lawsuits related to the event.

Invitation suite: The complete set of wedding stationery, including the invitation, RSVP card, details card, and any additional inserts.

Itinerary: A detailed schedule outlining the sequence of activities, times, and locations, guiding the flow of the event.

Limited bar: A bar that offers a selection of specific types of alcohol (e.g., only beer and wine or a few chosen cocktails) rather than a full range of beverages.

Linens: Fabrics used for tablecloths, napkins, and chair covers at events, often selected to match the event's color scheme or theme.

Load-in: The process of moving equipment, décor, and other materials into an event space before the event begins. (Load-out refers to removing these items after the event.)

Logistics: The planning and coordination of operational details, such as transportation, setup, and schedules, to ensure the event runs smoothly.

Marriage certificate: A legal document that proves a couple is married. It includes the couple's names, the date and time of the wedding, and the location.

Marriage license: A legal document that authorizes a couple to marry, issued by a government official.

Memory Plane: The conceptual space where an event is imprinted in the minds of attendees. It's shaped by the event's atmosphere, the emotions it evokes, and the sensory details it presents.

Micro wedding: A small, intimate wedding ceremony with fewer than 50 guests. The emphasis is a close, meaningful gathering rather than a large celebration.

Milestone celebration: An event held to mark a significant life event, such as a birthday, anniversary, or retirement.

Minimony: A small, intimate wedding ceremony that usually takes place before a larger celebration.

Mocktail: A non-alcoholic drink, often crafted to resemble a cocktail, suitable for guests who prefer alcohol-free options.

No-show: A guest who RSVPs to attend an event but does not show up, often affecting seating and meal counts.

Officiant: The person who performs the wedding ceremony and legally binds the couple by signing the marriage license.

Open bar: A bar setup where guests can enjoy complimentary drinks, with the host covering the costs.

Passed hors d'oeuvres: Appetizers served by waitstaff who circulate the room, offering guests small bites from trays.

Place card: A piece of paper that indicates a guest's assigned seat at an event. They are typically used for formal events with assigned seating arrangements so guests can easily locate their designated place at the table.

Place setting: The arrangement of tableware, including plates, glasses, silverware, and napkins, set at each guest's seat.

Plated meal: A service style where guests are served individually plated courses at their seats by the catering staff.

Plus-one: An additional guest invited to accompany an attendee.

Post-event feedback: Comments and evaluations from attendees, vendors, or team members about the event's success and areas for improvement.

Post-event report: A comprehensive summary of the event, including successes, challenges, attendance, and budget details, used for future planning.

Prenuptial agreement: A legal document signed by a couple before marriage outlining the division of assets in case of divorce.

Prix fixe: A menu with a set price for a multi-course meal, often with limited options for each course.

Processional/recessional: The formal entrance (processional) and exit (recessional) of the wedding party and couple during the ceremony.

Reception card: A card that provides guests with information about the reception that takes place after a wedding ceremony.

Reception: The celebration that follows the wedding ceremony, when guests enjoy food, drinks, dancing, and other festivities to honor the newly married couple.

Registry: A curated list of desired gifts created by individuals or couples for special occasions such as weddings, showers, or anniversaries. Guests can refer to the registry to select gifts that align with the recipient's preferences.

Retainer: An upfront fee paid to secure the services of a vendor or professional, often credited toward the total cost of the service.

RSVP card: A request for a response to an invitation to an event, such as a wedding, birthday party, or business function. The acronym RSVP comes from the French phrase répondez, s'il vous plaît, which translates to "please reply."

Rustic: A celebration that emphasizes natural simplicity, and a personal touch.

Save-the-date: A pre-invitation announcement sent to guests to inform them about an upcoming event and request they mark the date on their calendars. It typically precedes formal invitations and provides essential details such as the event date, location, and the names of the hosts or honorees.

Seating chart: A visual representation of where guests will be seated at an event.

Signage: Signs used at a venue to help guests navigate the event, share information, and set the mood.

Signature cocktail: A specially crafted alcoholic beverage served at an event, often reflecting the theme, personality, or preferences of the host or honoree. It adds a personalized touch to the bar service and provides a memorable element for guests to enjoy.

SLAM: An acronym for "sound, light, air/climate, and music," representing the foundational elements contributing to the "Vibe Dimension" of an event. Carefully orchestrating these elements creates a specific atmosphere and mood, influencing the overall guest experience and the memories formed.

Sweetheart table: A reception table just for the bride and groom.

Tablescape: The overall decorative arrangement on a table, including centerpieces, linens, tableware, and other design elements.

Tasting: A session when couples or event organizers sample potential menu items to help them select the final menu.

Vendor buyouts: Fees imposed for bringing in outside vendors not on the venue's approved list.

Vendor: A business or individual that provides goods or services for an event.

Vibe Dimension: A combination of elements, including sights, sounds, food, aromas, and other sensory elements, that create the overall atmosphere and mood of an event. A well-crafted Vibe Dimension leaves a lasting impression on guests, influencing their emotions and memories associated with the occasion.

Wedding website: A custom site created by a couple to share wedding details, such as the schedule, venue information, RSVP options, and registry links.

Wine service: Serving wine directly to guests at their tables during a meal, often coordinated with the food courses.

Index

-A-

about the author, VII
accessibility, 9–11, 40, 50, 344, 351
adults-only weddings, 4, 158
after-party, wedding, 173–178, 351
alcohol, whether to offer, 126–127
allergies, food, 106, 109, 163
anniversary celebrations, 52–56
appetizers, 20, 313, 316–317
    see also hors d'oeuvres
audio:
    outdoor event, 284
    venue for charity event, 257

-B-

baby shower, 70–72
bachelor party, 189, 203
bachelorette party planning, 165–167
backup plan, 283, 297, 339, 352
band, music, 40, 175, 295, 334–339
bar ideas, events, 122–123
bathroom, 10, 85, 257
best man, 190–191, 203, 226, 229
beverages, nonalcoholic, 29, 36,
    70, 126–127, 307, 315
bridal bouquets, 180–183
bridal party, 132, 162, 175
bridal shower, 133, 162–165
bridal portrait, 9, 183–186, 351
bride's entrance, 227–230
brunch event, 18–20, 71, 112, 117,
    123, 177, 352

budgets:
    band or DJ, entertainment budget,
        335
    bridal shower, 162
    cut costs, parties and special events,
        4–5
    double wedding, 138
    family reunion, 57
    favors, 78, 281
    flowers, weddings, 181–182
    hidden fees, 74–78
    how to plan a reception, 142–143
    how to involve your partner, 135–137
    prom, 37, 39
    rehearsal dinner, 172–173
    quinceañera, 43

-C-

cake:
    cake alternatives, 118–121
    cutting, cakeage fees, 75
    retirement party, 45
cards:
    escort, 14, 16, 17, 93, 352
    place, 17, 92–94, 356
    rsvp, 48, 98, 101, 354
    save-the-date, 94–98
cash bar, 122, 127, 155, 351
catering:
    brunch, 20, 112
    buffet, 108–109, 308, 351
    caterers, 6, 74,

corporate events, 296, 308–310
dietary needs, 114, 296
food station, 118
grazing tables, 110
luxury menu ideas, 111–112
menu selections, 108–113
specialty foods, 106
tastings, 106–107
see also food
celebrations:
accessibility, 9–11, 50, 344
brunch gathering, 18–20
cut costs, 4–5
family reunion, 56–60
planning strategies, 7–9, 82–86
summer celebrations, 32–37
thank-you note, 88–90
see also parties
centerpieces, 19, 29, 35, 81–82, 276, 351
ceremony order, 226–30
certified copies, marriage certificate, 240
chair options, 280–81
charities:
charity events, 256–58
gift registries, 69
change name
see name change
children at events:
activities, 17, 19, 37, 81
flower girl/ringer bearer, 172, 211–17, 227, 229
food, 81
second weddings, 132
cocktail hour, 312–15, 351
cocktails, signature, 64, 124, 313–14, 357
communication plan, 260–63
corporate events/parties:
catering trends, 308–10
entertainment, 332–34
favors, 281–82, 325
high-tech options, 325–26
mindfulness and wellness, 310–12
minimizing no-shows, 288–92
mistakes to avoid, 294–97
planning advice, 258–60

team building/trust-building, 263–69
themes, 269–70
time management, 273–75
when something goes wrong, 292–94
see also event planning

-D-
décor:
bridal shower, 164
bar décor, 124–25
centerpieces, 19, 29, 35, 81–82, 276, 351
holiday celebration, 28–29, 31–32
linens, 277–80, 355
lighting tips, 28, 36, 346–48
rustic, 345
summer celebrations, 32–36
wedding after-party, 175
dietary restrictions, 20, 72, 163, 262
see also allergies, food
dinners, rehearsal
see rehearsal dinner
disabled guests
see accessibility
DIY, downsides, 5–7
DJ, 5, 40, 334–36
double wedding, 137–41
drinks:
children's, 37
summer events, 35–36
see also alcohol; non-alcoholic drinks

-E-
eco-friendly invitations, 90–92
see also invitations
emergency kits, 85–86
engagement party, 167–70
entertainment:
accessibility, 51
brunch entertainment, 19
cocktail hour, 314–15
corporate events, geared for, 332–339
corporate event planning mistakes, 296
live music options, 337–39

micro wedding, 147
prom, 38–40
rehearsal dinner, 173
wedding after-party, 174–77
envelopes, invitation, 101–103
escort cards, 14, 17, 93, 352
etiquette:
cocktail hour, 315
graduation party, 47–52
groom, 192
save-the-date, 96–97
seating chart, 18
second wedding, 132–33
shower, 153–54
thank-you card, 88
tipping, vendors, 78
wedding after-party, 176
wedding planning, 152–55
wedding registry, 68
wedding send-off, 237–38
event planning:
apps, 320–21
back-up plans, 283, 297, 339, 352
band or a DJ, 334–339
budget, 37, 43, 57, 135–137, 138, 143, 162, 172–73, 335
communication plan, 260–63
crunched for time, 78–80
dos and don'ts for event doers, 7–9
event professionals, 270–73
event website, 323–24
hashtag, 327–30
lighting tips, 28, 36, 346–48
logistics, 237–38, 339, 355
marketing, 323
scheduling, 47, 57, 143, 295
signage, 51, 314, 342–44
social media, 48, 262, 291–92, 324
strategies for what ifs, 76, 84, 139, 259, 293
table shapes, 275–77
technological tools, 301, 320–323
timeline, 273–75
transportation, 11–14, 176, 297
vendors, 7, 9, 77, 139, 143–44, 149–50, 155, 301–303, 358

venue selection, 8, 10, 39–40, 57–58, 139, 168, 174, 256–58, 265, 295

-F-
fabric, men's suits, 195
families: disputes and seating arrangements, 16
family reunion, 56–59
favors, 20, 78, 93, 281–82, 325
fees, 9, 24, 74–78, 186, 238, 358
first look, wedding, 230–35
flower girl, 172, 211–17, 227, 229
flowers:
centerpieces, 19, 29, 35, 81–82, 276, 351
bouquets, 180–83
flower expenditures, 181–82
food:
accessibility, events, 11
allergies, 106, 109, 163
appetizers, 20, 313, 316–317
baby shower, 70–72
bridal shower, 164
brunch, 20
corporate events, 308–10
dessert ideas, 112, 114, 118–21
dos and don'ts for event doers, 7–9
engagement party, 168–69
food costs, 142–43
food theft, 151
for children, 81
flexitarian, 309
gluten-free options, 72, 106, 113–16
graduation party, 49
holiday party, 29, 32
micro wedding, 146–47
mistakes to avoid, corporate gathering, 296
rehearsal dinner, 172
self-care, 286
vegan/vegetarian options, 309, 315–18
wedding after-party, 175
see also catering
food stations, 116–18
friend/family, conducting wedding ceremony, 224–25

-G-

games:
engagement party, 170
holiday party, 30–31
retirement party, 46
summer celebrations, 35, 37
gift registries, 67–69
charitable giving, 69
etiquette, 68
scams, 150–51
gifts:
bridal shower, 163–64
for flower girl/ring bearer, 216–27
reception-only wedding, 144
second wedding, 144
glossary, 351
gluten-free options, 72, 106,
113–16
graduation party, 47–52
grand exit, 235–38, 355
groom:
bachelor party, 203
etiquette tips, 192
supporting your bride, 190
wedding day style, 193–97
wedding planning, 188–90
groomsmen, 190, 197 202–205
guest list, 16
bridal shower, 163
double wedding, 140–41
graduation party, 47–48
micro wedding, 145
mother of the bride, 209
save-the date, 96
reception-only wedding, 143
rehearsal dinner, 172
wedding after-party, 176

-H-

handwritten thank-you, 52, 88–90
hashtag, events, 324, 27–30
hidden fees, 74–78
holiday party, 28–32
honeymoon scams, 150
honoring loved ones, 65–67
hors d'oeuvres, 168, 256, 316–17, 357

-I-

invitations:
affordable, 102–103
digital, 4, 99
eco-friendly, 90–92, 99
family reunion, 58
invitation providers, 101–102
invitation suite, 100–101
options, 98–101
reception-only, wedding, 143–44
save-the-date, 94–98, 357
wording, 133, 141, 155–59, 263

-J-

Jewish wedding processional, 227–28

-L-

last name, changing
see name change
letters, thank you, 88–90, 217
see also handwritten thank-you
liability insurance, vendor, 297, 301–303
lighting tips, 346–48
linens:
chair covers, 279
event linens, 277–80
liners, 278
materials, 277–78
overlay, 278
sizes for rental, 279
locations, events, 143
see also venues

-M-

maid/matron of honor:
releasing from duties, 205–208
what's expected, 200–202
makeup artists, 186–87
marketing, event, 259, 261, 323
marriage certificate, 240–45, 355
marriage license, 240, 355
menus:
brunch, 20, 71, 112
rehearsal dinner, 172
creating a menu, 70–72, 108–13
luxury menu items, 111–12

tasting, 106–107
see also catering; food
menu signs, 112–13
mocktails, 306–307
mother of the bride, 208–211
music:
band or DJ, 334–36
bridal shower, 164
cocktail hour, strategic approach to
live music, 314
corporate gathering, mistakes to
avoid, 294–297
live music options, 337–39
wedding after-party, 174–75, 177

-N-
name change, after marriage, 240–46
non-alcoholic drinks, 126–27
see also mocktails

-O-
objection, during ceremony, 249–52
officiant, weddings, 221, 222–25
open bars, bar types, 122
outdoor bars, 125
outdoor events, 34, 76, 84–85, 283–84
outdoor wedding considerations, 194
overlay, linen, 278

-P-
parking:
easy access to parking, 256
event doer dos and don'ts, 8
event transportation, 14
graduation party etiquette, 50
hidden fees, 76
prom venue, 40
parties, celebrations
anniversary party, 52–56
engagement party, 167–69
graduation party, 47–52
holiday party, 28–32
quinceañera, 42–44
retirement party, 44–46
party, bridal
see bridal party

partner, in wedding planning, 134–37
pets, 60–65
photo booth:
cocktail hour, 315
high-tech options, 325
photo booth for events, 22–26
photographer:
engagement party, 170
ditch your DIY ideas, 5–6
double wedding, 138–39
first look, capturing on camera,
234–35
grand exit, 238
micro wedding, 146
photos with pets, 64–65
quinceañera, 43–44
timeline, plan with photography in
mind, 275
wedding scams,149–50
photo display:
anniversary party, 53
engagement party, 169
place cards, 92–94, 356
plus-one:
cut costs, 4
rehearsal dinner, 172
postcards, save-the-date, 96
postponement and cancellation
insurance, 297–99
prenuptial agreement, 246–49
processional, wedding, 226–30
prom, 37–40

-Q-
quinceañera, 42–44

-R-
reception, wedding
see wedding reception
recessional, wedding ceremony, 229
registries, gift
see gift registries
rehearsal dinner, 170–73
reservations, RSVPs, invitation
wording, 158
ring bearer, 172, 211–17, 227, 229

runners, linens, 279
rustic events, 345, 357

-S-
safety:
 signage, 342
 team-building events, 266
save-the-date:
 destination weddings, 95
 digital versus paper, 79, 96
 environmentally friendly, 91
 etiquette, 96
 information to include, 95–96
 postcards, 96
 texts, 97–98
 timing, 95
seating:
 assigned, 14, 17, 94
 seating charts, 14, 16–18
 seating plan, 14–18
 strategies, accessibility, 11
second wedding, 132–34
self-care, 67, 286–87
send off
 see grand exit
servers, hidden wedding costs, 74
shower
 see baby shower; bridal shower
signature cocktail, 124, 313–14, 357
signs:
 menu signs, 112–13
 signage tips and ideas, 342–44
 signature cocktail signage, 314
social media:
 event hashtag, 324, 27–30
 event tech, 323, 324–25
 graduation party invitation, 48
 minimizing no-shows, events, 291–92
 photo booth, GIFs, 25
speaker, event:
 contingency plan, 292–94, 297
 corporate comedian, 332
special events
 see celebrations; parties

speeches:
 best man, 190–91
 graduation party, 51–52
 maid/matron of honor, 201
 mother of the bride, 210
 rehearsal dinner, 171
 retirement party, 45
suits, groom, 193–96
Sunday weddings and events, 21–22, 158

-T-
tablecloths, 76, 125, 277–79
table shapes, 275–77
team-building events, 263–69
technological tools, 325–26
thank-you notes, 52, 83, 88–90, 155, 185, 201
themes:
 anniversary party, 52–53
 baby shower, 70
 bridal shower, 164
 corporate event, 269–70
 grand exit, 237
 holiday party, 31
 photo booth, 23
 retirement party, 44–45
 second wedding, 134
 summer celebrations, 33–34
 Sunday events, 22
 team-building, 268
 wedding after-party, 175, 177
time management, corporate event planning, 287, 299–301
timeline, event, 273–75
toasts, 45, 126, 141, 170, 171
transportation, 11–14, 22, 176, 297
tuxedos, 193–96

-U-
uplighting, 347

-V-
vegan/vegetarian options, 35, 72, 106, 116, 256, 269, 296, 309, 315–18
vendors:
 bridal portrait, 185

buyouts, 9
double wedding, 139
groom's guide, wedding planning, 189–190
liability insurance, 297, 301–303
micro wedding, 145–47
pets at celebrations, 62–63
post-event cleanup, 76
reception-only, weddings, 141–44
Sunday events, 21–22
vendor meals, 77
venues:
  bar packages, 75
  bridal portrait, 9, 183–86, 352
  bridal shower, 163
  double wedding, 139
  engagement party, 168
  outdoor events, 284
  reception-only wedding, 142–43
  rehearsal dinner, 171–73
  taxes and service charges, 77
  wedding after-party, 173–75
  wedding scams, 149–50
vibe dimension, IX
videographer:
  DIY disadvantages, 6
  high-tech options, 325
  micro wedding, 146
  timeline, 274
  wedding after-party, 175–76
virtual reality, events, 326, 332
vows, wedding, 134, 146–47, 192, 220–22, 224, 229, 251, 352

-W-
website, 10, 19, 22, 96–99, 101–102, 153, 158–59, 163, 189, 289, 323–24
weather:
  cocktail hour, 312
  contingency plan, 84, 353

event communication plan, 260–63
fabrics, suits and tuxedos, 194–95
family reunion, 59
grand exit, 238
outdoor bar, 125–26
outdoor event, 283–84
planning strategies, 84–85
weddings:
  after-party, 173–78, 351
  double wedding, 137–41
  etiquette tips, wedding planning, 152–55
  first look; 230–35
  guest list, 140–41, 143, 166
  invitation wording, 133, 141, 155–59, 263
  location/venue, 139, 142–43, 185, 194, 204, 238
  micro wedding, 144–48
  planning, involving partner, 134–37
  wedding cake, cakeage fee, 75
  wedding crashers, 84
  wedding dress, 134, 148, 182–83, 184–85, 200, 209
  wedding party gifts, 78
  wedding planner, 79, 146–47, 149
  wedding scams, 148–52
wedding ceremonies:
  bride's entrance, 228
  ceremony order, 226–30
  officiant, 221, 222–25
  processional, 226–28
  recessional, 229
  traditions, 136, 140–41, 180, 210, 227–28
  wedding objection, 249–52
wedding reception
  grand exit, 235–38
  reception-only wedding, 141–44

EXCLUSIVE SNEAK PEEK

rogerigo.com/exclusive

Download your complimentary copy of **Keep On Going** by Roger Igo.

From tragedy to triumph, **Keep On Going** chronicles the extraordinary history of Houston events venue The Bell Tower on 34th, from pioneering Texans to a disastrous betrayal to one man's fight for the future.

Founder and CEO Roger Igo candidly shares:

* The events that derailed the author's thriving company and forced him to find a new path

* Bold risks fueled by desperation and tenacity

* A guided tour of The Bell Tower on 34th and the elements that set it apart

From tragedy to triumph, **Keep On Going** is a story about never giving up, because sometimes, with faith and fortitude, it is possible to overcome great challenges.

Scan to download your copy!